Language Processing
and the
Reading of Literature

Language Processing and the Reading of Literature

Toward a Model of Comprehension

GEORGE L. DILLON

Indiana University Press
Bloomington & London

Manufactured in the United States of America

Library of Congress Cataloging in Publication Data
Dillon, George L   1944–
Language processing and the reading of literature.
Bibliography: p.
Includes index.
1. Discourse analysis.   2. Psycholinguistics.
3. Generative grammar.   I. Title.
P302.D54   1978   415   77-9861
ISBN 0-253-33195-1   1 2 3 4 5 82 81 80 79 78

For Fred and Jennifer
—they cheered

As a rule, all that you recognise as in your mind is the one final association of meanings which seems sufficiently rewarding to be the answer— 'now I have understood *that*'; it is only at intervals that the strangeness of the process can be observed.

William Empson

Contents

PREFACE

Quite a number of years ago Harold Whitehall declared that "criticism in English ought to have a hunger for a sound linguistics" and argued that this was so because "no criticism can go beyond its linguistics." These claims have not won universal assent. Indeed, twenty years later, there are many who remain unconvinced that linguistics has much to contribute to the understanding of literature or vice-versa. The unsettled status of Whitehall's claim notwithstanding, I would like to make a comparable one that criticism cannot go beyond its theory of reading, and that most critics operate with an implicit theory that might be characterized as 'watered-down Empson.' This is not a bad theory, by the way, except that it is very inexplicit, and I think criticism would benefit from an attempt to construct a model of reading as explicit and articulated as current knowledge will warrant. The pages that follow are an attempt to suggest the outlines of such an account.

The phrase *current knowledge*, however, is quite misleading in so far as it suggests a widely accepted, empirically based model of how we comprehend texts. In fact, there are hunches and hypotheses, small portions of which are supported by experimentally obtained data of arguable significance. The theory of language processing is in the very early stages of development, and a discussion of reading based primarily on the reading of difficult literary texts may contribute something to the general understanding of reading that one hopes will emerge from the current ferment.

I will concede at the outset the force of what might be the first axiom of reading research, namely that there are many ways of reading which vary with the type of text and the purposes of the reader—the notion of 'ordinary' or 'plain' reading is probably a chimera, the close relative of 'ordinary language.' What I will describe is an idealization of sorts—what we might do if we tied off every loose end and read not just for the gist but for as exact an account of the text as could be had. This first axiom leaves open the possibility that there may be certain strategies especially appropriate for certain types of texts, say for literary texts, but our procedure will be to assume not, until and unless the texts force us to admit such possibilities.

A few words about the examples: they are cited as proofs or evidence of the operation of certain strategies, but they will not function as such unless the reader struggles to read each of them and does not skip to the analysis. This study does not report the results of experiments; rather, it invites the reader to engage in analysis of his own cognitive processes, and the persuasive force of the book rests on whether the reader experiences the effects described. Read in this fashion, the book becomes quite dense, and so I have kept it as short as possible.

I would like to thank those who fed me examples and puzzled with me over them: my students Judith R. Palmer, Larry Platter, and Helen Twite, and my colleagues Walter Johnston and Philip R. Headings. Another colleague, Jeanette Clausen, gave the completed manuscript a very close reading and offered many useful comments that improved it both in content and in clarity, and the copy editor, Sharon Smith, patiently combed out numerous tangles. Finally I thank my friend and erstwhile collaborator Frederick Kirchhoff, who read and criticized early drafts and late and whose interest and enthusiasm provided me with vital stimulation.

NOTE ON THE TEXTS

Citations of Spenser are from *The Works of Edmund Spenser: A Variorum Edition*, edited by Edwin Greenlaw, C. G. Osgood, F. M. Padelford, et al. (Baltimore: Johns Hopkins Press, 10 vols., 1932–49). This text retains Spenser's punctuation in the 1596 edition of *The Faerie Queene*. Citations of Milton are from *The Works of John Milton*, edited by Frank Allen Patterson et al. (New York: Columbia University Press, 1931). This text reproduces the 1667 edition of *Paradise Lost*. In the citations, spelling and punctuation are unaltered, except that words originally italicized are printed roman— all italics are my italics. As the modern reader is likely to read Spenser and Milton in somewhat modernized texts, the main differences introduced by modernization should be noted. In most editions of Milton's and Spenser's works currently in print, editors modernize spelling and retain the original punctuation. Obviously, modernized spelling facilitates word recognition somewhat, though earlier spellings are generally 'phonetic' enough for the reader to recognize the word by 'sounding out' the printed form. We can look at it the other way too: Spenser's phonetic but non-standard spellings force us to decode to sound in order to recognize words—the spelling forces the reader to hug the phonetic surface of the work. The *u/v* and *i/j* reversals in Spenser give some difficulty to readers unfamiliar with Elizabethan orthography, but it is my impression that one works out the principles, at least roughly, in the first few hundred lines read.

Citations of Henry James's *The Wings of the Dove (WOD)* are from the New York Edition (New York: Charles Scribner's Sons) unless otherwise indicated; of *The Ambassadors (AMB)* from S. P. Rosenbaum's edition (New York: W. W. Norton and Company, Inc., 1964), which reproduces the New York Edition; of *The Portrait of a Lady* from the New York Edition. Citations of ''The Real Thing'' are from *The Complete Tales of Henry James*, edited by Leon Edel (Philadelphia: J. B. Lippincott Company) VIII (1963).

Citations of Faulkner are from *The Portable Faulkner*, edited by Malcolm Cowley (New York: The Viking Press, 1946), unless otherwise indicated; of *Absalom, Absalom! (ABS)* and *Light in August (LA)* from the Modern Library Editions (New York: Random House, 1951, 1950).

Citations of Wallace Stevens are from *The Collected Poems of Wallace Stevens (CP)* (New York: Alfred A. Knopf, 1964) by page number, and are quoted with the permission of the publisher.

Citations of Wordsworth's *Prelude* (1850 version) are from the edition of Ernest De Selincourt, revised by Helen Darbyshire (Oxford, Oxford University Press, 1959); of *The Excursion* from *The Poetical Works,* edited by Ernest De Selincourt and Helen Darbyshire (Oxford: Oxford University Press, 1959), Vol. V.

INTRODUCTION

Style and Processing

G ENERATIVE grammar, with its claim to represent the human mind and its activity, seemed a decade ago to promise a genuine insight into the function of language in literature. This hope was eloquently set forth in the concluding sentences of Richard Ohmann's now famous programmatic essay, "Literature as Sentences":

> Since critical understanding follows and builds on understanding of sentences, generative grammar should eventually be a reliable assistant in the effort of seeing just how a given literary work sifts through the reader's mind, what cognitive and emotional processes it sets in motion, and what organization of experience it encourages.[1]

Although there has been much progress in generative grammar in the last decade, it has not developed into the handmaiden Ohmann hoped for. Writing six years later, Roger Fowler cited Ohmann's words, but still found it necessary to ask, "What do transformations do to us?"[2] Fowler, however, had little to offer in answer to this question, and what he did suggest is vulnerable to the scathing strictures leveled against generative stylistics by Stanley Fish in his English Institute paper of 1973.[3] Fish saw that generative stylisticians had never systematically specified how sentences are understood and had indeed made contradictory assumptions about the effect of deletion, for example, on the reader. Fish is correct both in his description of the facts and in his identification of the critical weakness. Generative stylisticians never have sketched a model of how sentences are read, and, lacking that model, have described connections between syntax and cognitive processing which strike others as vague or fanciful, a mixture of inspired hunch, intimation, and bald assertion in no way more explicit or insightful than traditionally based analyses.

The reason that generative stylisticians did not specify a model of reading is to be found, I think, in a naive understanding of generative grammar that was endemic in the 1960s—one eminent grammarian has confessed to it, and Chomsky warned against it in *Aspects of the Theory of Syntax*.[4] That misunderstanding was to take the term *generative* psychologically—to assume that the model of surface structure, transformations, and deep structure was a direct replica of sentence production and perception. In reading a sentence, one parsed into surface structure, 'undid' the transformations to get a deep structure, and applied rules of semantic interpretation to the deep structure to get the semantic representation. Hence, one could assume that the transformations directly described some of the sifting done by the mind, some of the cognitive processes set in motion.

In the last decade, a body of evidence has accumulated which has raised doubts that the transformational model Ohmann assumed, or any of its descendents, is a direct rendering of the way we process sentences. Some sentences prove to be easier than their transformational derivation would predict, others harder. This research is summarized in Fodor, Bever, and Garrett's *The Psychology of Language* and in Charles and Helen Cairns's *Psycholinguistics*.[5] Fodor et al. conclude that psycholinguists thereby discovered that they had something to do, which is, among other things, to specify the "computational systems" whereby hearers and readers interpret sentences. Psycholinguists have made some headway in this specification, and attempts to simulate these 'computational systems' with computers have also clarified certain points. It appears that the model that is beginning to emerge is what is needed to realize the objective of generative stylistics. The way a writer chooses to frame sentences and place their elements does affect the reader's cognitive processes in predictable ways which analysis can explicate, but via the strategies of processing: a particular construction or preference of a writer is important insofar as it affects processing of the text. In this way, stylistics becomes concerned, as Fish argues it must, with the way texts and readers act on each other.

We will begin with the following assumptions and rudiments of a model of reading.

1. Reading has at least three levels, which we will call *perception, comprehension,* and *interpretation.* We will say we have perceived a sentence when we have specified its propositional structure. This includes identifying the propositions and the phrases that function in them, matching logical Subjects and Objects with the predicates that relate them, and associating modifiers with the elements they modify. These are relatively simple and uncontroversial notions, and we will not need any sophisticated logical formalisms to represent them. I thus assume no difference between the goal of perceiving sentences of literature and those of other discourses. Comprehension of a sentence involves the integration of its propositional content into one's running tally of what is being described or argued in the passage. It is on this level that one identifies the individuals referred to by the noun phrases and pronouns; the time and place of the actions represented in the sentence; possible motives, purposes, instruments, and consequences of the actions; and so on.[6] This integration may involve inferences establishing relations not explicitly stated in the sentences of the passage. Perry Thorndyke gives a simple example in the sequence,

John came into the room. The chandelier was beautiful.

where we infer the proposition 'there was a chandelier in the room' to link the second sentence to the first. Thorndyke states the general point nicely:

> Prose comprehension consists not only of comprehension of individual sentences [our 'perception'], but of the integration of sentences into a larger framework incorporating implicit causal, temporal, and motivational information. . . . A primary function of the inferential process is to generate from explicit information new propositions that incorporate the information into a more general contextual frame.[7]

The difference between perception and comprehension can be illustrated by a paragraph devised by J. D. Bransford and M. K. Johnson where the propositional structure of each sentence is easy enough to make out, but the sentences do not give us enough information to construct a 'frame' in which they will all cohere:

> The procedure is actually quite simple. First you arrange things into different groups. Of course, one pile may be sufficient depending on how much there is to do. If you have to go somewhere else due to lack of facilities that is the next step, otherwise you are pretty well set. It is important not to overdo things. That is, it is better to do too few things at once than too many. . . .[8]

Given any sort of clue to the frame, however, one finds that the paragraph falls easily into comprehensibility ("Washing Clothes").

Material in the contextual frame can constrain perception of new sentences. For example, the words in the following sentence can be grouped into phrases two different ways,

He put the block in the box on the shelf.

but if we had a context involving a block in a box we would not hesitate to group 'the block in the box' as a phrase in this sentence, and if the context has established a box on a shelf, then we would perceive 'the box on the shelf' as a phrase. This example suggests two major points: first, we may locate noun phrases not by looking for strings of words that could be grouped as noun phrases (with functions and reference to be decided later) but by looking for words that refer to things to which we can expect reference to be made. Second, we may not, therefore, construct all the possible parsings of the words before us if the first one we try is a plausible continuation of the contextual frame. We will examine many instances of 'garden path' phenomena in the following chapters which suggest that at least some of the time we choose one analysis rather than keep track of them all. This is an obscure and controversial point. All agree that many ambiguous strings are not *noticed* to be ambiguous—the question is whether the alternatives are momentarily constructed at some level beneath awareness. Such evidence as there is is conflicting and inconclusive, and it is also not clear what difference it makes. If these alternatives are never integrated into the networks of meaning one is constructing, they would seem to vanish as quickly as they arose (if they arose) and to be of negligible conceptual import.

Further, in the case of word recognition, we may be able to specify pretty closely the sense of a word before getting to it, and recognizing it then consists of determining that it has the right orthographic shape to bear the sense we have projected for it. In other cases, seeing its written shape will enable us to decide which of the possible concepts is in fact being invoked. This means that the sort of process envisioned by Empson where one retrieves or activates all of the senses of a written form which then reverberate in the subconscious while one sense is preferred by the conscious mind is an unusual or atypical one in general reading rather than the unavoidable basis of even the most practical kinds of reading (as Empson believed it to be). The view that skilled readers read word by word and from phonetic/graphic shape toward possible meaning is now generally doubted.[9]

Comprehension, then, synthesizes material into a world with actors, places, forces, and so on. In doing this it may be guided by conventions special to the type of discourse being processed. For example, there is a convention of narrative that descriptive material following a verb of perception is to be taken as specifying what was perceived. Hence the italicized *he* in the following sequence is not even momentarily ambiguous:

> Finally he saw a little old man come out of the side door and begin walking down the alley away from him. *He* was carrying a brown gym bag.

A more complex example would be the conventions of free indirect style in narrative, where one figure is referred to as *he* (or *she*) but must in some other respects be treated as an *I* if the passage is to cohere into a congruent scene.[10] The question of when one should stop searching for a character's motives is also settled in part by the type of work one is reading; inferences about physical causality may not be applicable in works of fantasy, and so on.

Interpretation, finally, is the most abstract level where we relate the sense of what is going on to the author's constructive intention—why he is saying what he says, or what he is getting at in terms of the themes and meaning of the work. In this sense of the term, all discourses require interpretation, and they must be interpreted by means of conventions to various degrees special to the type of discourse. Literary interpretation, then, is not something different from 'usual' interpretation but simply interpretation of literature according to the conventions appropriate to literary discourse.

Interpretation governs comprehension and perception in that we tend to see what we have inferred the writer wants us to see. Samuel Fillenbaum conducted a study in which subjects were asked to paraphrase sentences which included such 'perverse' items as

> John dressed and had a bath.
> Don't print that or I won't sue you.

In their paraphrases, over sixty percent of the subjects changed the sentences into the more likely sentences,

> John had a bath and dressed.
> If you print that, I'll sue you.

More than half were unaware of having changed the sentence, and many of those who were aware said that they knew what the original sentences were trying to say and so 'corrected' them.[11] Our capacity to take certain utterances as ironic and to respond to indirect speech acts, interpreting, for example,

> Can you take out the garbage?

not as a request for information as to ability but as a request for action, depends on this ability to infer the Speaker's probable intentions.[12] William Empson's sixth and seventh types of ambiguity furnish many other examples where the most obvious interpretation of lines taken out of context is inconsistent with the interpretation of the poem they occur in and so are 'adjusted' to conform. When we read the last line of Ben Jonson's "Drink To Me Only With Thine Eyes,"

> But might I of Jove's nectar sup
> I would not change for thine.

we do not read "If I could drink Jove's nectar, I wouldn't give it up for yours," but rather "I would not exchange yours for it." Again, this line may not send one scurrying off to the *OED* to find out whether there is an archaic sense of *change* that will warrant the reading that has to be right on the grounds of tone and intention of the lyric (there is). One may simply not notice and read "change thine (for it)." Similarly the odd possibilities Empson pointed out in the famous stanza from Lovelace's "To Althea"

> Stone walls do not a prison make,
> Nor iron bars a cage;
> Minds innocent and quiet take
> That for a hermitage.

namely, that the pronoun *that*, being singular, should be taken as referring to *prison/cage*, and hence we might get "minds innocent and quiet can take prisons and cages for hermitages (i.e., sentimentalize them), but they cannot do the same thing with (real) stone walls and iron bars." In another context, or century, these lines might well bear this force. It is so wildly inconsistent with the tone of the rest of the poem, however, that we may read *that* as referring instead to a general "imprisonment." There is a kind of dismissive aloofness conveyed by *that* (as opposed to *this* or a more accurate plural [*those, them*]) that does harmonize with the tone of the poem. Again, in context we may never notice, or indeed construct, the reading Empson says is there "on the face of it."[13]

Just as interpretation can shape comprehension and perception, so it may become the guiding consideration when a text is grammatically irregular, obscure, or elliptical: the processes of perception and comprehension do not get enough data, or enough consistent data, to select a reading, so one imposes a propositional structure or contextual frame which supports one's sense of what the passage should be saying. We will examine passages, especially in Chapters III, IV, and V, where reasoning from probable artistic intention is the most efficient way to set the text in order.

This three-way distinction (perception/comprehension/interpretation) is a useful one which we will employ throughout. Since everyone uses these terms differently, it is perhaps well to repeat the crucial basis of the distinction as we draw it, which is the goal of each level of processing (propositional structure/contextual frame/constructive intent). The three levels are not processes as such; rather, various processes may be carried out to achieve the goals of each, and the three levels may interact as described in achieving them. In what follows, we will be investigating the ways we may try to achieve the goals of propositional structure and contextual frame. How we arrive at constructive intent exceeds the bounds of this study, though E. D. Hirsch, Jr., argues that the process of arriving at the author's intention is of the same nature and a continuation of these 'lower level' processes of forming and testing hypotheses about the meaning of the text. His remarks succinctly characterize this process: "For that which we are understanding is itself an hypothesis constructed by ourselves, a schema, or genre, or type which provokes expectations that are confirmed by our linguistic experience, or when they are not confirmed, cause us to adjust our hypothesis or schema" (*Aims*, pp.

33–34). We proceed now to specify more narrowly our initial assumptions about perception and comprehension.

2. Readers have learned strategies for constructing propositional structure directly from serial order of words; they may not (re)construct a surface structure (a labeled bracketing into phrases) in all details (though I assume a grouping into basic phrases), nor pass through a deep structure representation by 'undoing' transformations. For example, if one is to process the following sentence correctly,

A person finally arrived who could answer their question.

a person must be identified as the antecedent of *who,* but this identification need not pass through an intermediate stage in which the entire relative clause is placed next to *a person* in some sort of mental representation.

3. These perceptual strategies can be semantically based (e.g., if one hypothesizes that a certain noun phrase is the Subject of a verb because it is the most semantically congruent noun phrase around) or syntactically based (e.g., if one hypothesizes a noun phrase as Subject because it is in a position often occupied by a Subject). One may use one sort of strategy or another, or use one as a check while relying on the other, and shift strategies as they prove to be more or less efficient and reliable. Psycholinguists have found evidence that some passive sentences are perceived somewhat more slowly than their active counterparts, but this is not the case if semantic clues identify the logical Subject and Object. For example,

The cookie was eaten by the dog.

is perceived as quickly as its active counterpart, though

The horse was followed by the cow.[14]

is not, presumably because the latter order and words would also constitute a possible active sentence (*The horse followed the cow.*). In other words, when either noun phrase could be the logical Subject, one must attend to whether the markers of passive voice (*be*, past participle, *by*) are present. Similarly, the first sentence of the next pair is easier than the second (though still very hard),

> The question the girl the lion bit answered was complex.
> The lion the dog the monkey chased bit died.

presumably because semantic clues help to identify *the lion* as the Biter, *the girl* as the Asker, and *the question* as the thing which is complex. It is still hard to get the structure of the first sentence into focus, but the semantic clues do assist us in getting our bearings. Semantic clues are not always available, but when they are, they facilitate perception.[15] Several different proposals have been made about the exact way semantic clues might function in perception, including John Kimball's suggestion that semantic compatibility is used as a check in initial parsing to help in choosing between alternative analyses (as it is in Terry Winograd's parsing program),[16] and the proposals of Langendoen, Kalish-Landon, and Dore and of Lakoff and Thompson that one might use semantic information to make initial hypotheses as to function.[17] Lakoff and Thompson, for example, propose that one might identify the following italicized noun phrases as logical Indirect Objects by a partially semantic strategy:

> *Who* did you give the bottle to?
> *Suzie* was given the bottle at 4 o'clock.

The strategy could be roughly phrased: "If you have a noun phrase which is not the logical Subject and which is animate, it is likely to be the logical Indirect Object (if the verb takes one)." This strategy will of course give some erroneous analyses, as it would to

> Suzie was given to Dr. Fishbein for surgery at 4 o'clock.

'Erroneous results' can be good, however, if they correspond to actual misunderstandings we experience—in that case, they *explain* how we misunderstood.

The notion of a semantic clue must be taken in the broad sense that includes pragmatic knowledge or assumptions and inferences drawn from the context. We did smuggle a piece of pragmatic information into the example with the lion, the girl, and the question: we assumed that *the girl* was incompatible as the Subject of *bit*, at least in the presence of a lion (i.e., given a choice between girl and lion as the Biter, take the lion), but this is not a true incompatibility, just an improbability. Further, in a given context, certain individuals are likelier to do certain things than others: in the case at hand, the probabilities change greatly if the lion has been shot full of tranquilizers. Thomas Bever speculates that, so enriched, semantically based strategies are very powerful:

> In the actual application of language, specific contexts must provide far stronger immediate constraints and basis for prediction of the most likely meaning of a sentence independent of its form. Thus, most normal perceptual processing of sentences is probably carried out with little regard to actual sequence or structure; rather, the basic relational functions . . . are assigned on the basis of temporary ('contingent') and generic ('constant') semantic probabilities.
>
> ["Cognitive Basis," p. 297]

We will see examples of contextual information clarifying formally obscure lines in the next chapter (especially examples 28, 29). One problem with exclusive reliance on semantic clues, however, is that the information they depend on is not always available, either because candidates are all roughly equal in eligibility (examples 30, 31, 41 of the next chapter) or because one has to look too far ahead or behind to check for compatibility (passim). Notice by the way that with this enriched definition of semantics we set up an interaction between comprehension and perception: entities can be eligible for a certain function in propositional structure because of their place, powers, or other attributes in the 'contextual frame' or

'world' we construct in comprehension. This means that the reference of a noun phrase may be determined before its function is
assigned; hence, in some cases at least, perception is not prior to
determination of reference.

4. We will examine many passages where clues of parallelism,
repetition, alliteration, rhythm, and rhyme assist perception of
propositional structure. Conceivably they might do this by being
the bases of perceptual strategies, but it is more likely that we
construct other sorts of groupings besides syntactic ones, and
when these groupings align with syntactic groups they may facilitate perception of propositional structure. Rhetoric books bear wit-
ness to the force of such non-grammatical indicators of patterning
by warning against using parallelism and repetition unless the
sense is truly parallel, the phrases logically alike.

5. (Implicit in 3 and 4): One evaluates and adjusts the strategies
one uses so that the particular structures favored by a writer can be
most efficiently processed. If, for example, one is reading an author
who inverts word order frequently, one might begin to give more
weight to semantically based strategies, though if he inverts just in
certain ways one might simply make certain adjustments in syntactically based strategies.[18]

6. (Follows from foregoing): Processing strategies are probabilistic in nature: they are based on expectations and likelihoods; they
are not categorical; they can cope with common but ungrammatical
constructions while being unable to cope with grammatical but
uncommon ones; in all of these respects they belong to the domain
of performance—they are indeed a quintessence or abstract of previous performances—rather than competence. Nils Erik Enkvist
has quite properly emphasized that insofar as a text is stylized it
departs from a norm, and it presents the reader with special problems insofar as it deviates from a norm of expectation:

For, if probabilistic levels are necessary, and if our sense of linguistic probabilities is determined by our past experience of language, this past experience becomes a very major force in shaping our ability to generate and to interpret linguistic texts. We carry with us not only a deterministic, all-or-nothing grammar, but also a body of statistical data which we extrapolate from past experience into current probabilities and expectations.[19]

As the word *generate* suggests, however, Enkvist is also somewhat confused about the status of generative grammar as a model of perception and production (see also his p. 43), and we must qualify his argument in one respect: a statistically uncommon construction is not necessarily a source of difficulty—it is so only if it cannot be readily processed by the strategies the reader is using. Further, passages can be difficult without involving any statistically rare features. Of course, the combination of common features that produced the difficulty might prove rare in some cases, but that is tendentious in the extreme. Fish's conclusion holds here: no profile of an author's syntactic proclivities, even if quantified along the lines Enkvist suggests, can directly predict how his style will shape our apprehension of his meaning.

7. Perceptual strategies are designed to accommodate limits of 'primary' or so-called Short Term Memory. Sentences are read linearly, with processing done as one reads, whenever possible before one gets to the end of the sentence. When a tentative analysis is assigned to an item, it can be removed from Short Term Memory, so there is a high value on strategies that assign an analysis quickly—with little 'look ahead', for example. In general, we experience difficulties in perceiving a sentence when a piece of information needed by the strategy we are using is not in its expected place but is either delayed or in a different place.

8. The fundamental condition that a perceived propositional structure must satisfy is that it be based on a grammatical analysis of the sentence. To illustrate with an absurdly simple example,

The man with the revolver shot the guard.

with the revolver cannot be perceived as modifying *the guard* even though it is semantically congruent as a modifier of *guard*. Similarly, whatever we take the referent of the pronoun in the next example to be, it cannot be the referent of *the boys* (by grammatical rule):

They left when the boys got back.

We must always choose propositional structures and reference assignments that are based on a grammatical parsing of the sentence over ones that are not. I will leave open for the time being the question of how one deals, or should deal, with cases where two propositional structures are grammatically possible (Empson's "double syntax") and cases where no grammatical analysis is possible, but we will touch on these matters at the end of Chapter Two and face them squarely in Chapter Five. A final point here is that perception is self-correcting: a hypothesized structure that leaves a piece of the sentence unanalyzed, or requires a piece that is not there, will automatically be questioned or rejected.

9. The notion of choice of an analysis must be treated with some delicacy. There are times when we may avoid making a choice, holding the point open as we read ahead in hope of further information that will aid in making the choice. Some choices are typically on-the-spot decisions (e.g., whether *have* or *be* is a main or auxiliary verb), primarily because the information needed to make the decision is usually found in close proximity. These decisions may be harder to delay than others which often require suspensions of decision (e.g., pronominal reference), and hence a writer whose style complicates an on-the-spot decision may give us an amount of difficulty disproportionate to the importance of the choice. Some critics, moreover, have suggested that if a writer makes a choice difficult for us and creates situations where either

choice fits into the interpretation of the work, perhaps we should not choose between alternatives but 'take both'. This suggestion involves fairly radical revisions in our model of reading which we will consider in Chapter Five.

Obviously these initial assumptions are very loose, allowing for variation within one's own practice, among the practices of different readers, and over particular texts being read. How, in practical terms, can readers discover what strategies they are employing? The key here is the experience of difficulty or confusion—in extreme cases, of incomprehension or miscomprehension. At such moments, the strategies jam, and we can become aware of the origin of the difficulty by noting what in the text is unusual. Normally we are not conscious of choosing or using a particular strategy, but when the results of the processes fail to tally as a well-formed structure, we shift to a more consecutively organized problem-solving routine, constructing and weighing alternative readings.

Usually this shift is accompanied by a sense of greater effort or concentration being expended. Paradoxically, we can learn about how we read simple texts by analyzing the sources of our troubles with difficult ones. Most of the sentences to be discussed in these chapters have given me difficulty. In some cases, the difficulty was only momentary; in other cases, I have repeatedly misread the example; in yet others, I am still uncertain what the best reading is. This is plainly a subjective and introspective way of proceeding, but, as I see it, the only practical one. I have tried to ensure that the sentences cited are typical of their authors' styles by drawing most of the examples from randomly chosen stretches of text, but I have also included sentences from outside those samples which other writers have cited as typical. I appeal to the reader to determine whether he finds the passages difficult, and in the ways described, bearing in mind that they are to various degrees 'pre-analyzed' by being cited in a certain context and by italic printing of the problematic element.

In each of the first four chapters, a particular task, or group of related tasks, will be examined: the first chapter will deal with identification of phrases and their functions; the second chapter, with identification of clause boundaries; the third and fourth chapters, with problems of reference, coreference, and attachment. Chapter Five will, as noted, consider whether we should modify the way we carry out these tasks when we read literature, but Chapter Six returns to ways that texts can present difficulties in the task of integrating material into its context.

Most of the examples are drawn from five writers with deserved reputations for difficulty: Edmund Spenser, John Milton, Henry James, Wallace Stevens, and William Faulkner. Each of these is difficult in some areas but not in others. We can in fact establish a taxonomy of difficulty: a principal source of difficulty in Stevens has to do with appositives; relations of Subject and Object are more problematic in Milton than in the others; identification of main verbs is unusually problematic in James, and so on. Further, we can describe which structural predilections of particular authors create difficulties of perception and comprehension.

The following pages are to be considered an exploratory and tentative account of some processes involved in reading literary texts. It is far from complete and does not consider some of the more complex constructions critics have called attention to such as the 'diabolical' logical syntax in Milton discussed by Stanley Fish or the long strings of adjectives, some of them contradictory, that Faulkner is fond of.[20] I would hope that the model sketched here could be extended to describe the processing of these and indeed numerous other constructions.

Asserting that the model outlined here will realize the objectives of generative stylistics leaves a major question having to do with the notion of an assistant unanswered. Does criticism need such a model? How has it fared without one? Many critics, relying only on tact, mother wit, and Empson's metaphors, have described the experience of reading various authors acutely and insightfully.

Studies which focus on the reader's experience of the writers and works that concern us include those by Paul Alpers on Spenser, Stanley Fish on Milton, and Helen Vendler on Stevens (and we will refer to Stephen Booth's work on Shakespeare's sonnets). These critics are among those who have anticipated psychologists and linguists in redefining the focus of their endeavor in terms of real-time experience of texts. With this focus on response has come an interest in the general principles which shape perception and comprehension. Stanley Fish, for one, sees the need for a model of processing which could specify responses by setting forth principles that "restrict (make predictable and normative) the range of response."[21] It is precisely these principles (some of them at least) that we undertake to provide and to give thereby some answers to the questions: what sorts of principles guide, or should guide, the reader and critic in reading literary texts?

Language Processing
and the
Reading of Literature

CHAPTER ONE

Phrases and Their Functions

MOST linguistic models take it as axiomatic that the words of sentences are grouped into phrases (and sometimes these phrases are grouped into phrases) in the process of perception, and further that the noun phrases are related to the predicate as arguments of the predicate.[1] The first place argument of the predicate I will call its logical Subject, the second its logical Object, and I will hereafter drop the *logical*.[2] Obviously the serial ordering of the noun phrases in English usually corresponds to their order as Subjects and Objects, and in the simplest cases a perceptual strategy for 'annotating' or recognizing Subjects and Objects can be based on this fact. We schematize:

If: N — V — NP . . .
then: S   O

The serial order of noun phrases in sentences, however, does not always yield to this principle, and, as we shall see, supplementary strategies are possible. In relative clauses, for example, the Object may precede the Subject:

the girl *whom all* adore
O   S

Note that in this example the case of the pronoun is a good clue to its logical function. In certain models of semantic structure, that would not be true all the time, but this controversial matter turns on constructions that will not concern us in the present study.

There is a limit to the practical importance of serial strategies: in context, semantic clues might often be most efficacious, with serial data operating as a check on a preliminary assignment of Subject and Object made on grounds of semantic plausibility. That is, one imagines serial and semantic strategies working simultaneously and in parallel fashion, but with primacy given to semantically based hypotheses. Perhaps the most neutral assumption, however, is that they normally work together. "If there is an initial noun phrase preceding the verb and if it is congruent semantically as the Subject of the verb, assign it the function of Subject." Problematic cases would arise when one condition or the other failed to hold, or if semantic information were inadequate. We will be examining just such sources of perceptual difficulty in this chapter. Before we consider how phrases are assigned functions, however, we should give some consideration to the processes involved in grouping words into phrases.

1. PHRASE BOUNDARIES

In general, the words of a phrase are contiguous: when one comes to a verb, for example, one can close off an initial noun phrase and assume that it is complete. This is as true of coordinate noun phrases as of simple ones and is reflected in part in the well known Coordinate Structure Constraint, originally described by John Robert Ross, that coordinate phrases cannot be 'chopped'—i.e., one conjunct cannot be moved out of the coordinate structure.[3] That is, the coordinate structure will always occur as a unit. Milton gives us occasional problems by splitting coordinate noun phrases, moving one part of the coordinate structure away and leaving the rest behind, or spreading the coordinate noun phrase. Here are a few examples:

(1)   his gestures fierce
    He mark'd and mad demeanour, ...

                                    [Milton, *PL.*, IV. 128–29]

(2)   Sea he had searcht and Land

                                    [Milton, *PL.*, IX. 76]

(3)   whose mortal taste
    Brought Death into the World, and all our woe, ...

                                    [Milton, *PL.*, I. 2–3]

(4)   Rais'd impious War in Heav'n and Battel proud
    With vain attempt.

                                    [Milton, *PL.*, I. 43–44]

(5)   when the Scourge
    Inexorably, and the torturing hour
    Calls us to Penance?

                                    [Milton, *PL.*, II. 90–92]

One might devise a strategy based on the meaning of words to help put back together a split coordinate noun phrase—the parts must be put back together in the sense that they must be seen as performing the same function and performing it jointly. Most co-ordinated noun phrases share some degree of similarity: hence if the noun phrases have many features of meaning in common, they may belong together as parts of a single phrase. Here the strategy works by grouping *gestures + demeanour, Sea + Land, death + woe, war + battle,* and *scourge + torturing hour.* A similar problem of split conjuncts occurs in the next example from Faulkner, where the italicized noun phrase is coordinate to *dim coffin-smelling gloom . . .* but stupefyingly far away from it:

(6)   There would be the dim coffin-smelling gloom sweet and over-sweet
    with the twice-bloomed wistaria against the outer wall by the savage
    quiet September sun impacted distilled and hyperdistilled, into
    which came now and then the loud cloudy flutter of the sparrows like
    a flat limber stick whipped by an idle boy, and *the rank smell of female
    old flesh long embattled in virginity* while the wan haggard face watched

him above the faint triangle of lace at wrists and throat from the too tall chair in which she resembled a crucified child. . . .

[Faulkner, *ABS*, 8]

There is a semantic relatedness between the coordinate noun phrases ("smelly atmosphere"), but there is evident here some limit on how long a noun phrase can be held for matching purposes. In the next example, the second member of a coordinate prepositional phrase (italicized) is relatively near the first, but appears semantically unlike the first (because it appears to be abstract) and is for that reason hard to match to the first:

(7)   Her carriage, air, now was a little regal—she and Judith made frequent trips to town now, calling upon the same ladies, some of whom were now grandmothers, whom the aunt had tried to force to attend the wedding twenty years ago, and, *to the meager possibilities* which the town offered, shopping—as though she had succeeded at last in evacuating not only the puritan heritage but reality itself. . . .

[Faulkner, *ABS*, 69]

The comma between *and* and the phrase in question makes it harder to see the phrase as coordinate to anything (instead, it looks parenthetical), but one eventually does realize that *possibilities* are actually places also and that there is a parallel structuring: *to town, calling . . . , and to possibilities . . . , shopping.*

The other principal boundary problem with noun phrases has to do with a prepositional phrase which properly belongs to the noun phrase. If the prepositional phrase is spread away, as in the following examples from James, we may close the noun phrase and have to reopen it as we encounter the prepositional phrase:

(8)   The perception of this became as a symbol for Densher of the whole pitch, so far as Densher himself might be concerned, of his visit.

[James, *WOD*, II. 297]

(9)   but he saw with it, straightway, that she was as admirably true as ever to her instinct—which was a system as well—of not admitting the possibility between them of small resentments. . . .

[James, *WOD*, II. 313]

(10) The court was large and open, full of revelations, for our friend, of the habit of privacy, the peace of intervals, the dignity of distances and approaches. . . .

[James, *AMB*, 145]

All of these nouns (*symbol, instinct, revelations*) are complement-taking, much as transitive verbs are, so that, perceiving them, one might scan ahead a bit looking for a possible complement. In the last two examples (9, 10), the scan is completed after just a few words, but the nine words intervening between the noun and its complement in (8) make it more attractive to close the noun phrase after the noun. That is, (8) should be the easiest to misperceive. (A similar problem occurs in example [9] of Chapter Four.)

Line division in Milton can also be a source of "premature closure" of a noun phrase since, as Milton warns us in the first line of *Paradise Lost*, he will split a noun + prepositional complement across two lines:

Of Mans First Disobedience and the Fruit
Of that Forbidden Tree . . .

The effect of this practice is more a double-take than confusion of any duration. In general, line ends probably do affect our perception of phrase groupings (and clause boundaries)—as usual, they are mainly noticeable when they do not work right (i.e., when they do not fall at a phrase or clause boundary). Many literary critics have noted particular instances of tricky enjambment.[4] The same sort of considerations apply to line medial caesura: one can expect a phrase or clause boundary about the middle of the line (for many poets). This is a rather specialized topic, and I will not pursue it further here.[5]

Spreading a conjunct or prepositional phrase complement away from the initial element affects perception more than enjambment, however. Partly this is so because the preposition or conjunction is delayed. In general, a preposition or conjunction following a noun phrase can be taken to signal 'consider attaching me to the previous noun phrase', where one would check the prepositional phrase or coordinated noun phrase for semantic compatibility with the preceding noun phrase. Such a check is necessary, for the prepositional phrase could be an Adverbial rather than a noun phrase modifier, as in the examples of (11), or coordinate to an earlier noun phrase, as in (6).

(11) Everything *in fine* made her immeasurably new, and nothing so new as the old house and the old objects.... The interested influence *at any rate* had, as we say, gone straight to the point—

[James, *AMB*, 146–47]

Here *in fine* does not make a congruent modifier for *everything,* nor does *at any rate* make one for *the interested influence,* so we can reject that possibility and consider that the prepositional phrases are Adverbials. The sequence ... NP — PP ... is very common, and we must have some such device for determining whether the two should be grouped as one phrase or not. Separating them by an amount of material sufficient to make 'look ahead' or 'look back' difficult in checking for compatibility will make them hard to process. Spread conjuncts present extra difficulties when the second conjunct could be coordinate to something in the intervening (i.e., 'spreading') material, as in (6), where *and* in *and the rank smell ...* sends us looking back to the left, checking first the immediately preceding noun phrase *an idle boy* (no good), then perhaps *a flat limber stick* (also no good), then *the loud cloudy flutter ...,* which is not so obviously incompatible with *the rank smell....* We can call this sort of initially plausible but incorrect alternative a *garden path* (see below, sec. 3). There are no tempting false alternatives in the cases of (8–10), and this is why (6) is much harder than any of (8–10).

We can summarize this section by saying that a writer who spreads conjuncts and complements from heads forces greater reliance on look-ahead and on semantic compatibility testing; writers who spread them over a considerable distance strain the reader;

and writers who intersperse other nouns which are semantically possible as heads run a serious risk of being misperceived.

2. SUBJECTS AND OBJECTS

Assuming that the phrases have been identified, their function must be assigned. Here, as noted, the position of noun phrases is a primary clue: the canonical order is Subject—Verb—(Object), and hence we can generally assign the first noun phrase preceding the verb the Subject function according to the scheme given above. There is, however, the possibility of the so-called Topicalized order, where an Object, or complement of a Preposition, is shifted to the front of the sentence, giving the ordering

$$NP - NP - V \ldots \text{(Prep)} \ldots$$

(12) *What had suddenly set them into livelier motion* she hardly knew. . . .
[James, *POL*, II. 188]

(13) the wilderness closed behind his entrance as it had opened momentarily to accept him, opening before his advancement as it closed behind his progress; *no fixed path* the wagon followed but a channel non-existent ten yards ahead of it and ceasing to exist ten yards after it had passed. . . .

[Faulkner, p. 231]

This order is fairly rare in Stevens, James, and Faulkner, but is quite common in Spenser and Milton. One way to process such a sequence is to set a strategy triggered by seeing a second noun phrase before the verb. This strategy would identify the second noun phrase as the Subject of the verb and hold the first until we find the site it was removed from (either the Verb is transitive and lacks its Object, or a preposition will be lacking its complement). This we schematize as

If: NP — NP — V . . .
then: (O)   S

(This is a modification of Bever's Strategy J in "Cognitive Basis," p. 337). Spenser and Milton sometimes prepose an infinitive, which is eligible as a Subject, so the recognition of a second noun phrase before the verb must trigger a similar strategy putting the initial infinitive on hold for matching to its site later:

(14)   To suffer, as to doe,
       Our strength is equal, . . .

[Milton, *PL*, II. 199–200]

(15)   him to unthrone we then
       May hope. . . .

[Milton, *PL*, II. 231–32]

(16) That hand or foot to stirre he stroue in vaine:

[Spenser, *FQ*, I.i. 18]

(17) That which of them to take, in diuerse doubt they been.

[Spenser, *FQ*, I.i. 10]

Note that (17) may be a little harder to perceive than the others because we are made to wait longer before getting the second noun phrase (*they*), which signals that the initial infinitive is not the Subject. This indeed may be the functional explanation of the fact I have elsewhere observed[6] that when Object and Adverbial are both shifted to the front, the Adverbial in the great majority of cases precedes the Object (A O S V): the signal that the first noun phrase may be an Object is the presence of a second noun phrase immediately following. Also, of course, if the Adverbial were a prepositional phrase and followed the Object (O A S V), one might mistake the Adverbial as a complement of the Object noun phrase, as in the following example:

(18) And that new creature borne without her dew,
       Full of the makers guile, with vsage sly
       He taught to imitate that Lady trew,

[Spenser, *FQ*, I.i. 46]

With vsage sly can be taken as modifying *that new creature,* but may also be taken to modify *taught* or *imitate.* Usually, however, the Adverbial is incongruent as a modifier of the noun phrase, and this misperception would be quickly rejected on semantic grounds:

(19) The holy Saints of their rich vestiments
    He did disrobe,

[Spenser, *FQ,* I.iii. 17]

The notion of holding an element until we find the site need not be taken too literally: the sense of the process is that we must find the governing element or phrase that the initial element is in construction with: it is not necessary to assume that we 'move it back' to where it would have been, though I do assume that we notice 'something missing' following a preposition or transitive verb. In these sentences with initial infinitives (13–16), we are looking for verbs or nouns that will take an infinitive complement and find them in *hope, stroue,* and *doubt* (and, with a little forcing, *equal*).

In the case of the construction Ross has called "Left-Dislocation," the Subject, Object, or complement of a preposition is moved to the left and a definite noun or pronoun appears in its 'original' place. Perceiving these correctly does not involve perception of a 'hole' but rather matching the shifted Object with the nominal or pronominal place-holder. Most commonly it is the Subject that is dislocated to the left, as in these examples (the place-holder is italicized):

(20) That cunning Architect of cancred guile,
    Whom Princes late displeasure left in bands,
    For falsed letters and suborned wile,
    Soone as the Redcrosse knight he vnderstands
    To beene departed out of Eden lands,
    To serue againe his soueraine Elfin Queene,
    His artes *he* moues, and out of caytiues hands
    Himselfe he frees by secret meanes vnseene;

[Spenser, *FQ,* II.i. 1]

(21)   To bow and sue for grace
    With suppliant knee, and deify his power

> Who from the terror of this Arm so late
> Doubted his Empire, *that* were low indeed,
> *That* were an ignominy and shame beneath
> This downfall;

> [Milton, *PL*, I. 111–16]

(22) That he was prepared to be vague to Waymarsh about the hour of the ship's touching, and that he both wanted extremely to see him and enjoyed extremely the duration of delay—*these things*, it is to be conceived, were early signs in him that his relation to his actual errand might prove none of the simplest.

> [James, *AMB*, 18]

Objects, however, can also be left-dislocated:

(23) All strength—all terror, single or in bands,
That ever was put forth in personal form—
Jehovah—with his thunder, and the choir
Of shouting Angels, and the empyreal thrones—
I pass *them* unalarmed.

> [Wordsworth, *Works*, V. 3–4.]

Although, technically, correct perception in these cases involves perception of coreference between the fronted Object and the place-holder, I do not think these are perceived by the usual process of determining coreference, but rather along lines similar to the ones under consideration for identifying the function of initial noun phrases: one has an 'extra' noun phrase and is looking for a 'place' to put it, which in this case is filled by the coreferring noun or pronoun. We might then elaborate our scheme to:

$$\text{If:} \quad \text{NP} - \text{NP} - \text{V} \dots \left\{ \begin{array}{c} \emptyset \\ \text{def} \\ \text{pro} \end{array} \right\}_i \dots$$

then: O   S

What is difficult about the following passage from Spenser's "Prothalamium" (cited by Paul Alpers[7]) is that the identical noun phrase is not exactly identical, and the effort of perceiving it as the 'hole' for the fronted noun phrase is unusually great:

(24) When I whom sullein care,
   Through discontent of my long fruitlesse stay
   In Princes Court, and expectation vayne
   Of idle hopes, which still doe fly away,
   Like empty shaddowes, did aflict *my brayne*,
   Walkt forth to easy my payne....

[Spenser, "Prothal.," 5–10]

The fronted Object is in this case the relative pronoun *whom*, which is a subpart of *my brayne* (i.e., *whom* = "I").

Note by the way that left-dislocated constructions are commonly said to be non-standard (*My brother in St. Louis, he got laid off.*) but the perceptual motive for them is clear: the Subject noun phrase becomes so complex and unwieldy and so separated from the main verb by modifiers that it seems best to indicate again its place in the sentence when the main sentence is resumed.

Identifying the function of initial noun phrases in Milton and Spenser is again more complicated because they also allow the order Subject—Object—Verb, so that the modified serial-ordering strategy described above will not work. That is, an NP — NP — V sequence could be either Subject—Object or Object—Subject. It turns out, however, that Spenser and Milton provide a pronominal clue in most O S V cases. That is, either the first noun phrase or the second is a personal pronoun, which, being marked for case, makes identification of functions easy. The following illustrate:

(25)   Him the Almighty Power
   Hurld headlong flaming from th' Ethereal Skie...

[Milton, *PL*, I. 44–45]

(26) For whose sweete sake that glorious badge he wore,...

[Spenser, *FQ*, I.i.2]

(27) For her he hated as the hissing snake ,...

[Spenser, *FQ*, I.ii.9]

Either the first or the second noun phrase is a case-marked personal pronoun in 77 percent of the instances of O S V order in the first three cantos of *The Faerie Queene* (60 of 78 occurrences) and in 78 percent of the instances (18 of 23) in the same number of lines from the beginning of *Paradise Lost*. The minority of cases where there is no pronominal clue is fairly substantial, and we would like to know whether there is any strategy that would help discriminate the O S V from the S O V cases beyond that of semantic compatibility since semantic clues are not always available: in the next four examples, the verbs do not select one noun phrase or the other as their Subjects or Objects:

(28) Then seemed him his Lady by him lay,
     And to him playnd, how that false winged boy,
     Her chast hart had subdewd, to learne Dame Pleasures toy.
                                                [Spenser, *FQ*, I.i. 47]

Here the verb *subdew* takes an animate Subject and Object, so that *boy* and *hart* are each possible as Subject or Object. Reading forward, however, we see an infinitive complement (*to learne Dame Pleasures toy*), and the logical Subject of *learne* must be her heart (since the false winged boy is already an adept). If we decide that *subdew* is being used like *coerce* or *induce*, then the Subject of *learn* must be the Object of *subdew* and the Subject of *subdew* must be *boy*. This reading makes sense in the context of her lying down beside the knight and "playning"—indeed, given the scene, we probably do not even consider the other possible reading. Similarly in (29), either *Vna* or *Archimag* could be semantically congruent as the Object of *seek:*

(29) And in the way, as shee did weepe and waile,
     A knight her met in mighty armes embost,
     Yet knight was not for all his bragging bost,
     But subtill Archimag, that Vna sought
     By traynes into new troubles to haue tost:
                                                [Spenser, *FQ*, I.iii. 24]

In context, however, we know enough of the characters of Una and Archimago to reject immediately the possibility that Una is seeking to toss Archimago into new troubles. These two examples provide illustrations of Bever's point that information from context will facilitate perception even when the inherent semantic properties of the nouns and verbs are not sufficiently obvious to identify their functions.

No such ready contextual clues are available in the next two examples and consequently it is harder to identify the Subjects and Objects of *bereaue* in (30) and *riue* in (31):

(30) Your owne deare sake forst me at first to leaue
My Fathers kingdome, There she stopt with teares;
Her swollen hart her speach seemd to bereaue,

[Spenser, *FQ*, I.i. 52]

(31) Who threat wondrous wroth, the sleeping spark
Of natiue vertue gan eftsoones reuiue,
And at his haughtie helmet making mark,
So hugely stroke, that it the steele did riue,
And cleft his head.

[Spenser, *FQ*, I.ii. 19]

Upon consideration one concludes that, in (30), her stopping means that her speech has been bereft and infers that her heart is swollen with grief; hence *her swollen hart* must be the Subject of *bereaue*, *her speach* the Object. In (31) we must decide what *it* and *the steele* refer to in order to decide which is more congruent as the Subject of *riue*. One might try to get *stroke* as the antecedent of *it* (as an unexpressed cognate Object of *strike*: strike a stroke), taking *the steele* to refer to his helmet, but, on further reflection, I decide that *it* refers instead to *helmet* (and is Object) and *the steele* refers to his sword (and is Subject): I do not know whether knights in Faery Land have steel helmets, but I do strongly associate *the steele* with swords (as in "four inches of cold steel in the guts"). In this last example, and perhaps in the previous one, normal, rapid perception breaks down, and we must adopt a problem-solving routine, consciously considering alternative possibilities.

There is, however, a further sort of clue that we can make use of

in discriminating the O S V from S O V sequences when pronominal clues are absent. This clue is based on the relation of the clause
to its context and thus involves processing of a somewhat different
order, which we will take up in Chapter VI, but I will introduce the
relevant notion here, for I think this is a point at which comprehension and perception intersect. The clue can be developed from the
principle that the beginning of a clause (the "theme" or "frame"—
see Clark and Clark, pp. 34f.) is generally expectable information,
and the fronting of an Object is governed by this constraint. Hence
if we suspect that an initial noun phrase is a fronted Object (because it is semantically unlikely as a Subject), we may identify it as
such if it is not novel—i.e., if it is relatively expectable in the context. Examples will follow momentarily, but first a general definition of expectability is in order. The basic notion is simply that the
scene and matter under discussion give rise to a set of expectations
on the reader's part about what might be mentioned next. This set
includes the individual most recently mentioned (which could appear as a definite pronoun or noun phrase in the new sentence),
other individuals already mentioned (which might appear as demonstrative noun phrases), parts of things already mentioned, and
other things customarily linked to the things mentioned such as
purposes, instruments, and results of actions (murder→ motive,
weapon, etc.).[8] Following are six examples of this latter type of
expectable theme:

(32)   Who all this while with charmes and hidden artes,
       Had made a Lady of that other Spright,
       And fram'd of liquid ayre her tender partes,
       So liuely and so like in all mens sight,
       That *weaker sence* it could haue rauisht quight:

[Spenser, *FQ*, I.i.45]

What is being described is a luscious image which is being fash-
ioned by the evil Archimago to tempt and delude the hero. In
Renaissance psychology the target of such titillating sensation is

the faculty of sense, which is weaker than the will. Hence one can expect *weaker sence* in the context of temptation.

(33) Her neather partes misshapen, monstruous,
    Were hidd in water, that I could not see,
    But they did seeme more foule and hideous,
    Then *womans shape* man would beleeue to bee.

                                         [Spenser, *FQ*, I.ii.41]

This is part of a description of a naked witch, concentrating on the parts which would most identify her as a woman, hence *womans shape* is anything but novel. The next two examples introduce a particular aspect of what is being generally discussed:

(34)   She of nought affrayd,
    Through woods and wastnesse wide him daily sought;
    Yet *wished tydings* none of him vnto her brought.

                                     [Spenser, *FQ*, I.iii. 3]

(35)   Dark'n'd so, yet shon
    Above them all th' Arch-Angel: but *his face*
    Deep scars of Thunder had intrencht, . . .

                                   [Milton, *PL*, I. 599–601]

In (34), if she is seeking him, then one expects her to wish tidings of him—*wished tydings* are a particular aspect of her search. Similarly in (35), the shift to *his face* is a shift to a particular aspect of the appearance of the Arch-Angel. The next two examples involve a different sort of refocusing on the general topic which may have gotten lost in the preceding particulars:

(36) Regions of sorrow, doleful shades, where peace
    And rest can never dwell, hope never comes
    That comes to all; but torture without end
    Still urges, and a fiery Deluge, fed
    With ever-burning Sulphur unconsum'd:
    Such place Eternal Justice had prepar'd
    For those rebellious. . . .

                                     [Milton, *PL*, I. 65–71]

(37) *Warr* therefore, open or conceal'd, alike
    My voice disswades;

                            [Milton, *PL*, II. 187–88]

In none of these examples does the italicized noun phrase introduce an entirely new or novel (i.e., unexpected) entity. The 'marked' or stylistically unusual fronting of an Object in these examples (and see [12–19]) seems to correlate with this sort of refocusing on one aspect of the matter at hand.

If indeed this is the way a particular writer is using the O S V order, then we can refine our basic strategy for annotating the two noun phrases before a verb by placing the condition on the first noun phrase that to be identified as an Object, it must not only be incompatible as a Subject but must not be novel as well. Schematically,

If: NP — NP — V . . .
and: -S   (on compatibility check)
and: -novel
then: O   S

Note that this strategy will not incorrectly identify the S O V examples (28–30) as O S V unless they meet the conditions of the strategy. It will not apply in (28) and (29) because they do not meet the first condition (-S): in (28), *that false winged boy* may well be the Subject of *subdewd*; in (29), *that* as a relative pronoun could be the Subject of *sought*. In (30), however, *her swollen hart* seems unlikely as the Subject of *bereaue* and is scarcely novel, given that she is weeping, so the line satisfies the requirements of this strategy, which then assigns *her swollen hart* the Object function, *her speach* the Subject function—and we misperceive the clause. I do find (30) easy to misperceive, and this is evidence that I must be employing some such strategy as this one.

An extension of this strategy is warranted for Milton, who uses the order O V S rather more often than Spenser or most writers. Needless to say, such ordering would be very likely to be misperceived as S V O unless it were marked in some way. Some instances are marked by a pronoun, as, for example,

(38) And him thus answer'd soon his bold Compeer.
[Milton, *PL*, I. 127, see also I. 238]

In most other cases, the initial noun phrase is highly marked as theme:

(39) *That Glory* never shall his wrath or might
Extort from me.

[Milton, *PL*, I. 110–11]

(40)   *that proud honour* claim'd
Azazel as his right, a Cherube tall:

[Milton, *PL*, I. 533–34]

Note too that on a quick check for semantic compatibility the verbs pretty clearly signal that the initial noun phrases are not their Subjects. One might suppose that the dual perception of the first noun phrase as an unlikely Subject and as a possible theme would trigger the assignment of Object to it. The scheme is identical to the preceding one, except that the linear input has the second noun phrase following the verb:

If: NP — V — NP
and -S   (on compatibility check)
and: -novel
then: O   S

We are now in a position to explain a passage from Spenser that intrigued William Empson (*Ambiguity*, p. 208) (the passage overlaps two stanzas):

(41) And at the point two stings in-fixed arre,
Both deadly sharpe, that sharpest steele exceeden farre.

12

But stings and sharpest steele did far exceed
The sharpnesse of his cruell rending clawes;
Dead was it sure, as sure as death in deed,

> What euer thing does touch his rauenous pawes,
> Or what within his reach he euer drawes.
>
> [Spenser, *FQ*, I.xi. 11–12]

On semantic grounds, the clause beginning stanza 12 could be S V O or O V S. On interpretive grounds, however, the passage seems to be trying to set up a series of increasingly sharp and menacing things (*steel-sting-claws*), the continuation suggesting that the last is the worst. This works syntactically if we allow the interpretation to impose the propositional structure O V S. Note that the O (*stings and sharpest steele*) is a good example of expectable theme here. (Empson's difficulties were enhanced by an apparent corruption in his text, which had *exceedeth* in place of *exceeden*—singular instead of plural agreement—which made it appear to him on first reading that *sharpest steele* had to be the Subject of *exceedeth*—since *two stings* looks plural—and hence that steel was sharper than the stings, getting the order of ascending sharpness off to a bad start.)

Such a perceptual strategy assumes that an O V S sequence would have a thematizing motive, and this it very clearly does in Milton. I can find no instances of O V S order where the initial noun phrase is not an obvious, expectable theme. This is a remarkable fact and should be pursued a little further in relation to the more numerous O S V constructions. Even when pronominal clues are available in Milton, a fronted Object is usually expectable information if one is reading closely and informedly enough. I will consider a few of the less obvious examples:

(42) [context: description of Satan's shield]
> *His Spear*, to equal which the tallest Pine
> Hewn on Norwegian hills, to be the Mast
> Of some great Ammiral, were but a wand,
> He walkt with to support uneasie steps. . . .
>
> [Milton, *PL*, I. 292–95]

Here the pronominal clue (*he*) is delayed so long as to render it useless (as also in [45]). In a conventional epic description of a hero—which Milton is evoking and parodying—description of the hero's spear is highly to be expected. In the next example, a view of human history is assumed, making the fronted Object expected (*they* = the fallen angels):

(43) Nor had they yet among the Sons of Eve
Got them new Names, till wand'ring ore the Earth,
Through Gods high sufferance for the tryal of man,
By falsities and lyes *the greatest part*
Of Mankind they corrupted. . . .

[Milton, *PL*, I. 364–68]

The greatest part of mankind is of course linked to *the tryal of man* and is expectable given what we 'know' of how the trial turned out. Occasionally Milton will treat particular facts of biblical history as known in the sense that the theme is expectable, but only if you know the story (here *I Kings* xi. 7; *he*=Moloch):

(44)   Nor content with such
Audacious neighbourhood, *the wisest heart*
Of Solomon he led by fraud to build
His Temple right against the Temple of God. . . .

[Milton, *PL*, I. 399–402]

This sort of drawing on knowledge of Scripture (and classical mythology in other cases) is typical of Milton. Spenser also normally fronts Objects which are expectable, though we need less erudition not to be surprised by them. This is an interesting contrast. Spenser draws on an elaborated and complex body of knowledge (Arthurian romance and allegory), but it remains in the background as a kind of superstructure (e.g., Knight of Holiness = Red Crosse Knight = St. George/ wears armour of faith . . . .), where Milton insists on explicit connection. Thus where *The Faerie Queene* seems richly allusive and open-ended, *Paradise Lost* seems all encompassing and containing. In general, then, it is often interesting to ask, when encountering a fronted Object, "How is this expectable, given what I have already comprehended?" We will examine several further cases involving this sort of compatibility of material with its context in Chapter VI.

Perceptual strategies, we have postulated, are useful for making quick decisions on limited information. As noted above, a pronominal clue delayed too long can come too late. This may explain why I fairly consistently misperceive the next example even though I do eventually get to the pronominal clue of *he*:

(45)   There *the companions of his fall,* o'rewhelm'd
        With Floods and Whirlwinds of tempestuous fire,
        He soon discerns, and welt'ring by his side
        One next himself in power, and next in crime,
        Long after known in Palestine, and nam'd
        Beelzebub.

                                        [Milton, *PL,* I. 76–81]

The *there* may also be part of the problem: it appears to be the theme, the verb is quite far away for checking compatibility, there is only one theme per sentence, the noun phrase following *there* (*companions*) therefore is unlikely to be a thematized Object, so I assign it the tentative function of Subject (erring). (Note by the way the split Object: *companions + one next himself.*)

We have thus considered four kinds of strategies for identifying Subjects and Objects: strategies based on serial order, on pronominal clues, on semantic compatibility (enriched by context), and on perception of theme. Each has its limitations. I have described them working in concert in certain ways, but they are probably not all equally important: the absence of semantic clues seems to be the most fertile source of serious perceptual difficulty. We have also begun to see the importance of 'look ahead' to the material following the initial noun phrase (is it a noun? a pronoun?) and to the main verb to check whether the first noun phrase is semantically compatible with the verb as its Subject. In the next section we will see why finding the main verb is not always easy.

3. MAIN VERBS

Thus far I have been assuming that the main verb at least could be readily identified. There are two situations, however, which render recognition of the main verb difficult. The first is when the Subject is followed by a participial clause where the participle is identical to the past tense of the verb. In all the examples following, the italicized form appears to be a main verb:

(46)   As when the potent Rod
Of Amrams son in Egypts evill day
Wav'd round the Coast, up call'd a pitchy cloud
Of Locusts, warping on the Eastern Wind,

[Milton, *PL*, I. 338–41]

(47) Say, Muse, thir Names then known, who first, who last,
Rous'd from the slumber, on that fiery Couch,
At thir great Emperors call, as next in worth
Came singly where he stood on the bare strand, ...

[Milton, *PL*, I. 376–79]

(48)   from the arched roof
Pendant by suttle Magic many a row
Of Starry Lamps and blazing Cressets *fed*
With Naphtha and Asphaltus yeilded light
As from a sky.

[Milton, *PL*, I. 726–29]

(49) a dimension free of both time and space, where once more the un-treed land *warped* and *wrung* to mathematical squares of rank cotton for the frantic old-world people to turn into shells to shoot at one another, would find ample room for both—

[Faulkner, p. 724]

(50) High broad clear—he was expert enough to make out in a moment that it was admirably built—it fairly embarrassed our friend by the quality that, as he would have said, it "sprang" on him. . . . but of what service was it to find himself making out after a moment that the quality *"sprung,"* the quality produced by measure and balance, the fine relation of part to part and space to space, was probably. . . .

[James, *AMB*, 69]

This sequence will turn up more in writers who use a lot of participials—as our writers do (there are other examples in Empson, pp. 76ff.). Such a sequence sets up what has come to be known as a *garden path*, though Henry Fowler had as good a term for it in *false scent:* "The laying of false scent, i.e., the causing of a reader to suppose that a sentence or part of one is taking a certain course, which he afterwards finds to his confusion that it does not take, is an obvious folly" (*Modern English Usage*, s.v. *false scent*). In psycholinguistic discussions, a garden path is considered a source of confusion or difficulty depending on how far it is pursued—how far from the main road one goes, hence how much one must retrace—and I will use the term *garden path* from here on because of this useful connotation.

Three or four considerations may function to indicate that a garden path is being pursued. First, one will scarcely get started on the path unless the Subject is semantically congruent as the 'Subject' of the putative main verb: the rod could wave in (46), the devils rouse in (47), but the lamps and cressets are unlikely to feed in (48), and the untreed land is an unlikely Warper and Wringer in (49). If the Subject passes this initial semantic screening, we may take the participial as the main verb, but if a 'second' verb follows hard upon the first, the recognition that the first is not in fact the main verb is fairly easy. This is the second consideration. So in (46), *up call'd* comes fairly quickly after *wav'd* and can trigger recognition that *wav'd* is not the main verb after all. Similarly in (48), *yeilded* comes fairly quickly after *fed*. But a long delay in getting to the true main verb like the one in (49) would allow the reader relying solely on this signal to go down quite a stretch of garden path. Third, the putative main verb will always be transitive and will always lack an Object; and noticing that it has no Object may trigger recognition that it is a (perfect, passive) participle. Fourth, if there is an Agent phrase with *by* or *with*, as in (48) and the second part of (50), it is a good clue that we have a participial, not a main verb. If one relied to some degree on all of these clues, (48) should be easier to perceive than (47).

Many things contribute to the difficulty in the next passage, but primary among them is the difficulty of spotting the Subject, Object, and verb because of the long and complex intervening material:

(51) Her sire Typhoeus was, who mad through merth,
   And drunke with bloud of men, slaine by his might,
   Through incest, her of his owne mother Earth
   Whilome begot, being but halfe twin of that berth.

[Spenser, *FQ*, III.vii. 47]

Even though *her* in the third line is obviously an Object, it is not easy to find the verb it should be matched to. One does not take *drunke* or *slaine* as the main verb, since *drunke* is obviously coordinate to *mad*, and *slaine* cannot be taken as past tense (*slew*)—one simply becomes uncertain when or whether one will ever reach a main verb. We depend so much on the verb to organize the sentence for us that when we must hold a Subject, three Adverbials, and an Object in mind before reaching the verb, we are in danger of 'losing the thread' entirely.

The second sort of mistake one can make concerning a main verb is to mistake an auxiliary for a main verb. Normally, auxiliaries immediately precede main verbs, and looking one word ahead (or two, if there is an adverb) suffices to reduce the first verb to auxiliary status. Two circumstances may separate the auxiliary from the main verb: for one, Milton and Spenser occasionally leave the auxiliary behind when they invert the verb and its Object. There is a kind of poetic constraint, however, that the verb normally goes to the end of the line, only very rarely beyond it, so that the look forward to check if there is a main verb yet to come is limited to a few words.[9] This general constraint also prevents problems like that in (51) where the verb is in the line following the one containing the Object. The second circumstance occurs when parenthetic material is inserted between the auxiliary and the main verb. Insertion in this position is a special preference of James in his later fiction. The material interposed is often of considerable length and complexity, as in the following examples, where we must wait quite a while to determine that the *have*s are auxiliaries but the forms of *be* are all main verbs:

(52) The principle I have just mentioned as operating had been, with the most newly disembarked of the two men, wholly instinctive....

[James, *AMB*, 17]

(53) Since, accordingly, at all events, he had had it from Mrs. Newsome that she had, at whatever cost to her more strenuous view, conformed in the matter of preparing Chad, wholly to his restrictions....

[James, *AMB*, 68]

(54) That note had been meanwhile—since the previous afternoon, thanks to this happier device—such a consciousness of personal freedom as he hadn't known for years....

[James, *AMB*, 17]

(55) But anything like his actual state he had not, as to the prohibition of impulse, accident, range—the prohibition, in other words, of freedom—hitherto known.

[James, *WOD*, II. 294]

(56) the quality "sprung," the quality produced by measure and balance, the fine relation of part to part and space to space, was probably—aided by the presence of ornament as positive as it was discreet, and by the complexion of the stone, a cold fair grey, warmed and polished a little by life—neither more nor less than a case of distinction....

[James, *AMB*, 69]

(57) but he had stolen away from every one alike, had kept no appointment and renewed no acquaintance, had been indifferently aware of the number of persons who esteemed themselves fortunate in being, unlike himself, "met," and had even independently, unsociably, alone, without encounter or repulse and by mere quiet evasion, given his afternoon and evening to the immediate and the sensible.

[James, *AMB*, 18]

One can test one's 'look-ahead' capacities on these examples. In cases like

(58) had been, he was quite aware, the first point. . . .

[James, *WOD*, II. 314]

(59) Poor Strether had at this very moment to recognise the truth. . . .

[James, *AMB*, 69]

it is perhaps possible to look ahead and across, and decide that the 'auxiliary' verb is in fact the main verb, but as the reader scans into a parenthesis like the ones in (54–57) he realizes that he must do something to avoid bogging down. He can skip ahead to the end of the parenthesis, since it is typographically marked, and promise himself to come back to the parenthesis after he has parsed the main clause, or he can put the parenthetical material into Short Term Memory as an unanalyzed chunk, or he can simply stop parsing the main sentence, process the parenthetical, and then return to the main sentence as close to the point where he left off as he can. I believe that I try each of these techniques at one time or another. The second, though the most mysterious to me, is one that might explain why sentences with two fairly long parentheses are much harder than those with one, as, for example, (53): there is 'room' in storage for one held parenthesis, but trying to put another one in before the first has been processed and removed is overcrowding. The density effect is particularly acute when the interrupting material is itself interrupted, as in the next two examples:

(60) What finally prevailed with him was the reflexion that, whatever might happen, the great man had, after that occasion at the palace, their young woman's brief sacrifice to society—and the hour of Mrs. Stringham's appeal had brought it well to the surface—shown him marked benevolence.

[James, *WOD*, II. 295–96]

(61) If she was different it was because they had chosen together that she should be, and she might now, as a proof of their wisdom, their success, of the reality of what had happened—of what in fact, for the

> spirit of each, was still happening—been showing it to him for pride.
> [James, *WOD*, II. 314]

Here the much discussed principle of self-interrupting processing seems to be involved. Roughly, the notion is that a perceptual process that is interrupted so that another instance of the same process can be executed will result in perceptual difficulty.[10] Whichever strategy the reader adopts will have to interrupt itself in these sequences. Note that the complexity of (61) is so great that James commits a very rare grammatical error—a *have* appears to have gotten lost.

One last, related perceptual difficulty is worth mention here. One cannot always be certain that a main verb will follow an auxiliary because the main verb may have been ellipsed under identity with the preceding main verb. Hence, when we read an auxiliary verb with no main verb in sight ahead, we may look back as well as (or instead of) forward to see if the previous verb could be plausibly inserted. This in fact is the correct solution in the latter portion of the following passage (the *cannot, can* part), but the 'main verbs' are tucked away in a relative clause and are hard to spot. The first part of the passage is a further example of the frustration of suspended *be,* and the whole thing is a nice little coda illustrating that a passage may be perfectly grammatical and in a certain sense quite simple but still be monstrously difficult to perceive if it baffles the strategies we try to apply. The passage is the beginning of a section of Samuel Beckett's *The Unnameable* (New York: Grove Press, 1970):

(62) I add this, to be on the safe side. These things I say, and shall say, if I can, are no longer, or are not yet, or never were, or never will be, or if they were, if they are, if they will be, were not here, are not here, will not be here, but elsewhere. But I am here. So I am obliged to add this. I who am here, who cannot speak, cannot think, and who must speak, and therefore perhaps think a little, cannot in relation only to me who am here, to here where I am, but can a little, sufficiently, I don't know how, unimportant, in relation to me who was elsewhere, who shall be elsewhere, and to those places where I was, where I shall be. [p. 18]

I have invoked the notion of limited look-ahead repeatedly in this chapter, and the examples do I think provide illustrations, not to say evidence, of its operation. It appears in the identification of phrase boundaries, in the recognition of a fronted Object, in the search for pronominal clues to assignment of Subject and Object, and to the assignment of auxiliary/main verb status to *have* and *be:* the longer an expected or needed clue is delayed, the more likely the reader is to slow down and adopt a deliberate problem-solving procedure, or simply to misperceive, arbitrarily choosing one path. Unfortunately, little is known about the limit of look-ahead—how fixed it is for an individual, or how it varies from individual to individual. No magical number exists, like George Miller's famous "seven plus or minus two" for the number of bits of information Short Term Memory can hold.[11] Still, the concept appears to have some value for predicting relative difficulty of perception.

A second general principle emerges from the discussions of passages in this chapter. One can call this the principle of functional compensation. Histories of English syntax often include the statement that word order (by which is meant, in part, order of Subject and Object) was 'freer' in Early Modern English, and we have seen many illustrations of that freedom in Spenser and Milton (it is a good bit freer in Milton's poetry than in his prose[12]). One would suppose, on the face of it, that Subjects and Objects would therefore be a great deal harder to perceive than they would be in texts of Modern English, but, as we have seen, the poets often provide a pronominal clue and restrict their freedom to the fronting of expectable elements. The point is that though some of the perceptual strategies the reader brings to the text may prove less reliable than usual, there are usually compensating strategies which he can develop. The sooner the reader learns to take the clues the text offers in place of the ones he expects, the sooner he will learn to read or 'get used to' the particular work.

CHAPTER TWO

Clause Boundaries

PSYCHOLINGUISTS have accumulated an impressive amount of evidence that the clause is a crucial unit of sentence processing. Once a clause is put together, it is removed from the immediate processing center, and material in it is no longer available for immediate recall. Again, the evidence has been nicely summarized in the surveys and continues to accumulate.[1] Research has concentrated on structural cues for clause boundaries, which will be discussed in the first section, and has largely ignored punctuation, which we will take up in the second section, particularly the much misunderstood semicolon. The third section will deal with perceiving boundaries between coordinate clauses. As in the previous chapter, we are concerned with the sources of perceptual complexity and the different types of strategies one might use to resolve them. We will add two new types of strategies to the repertoire: those based on punctuation and those based on parallelism.

1. STRUCTURAL CUES TO CLAUSE BOUNDARIES

The recognition of a clause is partly dependent on the recognition of the functional elements. We may not be sure whether we are reading a clause when we encounter the first noun phrase, but when we get to a main verb, we can be certain that we should be constructing a clause; similarly, if the verb is unequivocally transitive, or otherwise complement-taking, we will not close off the clause until we locate the Object or other complement—though once we have located the obligatory elements, we will close it off as quickly as we can. When a functionally complete (or apparently complete) clause aligns with a line boundary, the temptation to close the clause prematurely is even greater. Consider, for instance, these first lines from Shakespeare's *Sonnets* 15 and 33 cited by Stephen Booth:[2]

(1) Full many a glorious morning have I seen
     Flatter the mountain tops with sovereign eye

> [Shakespeare, *Son.* 33]

(2) When I consider everything that grows
     Holds in perfection but a little moment

> [Shakespeare, *Son.* 15]

The first line of (1) appears to be functionally complete when we get to the verb at the end of the line, which allows recognition of the initial noun phrase as a fronted Object, but the verb in the second clause forces reanalysis of it as the Subject of a clause, the entire contents of which are the Object of *seen*. Similarly in (2), lacking the complementizer *that*, we perceive *everything that grows* as the complete Object of *consider* and close off the clause, only to have to reanalyze it as the Subject of *holds*. To be sure, the garden path is very short in these cases and the perceptual effect a kind of double-take—I merely wish to show that apparent functional completeness combined with a line ending results in misperception.

It is not always obvious, however, that the verb is transitive, so the decision to treat it as such can depend on spotting a noun phrase likely to be its Object. Perhaps for this reason, insertion of adverbs or parenthetic material between the verb and its Object is generally felt to be awkward. Howsoever that may be, insertion in that position with a verb that is possibly intransitive will impede perception by promoting premature closure in just the way line ends do:

(3)   Each time she turned in again, each time, in her impatience, she gave him up, it was to sound to a deeper depth, while she tasted the faint, flat emanation of things, the failure of fortune and of honour.

                                                      [James, *WOD*, I. 3–4]

Sound could be intransitive (either "plunge" or "measure"), and it is not until we recognize that *the failure of fortune and of honour* is not really appositive to *the faint flat emanation of things*, but is in fact the Object of *sound*, that we are able to class *sound* as transitive. Further, a normally transitive verb can often occur with the Object ellipsed if it can be inferred from context, so that the absence of an Object does not automatically rule out the possibility that the verb is to be understood transitively. There is a rather unusual ellipsis of an Object in the next example:

(4)   He had already relinquished, of his will, because of his need, in humility and peace and without regret, yet apparently that had not been enough, the leaving of the gun was not enough.

                                                      [Faulkner, p. 243]

I experience an almost intolerable suspension following *relinquished* in searching for an Object which never comes. One further consideration is that certain orders of elements seem to be canonical for recognition. For example, if a verb takes an Object and an Adverbial, we expect the Object before the Adverbial, and will be inclined to close the clause after the Adverbial even if we have yet no Object (it might have been ellipsed). Here are two examples (omitting the well-known *Throw Mama from the train a kiss.*):

(5)   the planters with their gangs of slaves and then of hired laborers had wrested from the impenetrable jungle of water-standing cane and cyprus, gum and holly and oak and ash, cotton patches which, as the years passed, became fields and then plantations.

                                                    [Faulkner, pp. 710–11]

(6)   Shall she not find in comforts of the sun,
         In pungent fruit and bright, green wings, or else
         In any balm or beauty of the earth,
         Things to be cherished like the thought of heaven?

[Stevens, *CP*, 67]

In reading these, one tends to forget about the missing Object of *wrest* and *find*, reading the last noun phrase as appositive to the preceding. This misreading serves Stevens' purpose nicely (that is, *we* find them to be identical), and we might note that to unravel Faulkner's sentence (actually only the last part of a sentence) we must wrest the cotton patches from the preceding phrases. Similarly in the next three examples, once we complete the Adverbial and optional modifiers, we have a tendency to close the clause and be a little surprised by the Object (or Complement, in the case of [8]):

(7)   thir summons call'd
         From every Band and squared Regiment
         By place or choice the worthiest;

[Milton, *PL.*, I. 757–59]

The Regiment is not the worthiest—rather, the worthiest are called from every band and regiment.

(8)   [we are doomed] to remaine
         In strictest bondage, though thus far remov'd,
         Under th' inevitable curb, reserv'd
         His captive multitude:

[Milton, *PL.*, II. 320–23]

It is possible to read *his captive multitude* as appositive to *we*, but the sense is sharper as "remain. . . . reserved, his captive multitude."

(9)   his cousin McCaslin brought him for the first time to the camp, the big woods, to earn for himself from the wilderness the name and state of hunter. . . .

[Faulkner, p. 228]

With *earn*, as with *remaine*, one cannot be sure that an Object or Complement is to follow, and as the Adverbials accumulate, one begins to suspect not—and is slightly surprised when one does. It is important to note that interpolation of material between the verb and its Object does not necessarily produce perceptual difficulty. Such interpolations are characteristic of Joyce's style (or styles), for example, but, as Anthony Burgess notes in *Joysprick* (André Deutsch, 1973, p. 70), the interpolated matter is usually only an Adverb or a short phrase. As long as one can easily look across the material to check for an Object, interpolation of material between Verb and Object requires only a slight adjustment by the reader.

Certain forms, in general, indicate the beginning of a clause: nothing to the left of these forms is part of the clause initiated by the word. These forms include the subordinating conjunctions *if* and *when* and relative pronouns. John Robert Ross claims that a relative clause with an element shifted to the left of the clause is ungrammatical.[3] (Ross notes that we may regard the non-extractability of elements from adverbial clauses as coming under this constraint if we regard adverbial clauses as underlying relative clauses: *when* = at the time at which. . . .) However that may be, all of the following examples, culled from the early cantos of *The Faerie Queene*, are hard to perceive: we do not expect the italicized element to be part of the clause which follows and look in vain for a main verb after the subordinate clause to match with it:

(10)   . . . the labyrinth about;
      Which when by tract they hunted had throughout,
      At length it brought them to a hollow caue, . . .

                              [Spenser, *FQ*, I.i. 11]

(11) Deuoure their dam; on *whom* while so he gazd,
      Hauing all satisfide their bloudy thurst,
      Their bellies swolne he saw with fulnesse burst,
      And bowels gushing forth:

                              [Spenser, *FQ*, I.i. 26]

(12)   *of whose most innocent death*
      When tidings came to mee, vnhappy maid,
      O how great sorrow my sad soule assaid.

                              [Spenser, *FQ*, I.ii. 24]

(13) Like a young Squire, *in loues and lusty-hed*
    His wanton dayes that euer loosely led,
    Without regard of armes and dreaded fight:

                           [Spenser, *FQ*, I.ii. 3]

Note that the main source of difficulty is not that an Object or other argument is shifted to the left, since that occurs in Topicalized sentences—it is rather that our normal perceptual strategies are set not to integrate material outside a relative or adverbial clause into it or to seek missing phrases outside (i.e., to the left of) the relative pronoun or subordinating conjunction. There is an extra source of difficulty with these examples, however, which is that the subordinate clause is not obviously missing anything. Hence, should it occur to us that the relative pronoun does in fact belong in the clause, we cannot quickly see a place for it. This is most strikingly the problem in (12), where one must scratch one's head a bit before deciding that the fronted prepositional phrase is the complement of *tidings*, but it is also a problem in the others, where *gaze, hunt,* and *led* are not so obviously transitive as to attract the relative pronoun to them (actually, the *which* in [10] is probably the complement of *throughout*: "when by tract they had hunted throughout the labyrinth"). There are other examples at I.iii. 13 and 26. Contrast the following, where the verbs are obviously transitive or otherwise complement-seeking:

(14) That none did others safety despize,
    Nor aid enuy to him, *in need* that stands,
    But friendly each did others prayse deuize, . . .

                           [Spenser, *FQ*, I.ix. 1]

(15) The fift had charge sicke persons to attend,
    And comfort those, *in point of death* which lay;

                           [Spenser, *FQ*, I.x. 41]

(16) *Which* when the valiant Elfe perceiu'd, be lept
    As Lyon fierce vpon the flying pray,

                           [Spenser, *FQ*, I.i. 17]

(17) His forces faile, ne can no longer fight.
      Whose corage when the feend perceiu'd to shrinke,
      She poured forth out of her hellish sinke
      Her fruitfull cursed spawne of serpents small,

[Spenser, *FQ*, I.i. 22]

(18) *Which* when he saw, he burnt with gealous fire

[Spenser, *FQ*, I.ii. 5]

Stands in (14) and *lay* in (15) attract the preposed Adverbial to them, and *perceiue* and *see* attract the preposed Objects in (16–18). In (19) there is a special difficulty: *attaine* is obligatorily transitive, but it is incongruous to attain a person:

(19) To seeke *her strayed Champion*, if she might attaine.

[Spenser, *FQ*, I.iii. 8]

I have spent so much time on this particular construction because of its theoretical interest: it is probably ungrammatical and certainly rare in most reader's experience, so that readers presumably have no existing strategy for coping with it and a bias against it, but it is so common in Spenser that one must work out some strategy for it. If the reader does in fact find (14–18) easier than (10–13), he probably is adapting the strategy for identifying fronted elements outlined in the last chapter.

Spenser, by the way, so frequently inverts *to* + *verb* with its Object or an Adverbial that the usual function of *to* to signal the beginning of an infinitival Verb Phrase is virtually nullified:

(20) At last resoluing forward still to fare

[Spenser, *FQ*, I.i. 11]

(21) Therewith enrag'd she loudly gan to bray,
      And turning fierce, her speckled taile aduanst,
      Threatning her angry sting, him to dismay:

[Spenser, *FQ*, I.i. 17]

This case differs somewhat from the previous one in that the reader may well possess some perceptual principle for inserting material that appears before the *to* into the phrase following it, since one way not to 'split' an infinitive is to place the adverb before the *to*. In Spenser, we have only to add Objects to the list of things that can precede the *to*. The strain on perception is further mitigated by the fact that the material shifted out of the infinitival Verb Phrase is always shifted just to the immediate left of the *to*, or in the case of (20), one word over.[4]

Most of the last ten examples are noticeably harder to process than the initial set of ten. This is so, I think, because the first examples have mainly to do with premature closure of a clause rather than a radically false parsing involving misidentification of functions. One gets what appears to be a complete, well-formed clause, and correction of the error usually involves adding material to the preliminary structure rather than recasting it. The latter examples from Spenser involve a perceptual difficulty of an entirely different nature—namely, one cannot see how to construe the pieces into a clause at all. The experience is one of bafflement, not of committing a mistake that requires slight correction. We will examine the two other types and grades of difficulty in the next sections: the following section will examine uses of the semicolon that mislead by signaling that a clause is complete—the problem for perception is realizing that an apparent main clause is not independent of one that it precedes or follows but is dependent on it. This realization involves no restructuring of the basic clauses and is thus like the premature closure examples of this section. In the third section, however, we consider constructions where noun phrases appear to be part of one clause but are actually part of another: correction of such misperceptions does involve a major restructuring, and the examples do seem to be more difficult.

2. PUNCTUATION AS A CLUE TO CLAUSE BOUNDARIES

In the most general terms, marks of punctuation are used in writing to indicate groupings and closures of various types. Typically, different marks can be used to indicate the same syntactic boundary; for example, complete main clauses may be separated by a period, a dash, a colon, a semicolon, or a comma (plus a conjunction). Choice of mark in such cases conveys 'degree' of separation or integration of the clauses as units of comprehension: using a semicolon instead of a period, for example, suggests greater integration or cohesion between the material in the two clauses; use of a colon indicates an even tighter and more specific kind of integration (the second clause is a specification of, or [in my usage] a consequence of the previous clause); the dash indicates a discontinuity in the line of thought—possibly interrupting the main clause—though one that is prompted by the preceding clause. The degree of syntactic integration is the same in all of these cases—each clause must be a complete, main (i.e., not subordinate) clause—but the degree of cohesion differs in ways that would be signaled in speech by intonation (fall or half-fall or level) and pause. This function of punctuation, sometimes called 'rhetorical,' is not opposed to its function of marking syntactic boundaries and is in a sense based on it: a mark of a relatively light syntactic boundary (such as a comma) would never indicate a rhetorical separation greater than a mark of a heavier syntactic boundary (such as a semicolon) where both are possible. Thus the notion put forth by various critics that punctuation is either rhetorical or 'logical' (syntactic) is over-simplified from its outset. This dichotomy would hold only if there were some use of punctuation where each mark indicated a certain syntactic boundary uniquely: that would be a truly syntactic system. Marks in such a system would be very good clues to syntactic boundaries. In regard to real punctuation, we can say that a mark is useful as the basis of a perceptual strategy insofar as it regularly marks the same syntactic boundary.

Few marks of punctuation are as reliable a mark of a main clause boundary as the semicolon: most modern grammar books give the very simple and straightforward advice to use it to separate complete main clauses and only main clauses. However, reading the following passage by T. S. Eliot with this function of the semicolon in mind produces problems:

(22) Donne, I suppose, was such another,
Who found no substitute for sense;
To seize and clutch and penetrate,
Expert beyond experience,

He knew the anguish of the marrow
The ague of the skeleton;
No torments possible to flesh
Allayed the fever of the bone.

["Whispers of Immortality" cited
in Empson, *Ambiguity*, p. 79.]

The semicolon at the end of the second line signals the end of a complete clause, forcing us to find a place for the infinitive of purpose in the third line in the clause that follows it. Empson fits it in as the complement of *expert* (i.e., "expert at seizing, etc."), or it could be fitted in as the complement of *anguish* (i.e., "the anguish to seize and clutch"—which is rather nice, except for the *ague*). Neither parsing yields a perfectly idiomatic sentence, and Empson notes that the third line could go semantically with the second— the semicolon is the barrier. Interestingly, in the *Collected Poems, 1909–62* (Harcourt, Brace, and World, 1963), the semicolon does appear after the third line rather than the second, thus obviating the need for Mr. Empson's ingenuity and my own. Essentially, the semicolon in modern texts indicates that one main clause has been completed and another is about to commence. Hence what follows the semicolon cannot be subordinate to what precedes (or vice-versa) or appositive to it—rather, it must be construed as part of a new clause. The next examples suggest that in reading James, we must lower this expectation slightly:

(23) It was at this point, however, that she remained; changing her place, moving from the shabby sofa to the armchair upholstered in a glazed

cloth that gave at once—she had tried it—the sense of the slippery and of the sticky.

[James, *WOD*, I, 3]

(24) He pulled himself then at last together for his own progress back; not with the feeling that he had taken his walk in vain.

[James, *AMB*, 67]

The modification we must make when reading James is that what follows the semicolon may be some sort of loosely attached participial or supplemental clause or phrase, not another main clause, but we can at least rely on the material preceding the semicolon being a complete main clause. (Note by the way in [23] the parenthetical "—she had tried it—" splitting a verb and its Object: the sentence is easy to misread, since *gave* can be taken here as intransitive ["She tried the armchair and it gave at once"]. The optional Adverbial following *gave* also helps to induce this premature closure.) What makes these examples vexing, particularly (23), is the amount of time the reader can pursue the garden path assumption that a Subject and verb are yet to come. The next three examples are even worse, since what follows the semicolon is a noun phrase which apparently is the Subject of the next main clause—we search and search for the main verb:

(25)   He bad awake blacke Plutoes griesly Dame,
       And cursed heauen, and spake reprochfull shame
       Of highest God, the Lord of life and light;
       A bold bad man, that dar'd to call by name
       Great Gorgon, Prince of darkenesse and dead night,
       At which Cocytus quakes, and Styx is put to flight.

[Spenser, *FQ*, I.i. 37]

(26)   He scarce had ceas't when the superiour Fiend
       Was moving toward the shoar; his ponderous shield
       Ethereal temper, massy, large and round,
       Behind him cast; the broad circumference
       Hung on his shoulders like the Moon. . . .

[Milton, *PL*, I. 283–87]

This last one is frustrating because we can almost wrestle the material following the first semicolon into a clause, especially if we assume an ellipsed *he* ("he cast his shield behind him"), but there is no conjunction linking the two 'clauses', and it is therefore more regular grammatically to take *cast* as a participle, not a main verb ("his shield cast behind him").

(27) At first they had come in wagons: the guns, the bedding, the dogs, the food, the whiskey, the keen heart-lifting anticipation of hunting; the young men who could drive all night and all the following day in the cold rain and pitch a camp in the rain and sleep in the wet blankets and rise at daylight the next morning and hunt.

[Faulkner, p. 706]

After the fact, we can recognize the semicolon here as obeying the 'rule of weight'—*the young men . . .* is to be taken as appositive to the entire preceding series, and since that series is punctuated with commas, the next heavier mark must be used. But as we read, the semicolon looks like a clause boundary. Consider as a final example (28):

(28) She was handsome, but the degree of it was not sustained by items and aids; a circumstance moreover playing its part at almost any time in the impression she produced.

[James, *WOD*, I. 5]

It might be more obvious that the material following the semicolon depends upon the clause preceding it rather than initiating a new clause if it were clearer what *a circumstance* referred to.

It would appear, then, that we should not conclusively close off the first clause and open a new clause when we reach a semicolon, for the material following the semicolon may have to be integrated back into the first clause. Either we might check the material following the semicolon for completeness as a clause before clearing the first clause, or we might check the material for possible attachment to the first clause as we read (this would work well in [23] and [24], a little less well in [28]).

Whatever procedure we adopt, we will have to use it more when we read texts of Spenser and Milton with original punctuation, for they frequently use semicolons between main and subordinate clauses. As long as the beginning of the subordinate clause indicates that it is subordinate, however, the semicolon preceding it will not be too misleading. Usually subordinators do begin conditional clauses (*if*), comparative and result clauses (*as, so*) purpose (*for, to*), temporal (*when, till*), and relative clauses (the relative pronoun). So (29) is not too hard to make out:

(29)   For Spirits when they please
        Can either Sex assume, or both; so soft
        And uncompounded is thir Essence pure. . . .

[Milton, *PL.*, I. 423–25]

When the subordinate clause comes first, however, and is set off from the main clause by a semicolon, no mark of subordination is present to warn the reader that the subordinate clause is to be integrated into the one to follow:

(30) As gentle Shepheard in sweete euen-tide,
        When ruddy Phoebus gins to welke in west,
        High on an hill, his flocke to vewen wide,
        Markes which do byte their hasty supper best;
        A cloud of combrous gnattes do him molest. . . .

[Spenser, *FQ*, I.i. 23]

(31)   Or if Sion Hill
        Delight thee more, and Siloa's Brook that flow'd
        Fast by the Oracle of God; I thence
        Invoke thy aid to my advent'rous Song. . . .

[Milton, *PL*, I. 10–13]

Admittedly, for confusion to occur the subordinate clause must be long enough and complex enough for the reader to forget that it ought to be subordinated to something, but it is just when such a clause is long that a writer using Early Modern punctuation is inclined to set it off with a semicolon—and that is the source of the modern reader's difficulty.

The reader of Spenser and Milton, then, cannot assume that a clause is complete when he comes to a semicolon, since the material on one side of it may have to be integrated into the clause on the other side as an adverbial or nominal modifier. In setting off subordinate clauses, Spenser and Milton have a choice between a comma and a semicolon much like the choice moderns have between a comma or no comma: degree of heaviness can indicate degree of interpretive separation or cohesion. In their discussion of Spenser's revisions of punctuation in the 1596 edition of *The Faerie Queene*, the editors of the Variorum Edition of *Spenser's Works* cite certain lines where a semicolon emphasizes the discreteness of a clause, giving as an example the change of a comma preceding *till* in the 1590 edition to a semicolon in this passage:[5]

(32) [ancient Kings and Queenes], that had of yore
     Their scepters stretcht from East to Westerne shore,
     And all the world in their subiection held;
     Till that infernall feend with foule vprore
     Forwasted all their land, and them expeld:
     Whom to auenge, she had this Knight from far compeld.
                                        [Spenser, *FQ*, I.i. 5]

Spenser (and Milton) frequently do use a semicolon before *till*, and they may well mean to indicate a pause signifying duration. In any case, we must not close off the clause preceding a semicolon (or colon) until we have looked across it to see if the next material may possibly be a subordinate clause, and this should be easy to do if the next material begins with a subordinator.

We must look across the semicolon for another reason, which is that what follows may be a coordinated verb phrase:

(33) Halfe furious vnto his foe he came,
     Resolv'd in minde all suddenly to win,

> Or soone to lose, before he once would lin;
> And strooke at her with more then manly force....
>
> [Spenser, *FQ*, I.i. 24]

(34)   he praisd his diuelish arts,
> That had such might ouer true meaning harts;
> Yet rests not so, but other meanes doth make,
> How he may worke vnto her further smarts:
>
> [Spenser, *FQ*, I.ii. 9]

(35) O Prince, O Chief of many Throned Powers,
> That led th'imbatteld Seraphim to Warr
> Under thy conduct, and in dreadful deeds
> Fearless, endanger'd Heav'ns perpetual King;
> And put to proof his high Supremacy,
> Whether upheld by strength, or Chance, or Fate....
>
> [Milton, *PL*, I. 128–33]

(36) He trusted to have equal'd the most High,
> If he oppos'd; and with ambitious aim
> Against the Throne and Monarchy of God
> Rais'd impious War in Heav'n and Battel proud
> With vain attempt.
>
> [Milton, *PL*, I. 40–44]

A simple tactic for recognizing the coordinate verb phrase suggests itself in the first three examples: it is signaled by the sequence

$$...; CONJ — V...$$

The placement of the prepositional phrase *with ambitious aim*... before the verb in (36) may hinder this strategy, but such a look across the semicolon is sufficient to avoid being misled most of the time. Example (37) may also pose the same sort of delay of needed information (i.e., the verb) that (36) does (this continues [29]):

(37)   so soft
> And uncompounded is thir Essence pure,
> Not ti'd or manacl'd with joynt or limb,

Nor founded on the brittle strength of bones,
Like cumbrous flesh; but in what shape they choose
Dilated or condens't, bright or obscure,
Can execute thir aerie purposes,
And works of love or enmity fulfil.

[Milton, *PL*, I. 424–31]

We must scan across a line and a half from the time we see ; *but*
until we get to the verbs *can execute*. Interestingly, although
Spenser and Milton will sometimes place the Object before the
verb in a coordinate verb phrase (more on this below), they never
place a semicolon before such an inverted verb phrase, for a sequence like

$$\ldots; \text{CONJ} - \text{NP} - \text{V} \ldots$$

would be taken as beginning a new main clause by the strategy just
outlined.

These passages give us further illustrations of the principle of
compensation. After we recognize that we must not let a semicolon
trigger clause closure and removal from immediate processing, we
must develop some strategies that will give us a relatively quick
indication of what to do with the material that follows the semicolon. Checking to see whether the material might attach back, or
might itself constitute a clause, will help, as will noticing a subordinator which might link the clause across the semicolon. Further,
anything such as length or distance of the verb that impedes this
sizing up of the material will make the sentence hard to process. It
is interesting that Spenser and Milton for once assist us, in that
material looking like a Subject—verb sequence following a semicolon may be taken as such. Note that their avoidance of an O V
sequence following a semicolon and conjunction is especially helpful just because the semicolon leads us to expect a new clause. We
will see in the next section that they are not so careful about the
same situation with commas.

3. COORDINATE CLAUSE BOUNDARIES

The comma is of course less conclusively a clause boundary marker, since it may occur, for example, between coordinate or appositive phrases. Suppose we have an apparently complete clause ending with a noun phrase, followed by a comma, possibly a conjunction, and another noun phrase: should the second noun phrase (italicized in the examples) be taken as the Subject of another clause coming up?

(38) At once as far as Angels kenn he views
      The dismal Situation waste and wilde,
      A Dungeon horrible, on all sides round
      As one great furnace flam'd, . . .

                                         [Milton, *PL,* I. 59–62]

In this example, the decisive information is the verb *flam'd,* which is spread quite far from its Subject, *a Dungeon horrible.* This phrase, furthermore, is so semantically similar to *dismal Situation waste and wilde* as to be a likely appositive to *Situation.* In other words, it is easy to read it as an appositive, and the information that we need to decide that it is not is withheld. Hence it is easily misread. In the next example, the line end may induce the reader to misperceive *the Thunder* as coordinate to *fiery surge,* since the decisive verb (which is boxed) is again delayed for over a line:

(39)   the Sulphurous Hail
      Shot after us in storm, oreblown hath laid
      The fiery Surge, that from the Precipice
      Of Heav'n receiv'd us falling, and *the Thunder,*
      Wing'd with red Lightning and impetuous rage,
      Perhaps ⟦hath spent⟧ his shafts, and ceases now
      To bellow through the vast and boundless Deep.

                                         [Milton, *PL,* I. 171–77]

The same effect of uncertainty produced by a delayed verb occurs in the next two examples:

(40) the house, to his restless sense, was in the high homely style of an elder day, and *the ancient Paris that he was looking for*—sometimes intensely felt, sometimes more acutely missed— $\boxed{\text{was}}$ in the immemorial polish of the wide waxed staircase. . . .

[James, *AMB*, 145]

(41)   all access was throng'd, the Gates
And Porches wide, but chief *the spacious Hall*
(Though like a cover'd field, where Champions bold
Wont ride in arm'd, and at the Soldans chair
Defi'd the best of Paynim chivalry
To mortal combat or career with Lance)
Thick $\boxed{\text{swarm'd}}$, both on the ground and in the air,
Brusht with the hiss of rustling wings.

[Milton, *PL*, I. 761–68]

In this last example we do apparently have an appositive (*the Gates and Porches wide*) to *all access*, and we are tempted by the line end and parenthesis to group *the spacious Hall* with them—Milton makes us wait four lines before we can see that this is wrong. Semantic clues here are not too helpful because *Hall* could, on the face of it, be grouped with accesses, though in fact here it refers to the principal chamber of Pandemonium. Note that there is parallel structuring here which leaps out if the parenthesis is removed: *access . . . throng'd, Hall . . . swarm'd*.

Empson cites two instances where a noun phrase hangs perceptually between two clauses, appearing to be appositive or coordinate to the Object of the first clause, and his examples seem almost contrived to force this misperception by interposing material between the noun phrase and its governing verb:

(42) Sometimes 'tis grateful to the rich, to try
A short vicissitude, and fit of Poverty:
A savoury dish, a homely treat,
Where all is plain, where all is neat,
Without the stately spacious Room,

> The Persian Carpet, or the Tyrian Loom,
> Clear up the cloudy foreheads of the Great.
> [Dryden, in Empson, *Ambiguity*, p. 75]

(43)   Thou mak'st a Taper see
          What the sunne never saw, and what the Arke
          (Which was of Soules, and beasts, the cage, and park)
          Did not containe, one bed containes, through thee,
          Two Phoenixes, whose joyned breasts. . . .
                                    [Donne, in Empson, p. 51]

In the first, we read the colon as setting off an enumerating appositive ("fit of poverty, *viz.* a savoury dish, a homely treat") but four
lines later find a verb (*clear up*) without a Subject and must
reanalyze. In the second example, we tend to read *what the Arke . . .
did not containe* as coordinate to *what the sunne never saw* as Objects
of *see*, but when we finally get to *one bed containes*, we realize that
the *and* in the second line really marks the beginning of a coordinate clause ("and through thee one bed contains what the Arke . . .
did not contain, two Phoenixes . . ."). The *two phoenixes*, that is, is
not directly the Object of *containes*, as it at first appears to be, but is
appositive to the Topicalized Object, *what the Arke . . . did not contain.* The effort involved in reading across the parenthesis to put
what the Arke . . . did not containe together distracts one from the
falsity of the initial hypothesis. Milton achieves this effect at the
beginning of his Sonnet 18:

(44) Avenge, O Lord, thy slaughter'd Saints, whose bones
     Lie scatter'd on the Alpine mountains cold,
     Ev'n them who kept thy truth so pure of old
     When all our Fathers worship't Stocks and Stones,
     Forget not:

The *ev'n them* appears appositive to *thy slaughtered Saints,* and again
we must wait until the fifth line for the Objectless transitive verb
(*forget . . .*) to trigger reanalysis. To be sure, if we think about it, the
recently slaughtered Protestants cannot be the same as the ancient
saints, but the point is that perceptual mechanisms of the type we

have been studying operate prior to such higher-level processing; hence it does not save us from misperception here. If we do not think about it, we will 'forget' exactly who the sonnet is about, which is obviously the effect Milton is seeking.

Two aspects of Milton's syntax make commas more problematic as clause boundary markers than they are in other writers. First, Milton does not observe the constraint on split Subjects that, in Modern English, requires that if a second conjoined sentence is reduced down to just the Subject, the Subject must be inserted next to the Subject of the first sentence. Thus (a) can be reduced to (b) or (c), but (d), if reduced to (e), must then become (f):

a) John has thrown rocks, and Mary will throw rocks.
b) John has thrown rocks, and Mary will do so.
c) John has thrown rocks, and Mary will.
d) John cast stones, and Mary cast stones.
e)*John cast stones, and Mary.
f) John and Mary cast stones.

Note that (e) would be more ambiguous in speech than in writing: the comma should discourage one from reading *stones* and *Mary* as coordinate. However, commas may be present for several reasons if a noun phrase is complex or lengthy, so that a supplementary semantically based strategy is probably useful. As discussed in the first section of Chapter One, we can check the noun phrase following the *and* for semantic similarity to the preceding Object noun phrase. Thus *stones* and *Mary* are fairly unlike (inanimate objects versus the name of a human), and so the temptation to group them as coordinate is negligible. In practice, one might engage in a comparative feature matching with the Object and Subject of the preceding clause. Consider for examples:

(45)   Or if Sion Hill
Delight thee more, and *Siloa's Brook that flow'd*
Fast by the Oracle of God; I thence
Invoke thy aid to my adventrous Song. . . .

[Milton, *PL*, I. 10–13]

(46) Say first, for Heav'n hides nothing from thy view
      Nor the deep Tract of Hell, say first. . . .

[Milton, *PL,* I. 27–28]

Both examples can be misperceived by taking the trailing noun phrase (italicized) as the Subject of a new sentence (though this misperception is quickly recognized, since the search for a verb to go with it is quickly shut off—the semicolon does it in [45], the verb *say* instead of *says* in [46]). Additionally, (46) can be misperceived by grouping *Nor the deep Tract of Hell* with *nothing* as a split coordinate Object (if the reader reads *nor* as "not even": "for Heaven hides nothing, not even the deep tract of Hell, from thy view"). Again, the feature-matching strategy will help, provided the right features are noted (i.e., in the second, Heaven/Hell, which, as opposites, are semantically closely related), and it will quickly rule out any attempt to group *Siloa's Brook . . .* with *thee.* Matching semantic features can require a lot of attention to the meanings of the words, as the next example shows:

(47)   temperat vapors bland, which th'only sound
      Of leaves and fuming rills, Aurora's fan,
      Lightly dispers'd, and *the shrill Matin Song*
      Of Birds on every bough;

[Milton, *PL,* V. 5–8]

Here again the semicolon rules out taking *the shrill Matin Song . . .* as the Subject of a new clause, and it can be matched back to *sound* as coordinate with it once we realize that *the shrill Matin Song of birds* is a sound. If one is relatively in touch with the text, the next example is not too difficult:

(48) Regions of sorrow, doleful shades, where peace
      And rest can never dwell, hope never comes
      That comes to all; but torture without end
      Still urges, and *a fiery Deluge,* fed
      With ever-burning Sulphur unconsum'd:

[Milton, *PL,* I. 65–69]

In Hell, *the fiery Deluge* is a torture, so it links up with *torture* as a split coordinate Subject of *urges*. (We may thank Milton, by the way, for the comma after *Deluge*—otherwise we would take *fed* as a main verb and look in vain for its Object.) Example (49) is our last illustration:

(49)   and that strife
       Was not inglorious, though th' event was dire,
       As this place testifies, and this dire change
       Hateful to utter:

                                                    [Milton, *PL*, I. 624–27]

Here the second part of the split Subject (*this dire change*) is attracted to *this place* by repetition of *this* rather than by semantic similarity, though on reflection the place is the most obvious effect of this dire change.

To review briefly at this point, we may say that when we encounter a noun phrase following an apparently complete clause, we may look forward for a verb of which it could be the Subject while also considering whether it might belong back in the clause just processed. If for some reason the look forward does not give quick results, and if the noun phrase *could* be tucked back into the preceding clause, we tend to take this option. One reason that (43) is so difficult is that it is hard ever to find a place in the following clause for *what the Arke did not containe*. Notice that this uncertainty does not arise (45–47), where the look forward is cut off by punctuating or a non-agreeing verb: it is clear that the noun phrase must be a part of the preceding clause, unusual as the correct analysis as a split Subject is.

Matters are even a bit more complex in Milton (and Spenser) because of a second irregularity in syntax: they often invert verbs and their Objects in coordinate verb phrases:

(50) To winne him worship, and *her grace* to haue,
       Which of all earthly things he most did craue;
       And euer as he rode, his hart did earne

To proue his puissance in battell braue
Vpon his foe, and *his new force* to learne;

[Spenser, *FQ*, I.i. 3]

(51) Yet she her weary limbes would neuer rest,
But *euery hill and dale, each wood and plaine*
Did search, sore grieued in her gentle brest. . . .

[Spenser, *FQ*, I.ii. 8]

(52)   But he who reigns
Monarch in Heav'n, till then as one secure
Sat on his Throne, upheld by old repute,
Consent or custome, and *his Regal State*
Put forth at full, but still *his strength* conceal'd,
Which tempted our attempt, and wrought our fall.

[Milton, *PL*, I. 638–43]

(53) Such place Eternal Justice had prepar'd
For those rebellious, here *thir Prison* ordain'd
In utter darkness, and *thir portion* set
As far remov'd from God and light of Heav'n
As from the Center thrice to th' utmost Pole.

[Milton, *PL*, I. 70–74]

Example (52) suggests what is difficult about such an inversion: the
Object preceding the verb may be taken as its Subject ("his Regal
State put forth . . ."). Presumably one of the first decisions a reader
must make as he encounters a coordinating conjunction following
an apparently completed verb phrase is whether the next material
is conjoined as a clause or as a verb phrase, and the immediate
occurrence of a verb is the cue that the Subject of the first sentence
is to be carried over as the Subject of what follows. A noun phrase
between the conjunction and the verb, however, will be identified
as the Subject of the verb. We can schematize this as follows:

If: NP V (NP), CONJ NP V . . .
and: S   (O)
then: S

Placing the Object before the Verb baffles this strategy and would seem to invite misperception by setting up a garden path. There are again several tactics available to help the reader perceive particular cases correctly. Sometimes pronominal clues are present (i.e., the inverted Object is in the oblique or accusative case):

(54) Those two he tooke, and in a secret bed,
       Couered with darknesse and misdeeming night,
       Them both together laid, to ioy in vaine delight.

[Spenser, *FQ*, I.ii. 3]

Second, a running check on the rough semantic congruity of the noun phrase as the Subject of the verb should suffice to reject the misperception fairly quickly: in (53), for example, *thir Prison* can be quickly rejected as the Subject of *ordained*, and *thir portion* can be rejected as the Subject of *set*, on grounds of gross semantic incongruity. In (52), by contrast, *Regal State* and *his strength* just conceivably could refer to animate things suitable as the Subjects of *put forth* and *conceal:* semantic incongruity is not obvious enough here to reject the false analysis of the noun phrases as Subjects. (The situation here is roughly like that in examples [28–31] of Chapter One.) In (51), however, the semantic clues again work fairly well to reject *every hill and dale, each wood and plaine* as the Subject of *search*. Even if the semantic compatibility check fails to give a clear indication that the noun phrase is not the Subject of the verb, the perception of a transitive verb with a missing Object should trigger the re-analysis (i.e., when we get *to haue, to learne* in [50], or any of the verbs in [51–53]). Also, one might take advantage of the fondness of these writers for syntactic parallelism: Spenser and Milton often invert 'across the board', so that if the first clause is inverted, the second may also be (giving orders S O V + O V or O S V + O V). One might think of this tendency to parallel inversion as a warning to the reader, or as a warm up of the perceptual mechanisms needed to process the subsequent string. The pattern in (51), for example, is S O V + O V, in (52) it is S V A + O V + O V and in (53) it is O S V + O V + O V. Our writers also enjoy an occasional chiastic criss-cross, however, as in (50) (V O + O V; V O (A) (A) + O V). Note that (50) is not hard to process, since the Objects *his puissance* and *his new force* are so strongly similar that the parallel function is clear even though the order with respect to the verbs is reversed. In the next examples of chiastic order from Milton, the Objects again are linked together as contrasts:

(55) Consult how we may henceforth most offend
Our Enemy, *our own loss* how repair,
How overcome this dire Calamity. . . .
[Milton, *PL*, I. 187–89]

(56) Henceforth his might we know, and know *our own*
So as not either to provoke, or dread
New Warr. . . .
[Milton, *PL*, I. 643–45]

We should probably conclude that for Milton and Spenser the commitment to parallelism is not pronounced enough to base a perceptual strategy on, although it might provide confirming evidence for a certain analysis.

The next example illustrates the operation of these strategies in a more complex way:

(57) As when Alcides from Oechalia Crown'd
With conquest, felt th' envenom'd robe, and tore
Through pain up by the roots Thessalian Pines,
And *Lichas* from the top of Oeta threw
Into th' Euboic Sea.
[Milton, *PL*, I. 542–46]

Here the expectation of parallelism is violated (the structure is S V O + V A A O + O A V A). The only way to avoid misperceiving *Lichas* as the Subject of a new clause is to know the story as well as Milton does, since *Lichas* appears congruent enough as the Subject of *threw,* and we do not get to the transitive verb *threw* for several words. Again we brush up against Milton's learning—knowing the story helps not only to perceive the aptness of the simile, but the simile itself. One reason (43) is so hard to perceive correctly is that Donne sets up a misleading parallelism *what . . . what . . .*—they are both Objects, but they are not coordinate.

The punctuation adds to the difficulty of (58), where some fairly close reasoning about the total meaning is needed:

(58) By falsities and lyes the greatest part
     Of Mankind they corrupted to forsake
     God thir Creator, and *th' invisible*
     Glory of him that made them, to transform
     Oft to the Image of a Brute, adorn'd
     With gay Religions full of Pomp and Gold,
     And Devils to adore for Deities:

                          [Milton, *PL*, I. 367–73]

Th'invisible glory is in a position where it could be coordinate with *God,* and the two noun phrases are semantically similar enough and congruent enough as the Object of *forsake* to support that grouping. There appears to be an Object missing after *transform,* however, though one may seek it in the following lines for some time before giving up the search as fruitless. The comma before *to transform* still stands in the way of viewing *th'invisible glory* as the Object of *transform,* and, as noted earlier, we tend not to expect the Object of an infinitival verb to precede the *to.* After some pondering, semantic clues seem decisive: *the Image of a Brute* suggests that *th'invisible glory* refers to God's image in man—this he does not merely forsake, but actively perverts. Perhaps this can be viewed as a case of 'double syntax', yielding both senses: "forsake, and yet go further in their perversity." In the next example, we do not even have an obviously missing Object to trigger reanalysis:

(59) But what if he our Conquerour . . .
     . . .
     Have left us this our spirit and strength intire
     Strongly to suffer and support our pains,
     That we may so suffice his vengeful ire,

> Or do him mightier service as his thralls
> By right of Warr, *what e'er his business be*
> Here in the heart of Hell to work in Fire,
> Or do his Errands in the gloomy Deep;
>
> [Milton, *PL*, I. 143–52]

It takes some puzzling to identify *whate'er his business be* as the Object of *work*, partly because *work* is not obviously transitive (i.e., obviously missing its Object). In this elaborate set of (basically) coordinate purpose and result clauses, Beelzebub is trying to plumb the Divine Purpose, and if one does not get the Object matched to *work*, one misses the elegant twist that they will not merely work in fire in the heart of Hell, but work *his business*, whatever it be. It thus appears that the 'missing Object' tactic, which was the only clue in (41), is not always reliable—it fails for the same reason in the following:

(60)   our better part remains
> To work in close design, by fraud or guile
> What force effected not:
>
> [Milton, *PL*, I. 645–47]

Again, *work* appears intransitive, and the delayed Object which appears in the next line is a slight surprise. Also, as noted at the beginning of the chapter, when we have a verb followed by optional Adverbials, we tend to close the clause after the Adverbial. Finally, of course, line division invites us to close the clause after *guile*. There is a conspiracy to make the reader misperceive here.

Just as look-ahead was a recurrent explanatory concept in the first chapter (and in this also), so there is a general principle of perceptual difficulty that emerges from these examples, *viz.*, that a particular passage is not likely to be difficult unless it baffles several basic strategies at once. The notion of simultaneous operation of semantic strategies and those based on linear sequence implies that the failure of one set of strategies would not mean a breakdown in the process of comprehension as long as the other sorts of clues remained helpful. There is fairly good experimental evidence (mentioned in the Introduction) that structurally complex sentences are easier to perceive if there are semantic clues to the correct analysis, and many of our examples provide confirming instances. Indeed, our discussion suggests that the set of strategies operating simultaneously may well include clues of punctuation and parallelism, since these appear to make some passages easier or harder than others. A reader might of course take one type of strategy and ride it to the bitter end, but he would be a naive reader, and, in some of these passages at least, the end would be quick in coming.

An unexpected placement of a phrase or mark of punctuation, then, does not always result in misperception, and hence one cannot always assume a perceptual motive for every peculiarity of syntax or punctuation. Sometimes the motive can be found in the requirements of verse form[6] or of information structure. The tendency we have noted of Spenser and Milton to place the Object of an infinitival verb before the *to* can give rise to numerous misperceptions, one of which takes the Object to be the Object of the preceding verb. This may occur in (19), where *her strayed champion* appears to be the Object of *seeke*. However, such a motive is not present in every case of this inversion, since it occurs fairly often at the beginning of sentences, and of course the Object is not always congruent as the Object of the preceding verb.

Two further general points about the perceptual difficulty of garden paths can now be made. Almost any mistaken analysis can be called a garden path, including the premature closures discussed in the first section, but there is a marked difference in the felt complexity of various mistakes. Mistakes like the ones discussed in the third section can lead to considerable reanalysis, involving either the removal of a noun phrase from one clause and placement of it in another, as in (58) and in (38), (41)–(44), or the reassignment of the function of a noun phrase, as in (52), (57), and (59), where initially perceived Subjects are reassigned as Objects with the Subject of the preceding clause then being carried over as Subject. Such reanalysis gives rise to a greater sense of effort than the premature closures with which we began the chapter. So, for example, (59) involves more reanalysis than (60) since the Object of *work* in (59) can initially be misperceived as appositive to *service* in the preceding clause. The second point is a delicate one bordering on paradox. The notion of a garden path involves the recognition that it is a false path. We noted in the previous chapter that the longer it is pursued before it is discovered, the more serious the perceptual strain is. In the light (darkness?) of the examples in this chapter, we can add that the more obvious the final dead end is, the easier it is to escape, for the 'trigger' for reanalysis is often the clue to the right analysis. This is above all the case with a strongly transitive verb plainly missing an Object—it is the weakly transitive verbs like *work* that make the greatest difficulties. The paradoxical aspect is simply that if the clue to trigger reanalysis is weak, and the initial analysis is not awful, the garden path may never be perceived as such—in short, one experiences no perceptual difficulty at all! Literary critics and teachers often find themselves arguing that a certain reading is better than one initially arrived at: here it is no longer a matter of right and wrong, since the structure of the text does not *necessitate* reanalysis.

The garden paths described above are one type of what William Empson called double syntax. Empson found value where Fowler found only "obvious folly," though a particular instance does not qualify as a significant ambiguity of the second type unless the two readings, correct and erroneous, are "resolved into one" in an "ordinary good reading" (*Ambiguity*, p. 48). In Empson's practice, such resolution is often only that the aberrant reading also functions expressively. He clearly wants the reader to respond to double syntax by entertaining all possibilities rather than by excluding the less grammatical reading, and to be willing to find expressive function in the struggle with the text rather than to reject the by-ways with annoyance. Empson does discriminate between better and worse readings, giving some priority, at times grudgingly, to the 'main, grammatical' reading. He is right to hold fast to this principle, at least for the authors he considers, for one crucial reason—there is always a grammatical reading. A rather different attitude might be warranted for texts where a grammatical parsing is not always possible. If, for example, one had overlapping syntax where a single noun phrase played different functions in two clauses, a decision that it should go with one or the other would be misguided, since it would make the one clause grammatical at the expense of the other. Similarly, if one consistently had to choose between two somewhat ungrammatical parsings, one would gradually reduce the degree of priority given to the 'more grammatical' reading. Finally, if it frequently made little or no difference which clause an element went with, the reader might also begin to pay less attention to clause-boundaries as the basic unit of processing the text. The 'hovering' elements in so many of Empson's examples, which can go with the preceding or following clause, do not trigger reanalysis—either reading is right—and an acute awareness of sentence structure will only weary the reader with inconclusive comparisons of alternative parsings. All three of these conditions are considerably more prevalent in Spenser's works than in Milton's or in the later writers' and suggest a line of approach to Paul Alpers' claim that Spenser's syntax is 'permissive' and that attention to sentence structure never helps in reading *The Faerie Queene*. I will take up this matter in Chapter Five. If the great majority of a writer's sentences can be parsed into grammatical structures, however, the reader can aim for such a parsing and assume that his comprehension is correct if the sentence is grammatical. Whatever misperceptions he has made on the road may be interesting, valuable, and expressive, but they are, finally, misperceptions.

CHAPTER THREE

Reference, Coreference, and Attachment

I: PRONOUNS AND PARTICIPIALS

I N the Introduction, I treated finding the referents of noun phrases as a part of comprehension rather than perception. My basic reason for doing so is that we have a propositional structure when we have identified a function in the structure for each phrase—we do not need to know what they refer to in terms of our knowledge as shaped by context. The 'scene' under discussion is part of the contextual frame, and linking the noun phrase to entities in the 'scene' integrates the material into it: hence we are in the domain of comprehension.[1] It will happen in a stretch of text that the same individual is referred to by more than one noun phrase; hence those phrases will be coreferential, but comprehension may or may not proceed by identifying the coreference: one can find referents by noting that one noun phrase is coreferential to a preceding one (this I would call a structural strategy) and hence refers to the same individual, or by noting that the noun phrase refers to an individual previously introduced into the scene and hence that the second noun phrase is coreferential to the one that earlier introduced the referent or last mentioned it. This second procedure I would call a referential strategy. It is quite different from the first in that no notation of coreference as such is necessarily involved. What distinguishes definite noun phrases and pronouns from indefinites is that they explicitly indicate that they refer to an individual previously introduced, so that one might suppose they would automatically trigger a process of the first type—call it a process of leftward search. However, pronouns and definite noun phrases are often used more loosely to refer to things which have not been introduced by a noun phrase—that is, there is no antecedent to be found. One may call such uses of pronouns ungrammatical if one chooses, but they are so common that we have some means of coping with them perceptually. Consider, for example, these lines from *Paradise Lost:*

(1)   But he who reigns
Monarch in Heav'n, till then as one secure
Sat on his Throne, upheld by old repute,
Consent or custome, and his Regal State
Put forth at full, but still his strength conceal'd,
Which tempted our attempt, and wrought our fall.
[Milton, *PL,* I. 637–42]

Here the antecedent of *which* is, at the very least, "his concealing his strength," and it may be all the preceding material. *Which* here is said to have a "sentential" antecedent—which is to say that we must take the entire action or 'thought' of the previous clause as the 'thing' referred to. Such uses of pronouns have sometimes been cited as evidence that sentences or clauses are noun phrases at some level of representation, but this is at best just one way of modeling the perceptual process involved. There are other uses that may force us to dig out or cobble together an 'antecedent':

(2)   Whoever hath an Ambition to be heard in a Crowd, must press, and squeeze, and thrust, and climb with indefatigable Pains, till he has exalted himself to a certain Degree of Altitude above *them.* Now, in all Assemblies, tho' you wedge *them* ever so close, we may observe this peculiar Property; that, over their Heads there is Room enough. . . .
[Swift, *A Tale of A Tub,* Quintana Ed. 277]

Crowd and *assemblies* are said to function as anaphoric peninsulas here: one can find an antecedent in the paraphrase of their senses ("groups of *people* . . ."). Bever, Carroll, and Hurtig suggest that such sentences are easier to comprehend when the 'antecedent' is in a clause prior to the pronoun because the clause has been processed and its contents are accessible in the abstract form needed here.[2] (Hence, by the way, the second *them* should be harder to process than the first, since the clause with the 'antecedent' [*assemblies*] has not yet been processed, though I think in this case that the previous *them* facilitates repeating the move.) Such a process of inventing an 'antecedent' is presumably more a referential than a structural process, and it is conceivable that referential processes might be more efficient in identifying referents, so that we would use a structural strategy of leftward search mainly for confirmation: "I think this is the referent—can I find an antecedent which introduces it?" If we cannot, we might pause briefly to consider whether the "ungrammatical" reading is in fact the best one. Consider, for example, the following passage from Spenser:

(3)   They bene ymet, and both their points arriued,
       But Guyon droue so furious and fell,
       That seem'd both shield and plate *it* would haue riued;
       Nathelesse *it* bore his foe not from his sell,
       But made him stagger, as he were not well:

                                              [Spenser, *FQ*, III.i. 6]

Citing only the second and third lines as context, Sugden identifies the referent of *it* as "the general idea of the preceding verb . . . i.e., the drive, the stroke,"[3] but perhaps we could dig a singular *point* out of the plural since it is only Guyon's point involved in his 'drive'. This example is reminiscent of (31) in Chapter One, where one can extract *stroke* as a 'cognate Object' from *stroke* as the referent of *it*, but helmet is a somewhat more likely referent. (Examples [11] and [12] of Chapter Five are similar.) The general rule of thumb should be the analogue of that sketched at the end of the previous chapter: take the grammatical reading (i.e., the one with an actual noun phrase antecedent) as the right one.

As with other perceptual rules-of-thumb, however, this rule cannot be taken categorically but must be adjusted to particular writers and texts. In Swift's *A Tale of A Tub*, for example, (though not so much in his other writings) one must assume that a sentential antecedent is at least as likely as an actual noun phrase. Consider, for instance, the *which*'s in the following passage:

(4) Now, it usually happens, that these active Spirits, getting Possession of the Brain, resemble those that haunt other waste and empty Dwellings, which for want of Business, either vanish, and carry away a Piece of the House, or else stay at home and fling it all out of the Windows. By *which* are mystically display'd the two principal Branches of Madness, and *which* some Philosophers not considering so well as I, have mistook to be different in their causes, over-hastily assigning the first to Deficiency, and the other to Redundance.

[Swift, *TOT*, Quintana Ed. 344]

The first *which* must refer to two things, but not the active spirits and the ghosts, or the simile collapses (it suits Swift's satiric purpose, however, that this collapse should occur); rather, the two things are the two modes of operation of these ghosts (*vanish* . . . and *stay at home*. . .). The second *which*, following *and*, seems coordinate to the first and hence coreferential to it, but the two modes of operation can scarcely be said to be caused by deficiency and redundance; rather, the second *which* must refer to the two principal branches of madness. On this reading, which I think is the best, the *and* is just a piece of craziness.

In this chapter, we will consider definite noun phrases and pronouns separately because there are differences which might lead one to prefer one type of strategy for definite noun phrases and the other for pronouns. Finally, we will take up the attachment of participials to the noun phrases they modify because the principles involved are very similar, reserving comprehension of appositives for the next chapter.

1. DEFINITE NOUN PHRASES

Although both definite noun phrases and (definite) pronouns convey the assumption that their referents have already been introduced into the scene, locating the referent with definite noun phrases is usually easier than with pronouns because the definite noun phrase contains more information about the referent. We can determine the referent of *the father of our country,* that is, without regard to verbal context, but not so for *he, that, who,* etc. 'Elegant variation' in the noun phrases one uses to refer to the same individual can present a problem slightly different from that with pronouns: pronouns do not introduce a new mode of reference (i.e., new properties of the referent). With elegant variation, we must identify an individual previously described one way in terms of a different (but not a more general) description. Seymour Chatman notes that James's fondness for elegant variation creates considerable difficulty for the reader, who, for example, must in the first pages of *The Ambassadors* align the noun phrases *The same secret principle, this principle,* and *this happier device* as referring to the same thing.[4] In a paper presented to the Linguistic Society of America (Winter, 1976), Robert Kantor pointed out that there is a contrast between noun phrases that are merely definite and those that are also demonstrative. The demonstrative article or pronoun (*this/these, that/those, such*), he observes, signals to the reader that some extra effort may be required to locate the referent, either because the entity referred to is not at the moment in the foreground of attention or because it is receiving a new description. This seems to be the function of *this* in the phrases just cited from *The Ambassadors* and explains several of the examples in Chapter One where a fronted Object is demonstrative (e.g., [36], [39–40]). To see what is meant by a "new description," consider the contexts for examples (39) and (40):

(I.39)
    All is not lost; the unconquerable Will,
    And study of revenge, immortal hate,

> And courage never to submit or yield:
> And what is else not to be overcome?
> *That Glory* never shall his wrath or might
> Extort from me.
>
> [Milton, *PL*, I. 106–11]

(I.40)

> Then strait commands that at the warlike sound
> Of Trumpets loud and Clarions be upreard
> His mighty Standard; *that proud honour* claim'd
> Azazel as his right, a Cherube tall:
>
> [Milton, *PL*, I. 531–34]

In both of these, the demonstrative noun phrases bundle up the preceding propositions or action as single entities. Here we observe the link between a "new description" and a refocusing theme: the "new description" picks out certain aspects of what has been presented and hence constitutes a refocusing on what is already present in the scene. In other examples (e.g., I. 36, 34 below), the referent is hard to pick out because two are available or because the referent must be inferred (as in [34] below, where *that birth* must be inferred from the act of begetting, which is all that has been explicitly mentioned). Kantor noted that unskillful writers do not use these signals very effectively, but it appears that our writers do use them to indicate to the reader when special efforts to identify referents are necessary (see also [21, 23, 24] below).

As with pronouns, the referent of a definite noun phrase may not have been specifically introduced:

> My car failed inspection. *The muffler* is shot.

Here we make use of 'knowledge of the world' in establishing the link: introducing a car is tantamount to introducing a muffler. Violations of the principle that the referent of a definite noun phrase has been introduced are a source of difficulty in Wallace Stevens. Consider, for example, the definite noun phrases in the following poem, including those of the title:

(5)   The Sense of the Sleight-of-Hand Man

One's grand flights, one's Sunday baths,
One's tootings at the weddings of the soul
Occur as they occur. So bluish clouds
Occurred above the empty house and the leaves
Of the rhododendron rattled their gold,
As if someone lived there. Such floods of white
Came bursting from the clouds. So the wind
Threw its contorted strength around the sky.
Could you have said the bluejay suddenly
Would swoop to earth? It is a wheel, the rays
Around the sun. The wheel survives the myths.
The fire eye in the clouds survives the gods.
To think of a dove with an eye of grenadine
And pines that are cornets, so it occurs,
And a little island full of geese and stars;
It may be that the ignorant man, alone,
Has any chance to mate his life with life
That is the sensual, pearly spouse, the life
That is fluent in even the wintriest bronze.

[Stevens, *CP*, 222]

Some of the definite noun phrases may be taken as given in a scene (the leaves of the rhododendron, the clouds, the wind, the sky, the bluejay, the fire eye in the clouds); others may appear as drawn from a stock of general types (the ignorant man) or conventional entities (the gods). (Later in his career Stevens makes ever more frequent definite references to types and figures in his own system.) The effect of positing a scene in this way (the empty house) rather than describing it, and of drawing on general types and figures, is to treat the scene as an instance of something else, not the locus of attention: this is one source of the often remarked abstractness in Stevens' poetry. The title itself is a definite noun phrase—obviously without antecedent—but one may assume by a general convention governing titles that it will be specified by the poem which follows. There remain two definite noun phrases, however, that are difficult to identify if one is unfamiliar with Stevens. *The sleight-of-hand man* might be taken as coreferential to *one*, but one could not be sure of this without having some idea of what each phrase refers to. It is easier to be relatively sure of this if one is familiar with Stevens's (self-)deprecatory ways of referring to the poet and his poetizing impulse, a familiarity requiring some knowledge of his poetry beyond that available in the poem. Finally, *the sensual pearly spouse* is unexpectedly definite. The problem is that *mate* and *weddings of the soul* appear to be tossed in and are read metaphorically so that they do not introduce *spouse* into the scene, though as surely as cars have mufflers, weddings and matings have spouses (though not necessarily pearly, sensual ones). The whole noun phrase gives the impression that the reader is overhearing the poet in meditation rather than being addressed by him.[5]

The effect produced by Stevens with 'unintroduced definites' is in some ways similar to the effect obtained by certain of James's narrators: one enters their stories in mid-telling, as if one is in a conversation which has been going on for some time. Here is the first sentence of ''The Real Thing'':

(6)   When the porter's wife (she used to answer the house-bell), announced ''A gentleman—with a lady, sir,'' I had, as I often had in those days, for the wish was father to the thought, an immediate vision of sitters.

[James, *Tales*, VIII. 229]

The definite *the thought* precedes its 'antecedent', which is indefinite (*an immediate vision*), and we must infer from certain oblique references in the pages that follow what *the wish* refers to. One does not have to wait long, to be sure, to get some further information, but the definite article has just the opposite of its normal function here: instead of signaling that the referent has already been introduced, it signals that the reader must seek more information as he reads on. We will discuss this process of 'rightward search' in regard to pronouns below. The next example is even more unconventional:

(7) These things were true, but it was not less true (I may confess it
     now—whether because the aspiration was to lead to everything or to
     nothing I leave the reader to guess), that I couldn't get the honours,
     to say nothing of the emoluments, of a great painter of portraits out of
     my head. My "illustrations" were my pot-boilers; I looked to a dif-
     ferent branch of art (far and away the most interesting it had always
     seemed to me) to perpetuate my fame.

                                                     [James, *Tales*, VIII. 231]

We must look outside the parenthesis to the right to find out what
the aspiration refers to. As Dwight Bolinger observes in *Aspects of
Language* (2nd edition, Harcourt, Brace, Jovanovich, 1975, pp.
607–08), setting off material with parentheses usually signals that it
is relatively backgrounded (i.e., of lesser importance in context)—
in contrast to the dash—and is of course assumed to be a self-
contained unit, but here it is not self-contained, nor is the question
of incidental importance—in fact, it appears to be three questions
collapsed into one: "was it because of the outcome that he confes-
ses it?", "did the aspiration lead to either thing?", "if so, which?"
Notice that if the reader delays processing the material enclosed in
parentheses until he has processed the main sentence (a possibility
mentioned at the end of Chapter One), the antecedent will be
available (i.e., in mind) when the parenthetical material is processed. Thus the temporal order of processing would reverse the
serial order of presentation. I am indebted to Guy Carden for this
observation. There is, by the way, a difficulty of the opposite sort
with *a different branch of art,* which, being indefinite, appears to be
introducing a new thing but does in fact refer to 'portraiture'—
the sentence is, as it were, restating rather than advancing the
previous sentence and hence reintroduces portraiture.

  The largest and most ill-defined constraint on perception of reference is the imagination of the scene itself. Some of the disagreement among the readers of I. A. Richards' Poem 13 in *Practical
Criticism* turns on what is in the referential scene. The poem, given
without title, begins

(8) In the village churchyard she lies,
     Dust is in her beautiful eyes,

> No more she breathes, nor feels, nor stirs,
> At her feet and at her head
> Lies a slave to attend the dead,
>   But their dust is white as hers.[6]

Richards' students objected that either she has gone to dust or she has not: if she has, she does not have eyes anymore. Just possibly *her beautiful eyes* could be taken as referring to the eyes that we knew before she died, but the beginning of the third stanza raises the problem again:

> Who shall tell us? No one speaks;
> No colour shoots into those cheeks. . . .

which again seems an overwhelmingly trivial observation if she does not now have cheeks. Richards suggests that we could imagine a monument with her carven image in the churchyard, which certainly removes the objections, but the process by which one arrives at that scene, or does not, is very obscure. Some of my students not only have not seen, but refuse on demonstration to agree, that what is being described at the beginning of *The Sound and The Fury* is golf. Delaying information necessary for composing a scene becomes a kind of game with the reader for a writer like Pynchon (e.g., the beginning of *Gravity's Rainbow*). But to say what principles are involved here would require a separate, large scale study. In all of the discussion to follow, I will assume that the reader has got the scene right when he reads into the passage.

2. PRONOUNS

The traditional stylistic precept—that the first eligible noun phrase to the left of the pronoun should be the antecedent—implies a process of leftward search where one scans back to the first eligible (i.e., masculine, singular, or whatever) noun phrase to the left of the pronoun and takes it as the antecedent. Possibly this precept originates in the notion that the immediately preceding noun phrase is surest to be 'up' in the reader's mind. While there are doubtless times when one does engage in such a structurally based search, two other strategies may render it superfluous if conditions favor them: context may narrow the range of possible referents down to one, and the predicate may help pick out the individual of which it is predicated. In the following discourse, for example, one experiences little difficulty or even hesitation in identifying the referents of the pronouns:

(9)   The messenger approching to him spake,
       But his wast wordes returnd to him in vaine:
       So sound he slept, that nought mought him awake.
       Then rudely he him thrust, and pusht with paine,
       Whereat he gan to stretch: but he againe
       Shooke him so hard, that forced him to speake.

                                        [Spenser, FQ, I.i. 42]

We construct an imagined scene with two individuals, one of whom is in a deep sleep, so that only one individual (the messenger) is likely as the Speaker, Thruster, Pusher, and Shaker: we do not have to engage in a leftward search, which in this case would be very difficult to carry out. Here then, even with pronouns, the referentially based strategy is the more efficient.

For a second, more complicated example where referential 'scene' is our best clue, consider the following passage cited by Sugden as typical of Spenser's "careless, confused, and ambiguous manner" of handling his pronouns (p. 31). In the previous stanza Una and her lion have just left the hut of the blind Corceca and her deaf and dumb daughter Abessa:

(10) Whom ouertaking, they gan loudly bray,
      With hollow howling, and lamenting cry,
      Shamefully at her rayling all the way,
      And her accusing of dishonesty,
      That was the flowre of faith and chastity;
      And still amidst her rayling, she did pray,
      That plagues, and mischiefs, and long misery

Might fall on her, and follow all the way,
And that in endlesse error she might euer stray.

[Spenser, *FQ*, I.iii. 23]

Clearly the scene gives us one individual pursued and vilified and two pursuers—the problem is the shift from *they* to *she* when we get to the praying. But then we may remember that Abessa is incapable of speech (though she is presumably able to *bray*, etc.— this is quite realistic). S. K. Heninger helpfully supplies this observation in a note in his *Selections from the Poetical Works of Edmund Spenser*.[7] Another problem is that we do not expect the Rayler to be the same as the Prayer—that is, we suspect a shift in reference from *her* to *she* in the sixth line only to read in the next line that it is a wicked prayer. Thus Spenser is not really "careless" here, but he does demand that very close track be kept of the capacities of the individuals in the scene.

Often what is predicated of a pronoun will help pick out its referent. Garvey, Caramazza, and Yates give a simple example:

Rosemary trusted the secretary because she was efficient.[8]

We tend to identify *the secretary* as the referent of *she* because efficiency is commonly predicated of secretaries. (This example is a little more complicated than they suggest: the *because* clause gives an explanation of why one was either the Subject or Object of *trust*: efficiency is a reason that someone would be the Object of *trust*, but not the Subject; hence the Object of *trust* is the one who is efficient. I am indebted to Jeanette Clausen for pointing this out.) Thomas Bever has constructed more complicated examples of the way predicates specify the referents of pronouns: (a) is said to be easier to comprehend than (b) though they are structurally identical:

(a) The box it rolled out of scratched the ball it contained.
(b) The shovel it was below broke the rake it fell on.[9]

Given only the two noun phrases as possible antecedents and no context, it is easier to identify *ball* as the Subject of *roll* and *box* as the Subject of *contain* than it is to identify *rake* as the Subject of *was below* and *shovel* as the Subject of *fell on* because a ball is the likely Roller and a box the likely Container, while in (b) the predicates do not help to choose between shovel and rake as their Subjects. It appears that searching for antecedents involves a kind of 'plugging in' of candidates in place of the pronoun to see whether the resulting clause is congruent and likely. The problem with (b) is that even the plugging in is not decisive.

Often several phrases must be orchestrated into the likeliest reading of the whole. Comprehension of the following passage requires the reader to decide whether *the warning* refers to Chad's answer or to Strether's note:

(11) He had announced himself—six months before; had written out at least that Chad wasn't to be surprised should he see him some day turn up. Chad had thereupon, in a few words of rather carefully colourless answer, offered him a general welcome; and Strether, ruefully reflecting that *he* might have understood *the warning* as a hint to hospitality, a bid for an invitation, had fallen back upon silence as the corrective most to his own taste.

[James, *AMB*, 68]

The question of what *the warning* refers to is related to the reference of the italicized *he*. If James obeys the rule of first eligible antecedent to the left, the antecedent of *he* would have to be Strether, and *the warning* would have to refer to Chad's answer—which indeed from the description might be the sort of thing Strether might take as a warning. But the thing referred to as *warning* and *hint to hospitality* must also be the thing referred to as *a bid for an invitation* (since it is appositive), and Chad's answer could hardly be a bid for an invitation, since Chad is the resident, Strether the ambassador. The alternative analysis, where *he* refers to Chad and *the warning* to Strether's note, makes a better reading, since his note could be taken as a bid for an invitation. This example is particularly difficult because the reference of two noun phrases is uncertain: if *the warning* were replaced by the term *announcement*, the passage would be easier to perceive, since the only *he* who would be understanding the announcement would be Chad. The difficulty is certainly compounded by the first available antecedent to the left not being the correct one.

The way that particular decisions about referents are controlled by the need to compose the entire passage into a scene is further illustrated by the following two passages from Faulkner:

(12) It should have been later than it was; it should have been late, yet the yellow slashes of mote-palpitant sunlight were latticed no higher up the impalpable wall of gloom which separated them; the sun seemed hardly to have moved.

[Faulkner, *ABS*, 22]

(13) [sentence on previous page: When the shadow of the sash appeared on the curtains it was between seven and eight oclock and then I was in time again, hearing the watch.] . . . I got up and went to the dresser and slid my hand along it and touched the watch and turned it facedown and went back to bed. But the shadow of the sash was still there and I had learned to tell almost to the minute, so I'd have to turn my back to *it*, feeling the eyes animals used to have in the back of their heads when it was on top, itching.

[Faulkner, *SF*, 96]

In (12), if one looks leftwards for the first available noun phrase as the antecedent for *them*, one gets *slashes*, but why the wall of gloom would be said to separate the slashes is unclear, so we go to the context which gives us two figures sitting in the room with a wall of gloom between 'them' (on which the sunlight played). In (13), one may find oneself caught in a visualizing dilemma: if the shadow of the sash is projected by the morning sun, then for him to turn away from it would seem to mean turning toward the sun. Furthermore, if one imagines an erect animal with eyes in the back of its head, whatever was "on top" would not be seen anyway. These difficulties are almost enough to make one try *the watch* as the antecedent of *it*, but the business about the eyes is no clearer, since back in bed he couldn't see the hands of the dial anyway. The scene does cohere, however, if we imagine the shadow of the sash to be on the top of the curtain: then turning away is burying your head in the pillow, and eyes in the back of your head would still see the shadow when it was on top. Perhaps there are readers who visualize this scene correctly on first reading, but for the rest of us some careful weighing of alternatives is necessary: one sets up a possible interpretation and sees if it 'clicks'.

The process involved in these cases seems to be a kind of shuttling back and forth, reading new information and integrating it into the scene which may be only tentatively sketched in the mind. The final example of this sort of shuttling does not involve a literal spatial scene but rather a set of predications and inferences that allow one, finally, to select the best antecedent (which is sentential) for the italicized *which*, but only very slowly and as it were after the fact—that is, I find this passage impossible to process by any usual strategy and must tackle it with an analytic problem-solving routine:

(14) That even, I my self, the Author of these momentous Truths, am a Person, whose Imaginations are hard-mouth'd, and exceedingly disposed to run away with his Reason, which I have observed from long Experience, to be a very light Rider, and easily shook off; upon which Account, my Friends will never trust me alone, without a solemn Promise, to vent my Speculations in this, or the like manner, for the universal Benefit of Human kind; *which*, perhaps, the gentle, courteous, and candid Reader, brimful of that Modern Charity and Tenderness, usually annexed to his Office, will be very hardly persuaded to believe.

[Swift, *TOT*, Quintana Ed. 347]

The noun phrase immediately to the left of *which* is *the universal Benefit of Human kind*. This cannot be certainly rejected until we get to *believe* when it becomes obvious that it cannot be the Object of *believe*. 'That his friends make him promise to write' is next to the left, and is a proposition that could be the Object of *believe* (i.e., find it hard to believe), but in that case, the reader would be skeptical, not charitable: the proposition we are looking for is one that the author would consider damaging to himself, and the likeliest candidate is 'that he is a person whose imaginations run away with him' (the antecedent of *which Account* also)—they certainly ran away with him in this sentence!

These examples provide several instances where leftward search can lead us down a garden path if there is an eligible antecedent nearer the pronoun on the left than the correct one. I assume that the 'plugging in' or congruence testing is a kind of preliminary check and deals in such large categories as animate/inanimate, singular/plural, etc. Only if a noun phrase passes this initial screening does it qualify as a bothersome garden path. Further, one 'plugs in' to a structure that is not completely processed itself, and, as (14) shows, the information needed to force a reanalysis is often delayed. Finally, as Eugene Charniak points out, a reanalysis may never be 'forced' by an out and out incongruity: we must be ready to reject the nearest candidate to the left even if it is plausible, provided there is a more plausible candidate around (see the references of note 1). The general effect is that of working a puzzle where a piece seems to fit in a certain place and only appears not to after several other pieces are drawn in. The longer the mistake persists unnoticed, the greater will be the amount of puzzle torn up.

While writers may on occasion set up a garden path for their own purposes, the commoner case is for them to risk one now and then and hope the reader will not take it. Situations arise, for example, when one wishes to delay a relative clause so that it no longer immediately follows its antecedent. Milton, for one, does this quite a lot:

(15) All these and more came flocking; but with looks
Down cast and damp, yet such wherein appear'd
Obscure some glimps of joy, to have found thir chief
Not in despair, to have found themselves not lost
In loss it self; *which* on his count'nance cast
Like doubtful hue:

[Milton, *PL*, I. 522–27]

Loss it self is possible, if vague, as the antecedent of *which*, but the basic imagery is of light playing on Satan's face, and *glimps of joy* appears to give a better reading, given the usual association of joy with radiance. Again in the next example:

(16) Our labour must be to pervert that end,
     And out of good still to find means of evil;
     Which oft-times may succeed, so as perhaps
     Shall grieve him, . . .

[Milton, *PL*, I. 164–67]

Means of evil is marginally possible as the antecedent—if we are content to have means succeeding—but a better antecedent is *labour*. We might save ourselves the misperception if we take Milton's semicolon preceding the relative clause as a warning to the reader not to take the previous noun phrase as the antecedent (see also *PL*, I. 435). Faulkner is another heavy user of relative clauses who takes certain chances:

(17) And the librarian knew why he was laughing, who had not called him anything but Mr Compson for thirty-two years now. . . .

[Faulkner, p. 747]

In context, this is not very confusing: the librarian is a woman, and so by the time we get to *called him* we can see that *he* cannot be the Subject of *called*. The next example is also confusing only momentarily or for just a bit longer until we process the *his gifts* in the relative clause:

(18) For he whose daies in wilfull woe are worne,
     The grace of his Creator doth despise,
     That will not vse his gifts to thanklesse nigardise.

[Spenser, *FQ*, IV.viii. 15]

The one using "his gifts" must be the creature, not the Creator. The next example from Faulkner is a little more confusing out of context:

(19) the Negro woman, his sworn enemy since his birth and his mortal
one since that day in 1911 when she too divined by simple clair-
voyance that he was somehow using his infant niece's illegitimacy to
blackmail its mother, who cooked the food he ate.[10]

The Negro woman, not the mother, cooks his food, though this
may not be totally certain until the next page when reference is
made to the Negro cook. However, the attentive reader may have
been able to identify "the mother" of the infant niece as Jason's
sister Caddy, who, we have been told three pages earlier, had
abandoned her infant daughter to Jason's keeping never to return.
Hence she is not "in the scene" as a possible referent of *who*. (The
repetition of *infant* in the two noun phrases may help the reader to
perceive the coreference.) Interestingly, in *The Portable Faulkner* the
troublesome relative clause appears immediately following *the
Negro woman*, where of course it occasions no difficulty, the garden
path being avoided (p. 750).

Thus far a leftward search has always produced an antecedent or
at least a referent. It would seem that such a process would encounter most difficulty in cases of 'backward pronominalization'—
where the pronoun precedes its 'antecedent,' which is on the right:

After he recovered, John took his nurse to dinner.

He's a real character, that brother of yours.

The impression that one must search to the right in such cases may
be erroneous, however, for Susumo Kuno has argued that there is
a general constraint on discourses that the pronoun may precede
its 'antecedent' only if it is predictable from prior discourse—if,
that is, the individual the pronoun refers to has already been introduced and is 'on stage' or given in the situation of utterance.[11]
Hence, Kuno notes, the pronoun can never have an indefinite
'postcedent':

When he left, a man noticed the train was late.

Since an indefinite noun phrase is used to refer to a new individual, Kuno's constraint explains why it cannot be a postcedent: the individual must already have been introduced. Thus Bever's examples concerning the ball and the box, rake and shovel, are artificial insofar as no previous context is given: the reader must therefore really make a rightward search for the postcedent of *it*. Equally, Kuno's principle renders unnecessary Bever's perceptual principle devised to account for acceptability judgments in backwards cases ("Cognitive Basis," p. 319).

Kuno's principle appears to hold over the great majority of cases of apparent backward pronominalization in our texts, even in the following passage where the referent of *they* is represented to the left as well as to the right, though perhaps not obviously so, since the first occurrence of *afternoon and evening* does not set them up as 'things'—rather, the phrase tends to be read in terms of "spent time." Instead, *the immediate and the sensible* appears the likely antecedent, hence we have a garden path:

(20) he had . . . given his afternoon and evening to the immediate and the sensible. *They* formed a qualified draught of Europe, an afternoon and an evening on the banks of the Mersey, but such as it was he took his potion at least undiluted.

[James, *AMB*, 18]

Compare the following passage where there is no garden path to distract the reader:

(21) Such had at any rate markedly been the case for the precipitation of a special series of impressions. *They* had proved, successively, these impressions—all of Musette and Francine, but Musette and Francine vulgarized by the larger evolution of the type—irresistibly sharp:

[James, *AMB*, 67]

Notice by the way that (20) seems to involve a violation of Kuno's constraint, in that the specifying noun phrase is indefinite (*an after-*

noon. . . .). Clearly, however, the indefinite here is a special use meaning roughly "any such"—substituting *that* for *an* would insist too much on the specific afternoon and evening. Example (21) illustrates Kantor's point about demonstratives: James concludes that the reference of the pronoun *they* is not sufficiently clear (it refers to a subpart of the preceding noun phrase *the precipitation* . . .) and signals the extra effort by the demonstrative *these* (impressions). So also with (23) and (24) below. (On this construction, see Dwight Bolinger, "Pronouns and Repeated Nouns," pp. 25–26.)

Two factors make the following passage genuinely hard: it does violate Kuno's constraint, and it sets up a garden path: the leftward *these* ("shapes") is to be contrasted with the new *these* (things beneath the shadow of a shape):

(22) The bed, the books, the chair, the moving nuns,
 The candle as it evades the sight, *these* are
 The sources of happiness in the shape of Rome,
 A shape within the ancient circles of shapes,
 And *these* beneath the shadow of a shape

 In a confusion on bed and books, a portent
 On the chair, a moving transparence on the nuns,
 A light on the candle tearing against the wick
 To join a hovering excellence, to escape
 From fire and be part of that of which

 Fire is the symbol: the celestial possible.

 [Stevens, *CP*, 508–09]

The new *these*, that is, are the portent, transparence, and light. As before, the passage is confusing not just because the 'antecedent' can be found only to the right, but also because there appears to be a very likely antecedent to the left, which, according to the general strategy of leftward search, gets tried first.

We can explain the difficulty of these passages by assuming that leftward search has precedence over rightward search—if indeed one ever does make a rightward search. In general, I think one does not, but there are exceptions. The first is the pronoun *it* when sentence-initial (this is different from Bever's examples, where *it* is not initial). *It* does point to the right in both the cleft construction (*It was Oswald who killed Kennedy*) and in extraposed sentences (*It is surprising that you forgot his name*). James does use *it* rather loosely related to its context with a genuine specification following:

(23) [He] had presently strolled back to the Boulevard with a sense of injury that he felt himself taking for as good a start as any other. *It* would serve, this spur to his spirit, he reflected, as, pausing at the top of the street, he looked up and down the great foreign avenue, it would serve to begin business with.

[James, AMB, 57]

(24) She abounded in news of the situation at home, proved to him how perfectly she was arranging for his absence, told him who would take up this and who take up that exactly where he had left it, gave him in fact chapter and verse for the moral that nothing would suffer. *It* filled for him, this tone of hers, all the air;

[James, AMB, 60]

(25) His greatest uneasiness seemed to peep at him out of the imminent impression that almost any acceptance of Paris might give one's authority away. *It* hung before him this morning, the vast bright Babylon, like some huge iridescent object. . . .

[James, AMB, 64]

and this use of *it*, sometimes even without any preparation in context, is typical of Stevens also:

(26) It can never be satisfied, the mind, never.

[Stevens, CP, 247]

(27) It is a child that sings itself to sleep,
The mind, among the creatures that it makes.

[Stevens, CP, 436]

(and perhaps also the sentence cited in [5]: *It is a wheel, the rays/ Around the sun.*). The effect in all of these is that of the meditating mind making little leaps forward, and specification is never long delayed. The point is that the reader is prepared to look to the right for further specification when he sees a sentence-initial *it*, so these constructions are not hard to process.

The second exception are uses of pronouns (and definite noun phrases) at the beginning of stories and elsewhere in tales told in the free indirect style. Kuno stresses the beginnings of stories as points where his constraint does not hold, though of course confusion will not arise, as leftward searching is not possible. Beginning with a definite form has a kind of *in medias res* effect: the reader must scramble to find his bearings in a world that is, as it were, going on without regard for him. For example, the *they* at the beginning of (27) in Chapter Two has not yet been specified—it is the third sentence of the story. Note that the reader does not have to choose among possible referents already in the scene—rather, he craves more information about those that are being introduced. In the free indirect style, material is presented from the character's point of view, so that things are treated as 'in mind' by use of definites which have not been previously mentioned.[12] It should be noted, however, that rightward search will not necessarily pay off either: what the reader must do is imagine himself into the character's point of view as quickly as possible so that he will be able to share what the character is treating as 'given'.

The last exceptional situation, which is almost a trick rather than an exception, occurs in Faulkner when he presents the significance of a thing before naming it. Robert Zoellner cites one such sentence from *Absalom, Absalom!* where Sutpen "just walked on, erect, with the new hat cocked and carrying in his hand now that which must have seemed to them the final gratuitous insult. . . ." There follow nine printed lines before the final participial identifies what he was carrying ("carrying his newspaper cornucopia of flowers").[13] There is a similar sentence in (44) of the next chapter where lines and lines of ornate description precede the name of the thing described (the old bear).

None of these exceptions really requires the reader to innovate a strategy for rightward search. The reader already has a rightward strategy for initial *it*, and he simply will have to endure the suspension of beginnings and of Faulkner's delayed 'revelations'. There is a general sense in which we read ahead hoping that things which are yet somewhat unclear will fall into place with further information—we will see some further illustrations of this in the next section—and this is probably the way we read into a story or through a passage of suspended identification.

3. PARTICIPIALS

It is possible to regard the processing of subjectless participials as either a problem of perception (since one must establish a modifier-to-head relation called 'attachment') or one of comprehension (because of the similarity of participials to relative clauses). Though there is no relative pronoun present, participials usually immediately follow the noun phrase they modify (though they can precede the Subject if they modify it), but, like relative clauses, they can be shifted to the end of the clause and attach not to the preceding noun phrase but to an earlier one, usually the Subject. The parallelism with relative clauses is captured in a transformational framework by deriving participials from relative clauses via deletion of the relative pronoun and the form of *be:*

> A girl came in (who was) pursued by a bear.

It is not obvious, however, that comprehension involves restoring a relative pronoun and then searching for its antecedent, and so I treat the attachment problem as distinct from those involving coreference, although the parallel will be obvious.

It is quite crucial that we distinguish between reconstructions the reader must make to perceive a text from those he need not. Reconstruction (or identification) of a deleted Logical Subject in a passivized construction (i.e., the Logical Subject of the corresponding active sentence) has sometimes been treated as necessary, sometimes not—indeed, contradictory claims on this point provided Stanley Fish with some of his most telling arguments against transformational stylistics.[14] In a model of perception that involves reconstructing a deep structure of passivized constructions like

(28) Infinite goodness, grace and mercy shewn
      On Man by him seduc't, but on himself
      Treble confusion, wrath and vengeance pour'd.

                                                    [Milton, *PL*, I. 218–20]

by 'undoing' passive to get (in part),

      ... PRO show infinite goodness, grace and mercy on Man...
      ... PRO pour treble confusion, wrath, and vengeance on Satan...

the indefinite pronoun appears as a restored Logical Subject and presumably would have to have an antecedent assigned to it, or at least a referent from among the individuals in the world of the work. Thus Seymour Chatman claims that at some level we specify God as the deleted Subject and, as it were, unwittingly acknowledge His power.[15]

An alternative view is possible, however, which treats passivization as a way of making transitive (i.e., two-place) predicates intransitive (i.e., one-place). The logical form of a passivized construction would be satisfied even if the Subject of the corresponding active were not specified—it might appear as an optional modifier (as it does in *by him seduc't*), but the process of perception would be complete without it, as is the construction. This is roughly the view of passives presented by Ronald Langacker and Patricia Munro in their article "Passives and Their Meaning."[16] This does not mean that the reader may not go on on his own to specify a deleted Subject—only that passives are not "hidden persuaders" or inherently tools of "brainwashing" as Chatman among others assumed.[17] Certainly the traditional warning about the deviousness of passives is based on the assumption that we may *not* reconstruct the deleted Logical Subject.[18]

The question that we must ask in perceiving a participial, however, is to which noun phrase it is attached—which noun phrase, that is, would be the antecedent of the relative pronoun if it were present. When a participial is delayed and does not immediately follow the noun phrase it attaches to, other noun phrases may intervene, and the possibility of a garden path again arises. Consider, for example, the following two passages from *Paradise Lost:*

(29)   While smooth Adonis from his native Rock
        Ran purple to the Sea, *suppos'd with blood*
        Of Thammuz yearly wounded:

[Milton, *PL*, I. 450–52]

(30)   [scene: Uriel observing Satan] his gestures fierce
        He mark'd and mad demeanour, *then alone,*
        As he suppos'd, all unobserv'd, unseen.

[Milton, *PL*, IV. 128–30]

In (29) *suppos'd . . . wounded* could be attached to *the Sea,* since it is the immediately preceding noun phrase, but this reading does not make much sense, since there is no reason to think the sea is being viewed as having a body, so we must go back and try *rock* or *Adonis,* and of course *Adonis* is semantically congruent with *wounded*—the problem is really how it can also make sense as the name of a river, but one concludes that Milton is collapsing natural fact and its mythic explanation here. Example (30) is also momentarily difficult, since both *he*'s refer to animate beings. The context has Uriel observing Satan, and the best way to tell whether *then alone . . . unseen* is to be attached to *he* = Satan or *he* = Uriel is to note that Uriel would not suppose himself alone, since he is watching Satan. As long as the semantic incompatibility of the mistaken noun is fairly obvious, the mistake is quickly noticed:

(31)   where stood
        Her Temple on th'offensive Mountain, *built*
        By that uxorious King. . . .

[Milton, *PL*, I. 442–44]

The mountain cannot have been *built*—it must be the temple. Contrast the next example, where semantic clues to attachment are a bit more indirect:

(32) she loved him not only in spite of but because of the fact that he himself was incapable of love, *accepting the fact that he must value above all not her but the virginity of which she was custodian and on which she placed no value whatever:* the frail physical stricture which to her was no more than a hangnail would have been.

[Faulkner, p. 744]

Accepting the fact . . . could be attached to either *he* or *her.* But since love usually involves acceptance, the Lover ('she') is likely to be the Acceptor also. It is perhaps somewhat easier to find the noun to which *possessing* . . . *and being* . . . should be attached in the next example, since the alternatives *truck* and *horses* can be quickly ruled out:

(33) It was himself, though no horseman, no farmer, not even a country-man save by his distant birth and boyhood, who coaxed and soothed the two horses, drawing them by his own single frail hand until, backing, filling, trembling a little, they surged, halted, then sprung scrambling down from the truck, *possessing no affinity for them as creatures, beasts, but being merely insulated by his years and time from the corruption of steel and oiled moving parts which tainted the others.*

[Faulkner, pp. 712–13]

The sheer length of the participials appears to be one of the sources of difficulty in Faulkner. We could account for this if we supposed that we may wait to compose the entire participial before deciding what it is attached to, or, if we encounter uncertainty, to read forward into the participial hoping for further clues as to what was affected. The more we can find out about 'what happened', the easier it should be to infer whom or what it happened to. So in (34) (which repeats [51] of Chapter One) the final participial does not contain enough information to allow a certain choice among *mother Earth, her,* or even *him,* but the first line of the next stanza does:

(34) Her sire Typhoeus was, who mad through merth,
　　　And drunke with bloud of men, slaine by his might,

Through incest, her of his owne mother Earth
Whilome begot, *being but halfe twin of that berth.*

48

For at that berth another Babe she bore. . . .

[Spenser, *FQ,* III.vii. 47–48]

That berth, we conclude, is the consequence of the begetting just mentioned; therefore it must be her (Argante's) birth, but we cannot see why she (Argante) is just a half twin until we get to the next stanza.

Empson cites a number of cases where the attachment of participials is uncertain, among them the following lines from "The Waste Land"

(35) Reflecting light upon the table as
     The glitter of her jewels rose to meet it,
     From satin cases poured in rich profusion;

[Empson, *Ambiguity,* p. 77]

He comments: "What is *poured* may be *cases, jewels, glitter,* or *light,* and *profusion,* enriching its modern meaning with its derivation, is shared, with a dazzling luxury, between them; so that while some of the *jewels* are *pouring* out *light* from their *cases,* others are *poured* about, as are their *cases,* on the dressing-table." Empson nicely suggests the sort of shuttling back and forth the reader executes as he checks the compatibility of each of the likely candidates for attachment. This shuttling exactly parallels that described in the case of pronouns above.

The next passage again sets up this shuttling back and forth, which in this case is complicated by the length of the participial—one perhaps begins checking back before the participial is completely processed, or identifies the noun phrases to which the participial might be attached, hoping that by the time he finishes processing the participial he will be able to guess which among the candidates is right:

(36) For six years now he had heard the best of all talking. It was of the wilderness, the big woods, bigger and older than any recorded document—of white man fatuous enough to believe he had bought any fragment of it, of Indian ruthless enough to pretend that any fragment of it had been his to convey. . . . It was of the men, not white nor black nor red, but men, hunters, with the will and hardihood to endure and the humility and skill to survive, and the dogs and the bear and deer juxtaposed and reliefed against it, *ordered and compelled by and within the wilderness in the ancient and unremitting contest according to the ancient and immitigable rules which voided all regrets and brooked no quarter.* . . .

[Faulkner, p. 227]

Obviously the problem begins with the slightly uncertain reference of the *it* immediately preceding the participial in question. There appear to be two leading candidates: *the wilderness* and *the best of all talking.* The two are close, of course, in that the tale is of the wilderness, but *wilderness* seems more congruent with *juxtaposed against* since it has a physical location. We can tentatively conclude then that the participial does not attach to *it* (= the wilderness) but attaches to the long coordinate noun phrase *the men . . . and the dogs and the bear and the deer* (and is then essentially appositive to the preceding participial *juxtaposed . . .*). All of the members of this long coordinate noun phrase are congruent as the Subject of *ordered and compelled.* . . . But one may also wonder whether the participial attaches to *it* (= *the best of all talking*)—*it* too is congruent if we think of the story as shaped and necessitated by its subject and heard by the boy each year on the hunt. Perhaps the material immediately following the dash will help:

> the best game of all, the best of all breathing and for ever the best of all listening. . . .

The best game of all appears to be an appositive coreferential to *the ancient and unremitting contest,* but what are *the best of all breathing* and *the best of all listening* coreferential to? The last would seem to be *the best of all talking,* with the breathing as perhaps a bridge linking the hunt with the tale of the hunt. One senses that Faulkner is deliberately fusing the primary experience of the hunt with the verbal telling of it through difficult pronominal reference, uncertain attachment, and an obscure sort of summarizing appositive. I do believe that there is a 'best reading' here along the lines I have indicated, but I also believe that the other possibilities (a veritable maze of garden paths) contribute to the effect Faulkner is aiming at. One can see here, albeit darkly, how apposition figures in the pursuit of coreference, and we will return to the fusional effect in Faulkner at the end of the next chapter.

In this chapter again we have seen ways that processing involves both semantic and syntactic strategies. Comprehension of definite noun phrases and pronouns takes place in relation to an imagined scene: the referent must be identified from among those present in the scene, or those which can be imagined, as the case requires. In many instances, the range of possible referents is limited or narrowed down to one by the scene, so that no further strategies are needed. There does seem to be a process of leftward search, however, that gets underway in problematic cases involving a kind of trial-and-error matching of potential antecedents to the pronoun, and head nouns to participial, which can reject or continue to try candidates as the clause is processed. Thus (17) and (18) are relatively easy to make out, (29) somewhat harder, and similarly (31) and (33) may be easier than (32). There seems to be a clear tendency for the nearest candidate on the left to be tried first—hence the possibility of garden paths—though we should note that this tendency is most marked with relative pronouns and participials, since these generally do immediately follow the noun phrases they modify (other pronouns typically do *not* immediately follow their antecedents). I have assumed that when the immediately prior noun phrase proves unsuitable as the antecedent of the relative pronoun, one searches left for the antecedent just as one does with a personal pronoun (rather than pursue an integrative strategy of moving the entire clause back to its antecedent to create a 'canonical form' for perception of relative clauses). This may be incorrect, but it seems right to me. In the next chapter, which is a continuation of this insofar as comprehension of appositives also involves coreference, we will have further opportunity to explore strategies for perceiving delayed or strayed coreferential elements and once again to consider the interaction of semantic and structural processes.

CHAPTER FOUR

Reference, Coreference, and Attachment

II: APPOSITION

B ASICALLY, apposition is the juxtaposition of two or more like phrases or clauses without a conjunction. Semantically, the difference between coordination and apposition is crucial—coordinated elements are almost always understood as referring to different things, appositives to the same thing. Usually apposition is discussed in terms of noun phrases, but other elements can also be appositively juxtaposed. In the following example from Henry James's *The Ambassadors*, verbs are both conjoined and apposed, and the example illustrates the distinction between the multiple reference of coordination and the single reference of apposition:

(1)   Chad and Miss Gostrey had rummaged and purchased and picked up and exchanged, sifting, selecting, comparing;

[James, *AMB*, 146]

That is, *rummaging, purchasing,* and *picking up* refer to different (though closely related) actions, but *sifting, selecting,* and *comparing* refer to the same action.

Perceiving a phrase as appositive entails marking it as coreferential to some preceding phrase in the sentence and removing it from the list of items which must have some function assigned to them in the proposition (the function of the appositive being identical to that of the phrase it is appositive to). The misperception of examples (5) and (6) in Chapter Two occurs because the last phrases are read as appositive to the preceding and hence are not identified as the delayed Objects of the verbs (and see II.38, 44, where phrases are read as appositive and not as Subjects of new clauses). The problem of perceiving an appositive is primarily one of distinguishing it from a coordinated item in a series: both are items set off from the preceding like item by a comma, and it is not until we get to the last item that we can see whether a conjunction is present. Again we encounter 'look-ahead' limitations: the decision to treat an item as coreferential to the preceding or not waits for structural information that may be delayed quite a while. If the reader is deciding whether an item is appositive or not as he scans, he will experience difficulty when the structural clue is farther away than his look-ahead can reach. I will offer examples below which suggest that this difficulty does arise. However, the difficulty appears to be greatly reduced by certain semantic clues, again suggesting the use of a semantically based strategy along with a serial, structural one.

Comprehending an appositive involves the additional step of identifying which of the previous phrases of like type it is coreferential to. In the great majority of cases, the antecedent is the immediately preceding phrase of like type, and it would seem that a practical strategy for comprehending appositives could be based on simple linear precedence. Appositives may, however, be delayed, and this fact makes problems for a simple linear strategy, as we will see in sections two and three. Overall, the distributional possibilities are rather like those for relative clauses and participials, and some transformational grammarians have proposed a derivation of appositives from underlying relative clauses via deletion of the relative pronoun and copula:

George Washington, (who was/is) the father of our country. . . .

(Example [1] would require relative pronouns with verb and verb phrase antecedents.) If this derivation directly reflects the process of comprehension, then the task of identifying what the appositive is coreferential to becomes a case of (relative) pronominal reference. However, the range of possible referents for appositives is somewhat more restricted than that for relative pronouns since there must always be an antecedent phrase in the sentence— sentential antecedents are very rare. As in the case of participials, little insight into the processing of appositives is to be gained by regarding them as reduced relative clauses.

It is possible that some readers decide on apposition as they scan while others do not. Stanley Fish and Ralph Rader disagree about whether 'we' see one object ("the fiend-who-is-the spot") or two ("fiend" and "spot") as we read the following passage:

> There lands the Fiend, a spot like which perhaps
> Astronomer in the Sun's lucent Orbe
> Through his glaz'd Optic Tube yet never saw.
>> [Milton, *PL*, I. 588–90]

Rader apparently is one who notes apposition as he scans—he does not set up the *spot* as referring to a (possibly) distinct individual and therefore does not find the passage as confusing as Fish does.[1] Fish, however, appears not to decide on the appositive/ non-appositive status of *a spot* until the information contained in the relative clause is in: "in the first line two focal points (spot and fiend) are offered the reader who sets them side by side in his mind. . . . the detail of the next one and one half lines is attached to the image, and a scene is formed, strengthening the implied equality of spot and fiend. . . ."[2] Unfortunately, no experiments on the comprehension of appositives have been reported, so we will have to content ourselves (for the moment, but see the next chapter) with the apparent fact that some readers identify appositives as they scan and some do not.

1. STRUCTURAL AND SEMANTIC CLUES

To see what is meant by waiting for the structural clue, consider the following example:

(2)   Shall she not find (in comforts of the sun,)
      (In pungent fruit and bright, green wings,) or else
      (In any balm or beauty of the earth,)
      Things to be cherished like the thought of heaven?

                                                    [Stevens, *CP*, 67]

This has the structure

                ... find in x, in y, or else in z ...

As we read *in y*, we see that it could be appositive to *in x;* when we reach the conjunction *or else in z,* however, we see that it could be the second term in a three-term coordination. Reaching a coordinating conjunction, however, does not decide the question—it only indicates the possibility of coordination, and the decision must be made on grounds of the best reading in context. In context, the *pungent fruit and bright, green wings* have been established as the comforts of the sun, and there is a disjunction between *comforts of the sun* and *balm and beauty of the earth* that is the main ordering principle. Hence the disjunction is really two-way, not three-, and the term in question is a specifying appositive after all. (There is an asymmetry in that *balm or beauty* ... does not have an appositive to match against *pungent fruit.* ... This may explain why I tend to read *things to be cherished* ... as part of the preceding instead of the long delayed Object of *find* [see II.6]).

Because the structural signal of a conjunction may be delayed for some time, and because it is not decisive but only indicates possible coordination, some readers may employ a semantically based strategy to check items in a series for possible appositive relations before they get to the end of the series. Since appositives refer to the same thing, they are usually either synonymous with, or more or less general than, the initial term. The first example illustrates

the simplest case of synonymy (*sifting, selecting, comparing*); for a
more complex case, consider these lines:

(3)   Warblings became
        Too dark, too far, too much the accents of
        Afflicted sleep, too much the syllables
        That would form themselves, in time, and communicate
        The intelligence of his despair, express
        What meditation never quite achieved.

                                                        [Stevens, *CP*, 314]

Here *express* . . . is a verb phrase appositive to *communicate* . . . and is
easily recognized as such by the synonymous verb which initiates
it. We then recognize that the entire verb phrases are appositive
and establish an identity between *the intelligence of his despair* and
what meditation never quite achieved. In the next example, the semantic overlapping of terms, though less than exact synonymy, is a
comparable clue:

(4)   some glory, some prosperity of the First Empire, some Napoleonic
      glamour, some dim lustre of the great legend;

                                                        [James, *AMB*, 145]

Here are some other examples:

(5)   sights of woe,
        Regions of sorrow, doleful shades. . . .

                                                        [Milton, *PL*, I. 64–65]

(6)   Is this the Region, this the Soil, the Clime,
      Said then the lost Arch-Angel, this the seat
      That we must change for Heav'n. . . .

                                                        [Milton, *PL*, I. 242–44]

Notice that though the third appositive is separated from the preceding ones, Milton points out the relation by repeating the *this
the*.

    When the apposed term is narrower or more detailed than its
antecedent, we will call it a specifying appositive. Examples are
legion:

(7) a hint to hospitality, a bid for an invitation. . . .

[James, *AMB*, 68]

(8) She struck herself as hovering like a spy, applying tests, laying traps, concealing signs.

[James, *WOD*, I. 117]

(9) the air of supreme respectability, the consciousness, small, still, reserved, but none the less distinct and diffused, of private honour.

[James, *AMB*, 146]

(10)   that were low indeed,
       That were an ignominy and shame beneath
       This downfall;

[Milton, *PL*, I. 114–16]

In (10), full clauses are appositive, *ignominy and shame* specifying what *low* means. The next example is perhaps a little harder than the rest:

(11) intense little preferences and sharp little exclusions, a deep suspicion of the vulgar and a personal view of the right.

[James, *AMB*, 146]

What is tricky here is that the specifying appositives are in reversed order:

preferences and exclusions, suspicion and personal view

Here are some specifying appositives from consecutive pages in a Faulkner story ("Delta Autumn"), the last rather complex (appositives are marked with square brackets):

(12) he watched even the last puny marks of man—[cabin, clearing, the small and irregular fields which a year ago were jungle and in which the skeleton stalks of this year's cotton stood almost as tall and rank as the old cane had stood, as if man had had to marry his planting to the wilderness in order to conquer it]—fall away and vanish. The twin banks marched with wilderness as he remembered it—[the tangle of brier and cane impenetrable even to sight twenty feet away,] [the tall tremendous soaring of oak and gum and ash and hickory

which had rung to no axe save the hunter's, and echoed to no machinery save the beat of old-time steam boats traversing it. . . .]

[Faulkner, p. 713]

(13) it seemed to him that the retrograde of his remembering had gained
an inverse velocity from their own slow progress, [₁that the land had
retreated not in minutes from the last spread of gravel but in years,
decades, back toward what it had been when he first knew it: [₂the
road they now followed once more the ancient pathway of bear and
deer,] [₃the diminishing fields they now passed once more scooped
punily and terrifically by axe and saw and mule-drawn plow from the
wilderness' flank, out of the brooding and immemorial tangle,] [₄in
place of ruthless mile-wide parallelograms wrought by ditching the
dyking machinery.]]

[Faulkner, p. 712]

In (13), the first appositive *that*-clause explicates or specifies the
meaning of the first *that*-clause, and the second and third (verbless)
clauses in turn specify *what it had been like when he first knew it*. The
material inside the fourth set of brackets is attached either to *tangle*
or to the laboriously cleared fields (not exactly *the fields they now
passed*, but the fields as he remembered them). The repetition of
once more, by the way, is crucially helpful in guiding the reader to
the recognition of what is identical to what—it is a kind of clue of
parallelism.

The generalizing appositive does not so readily furnish a strategy
for running recognition, since it frequently comes only at the end
of a series of particulars, but it does signal quite conclusively that
the generalizing term is to be taken as appositive to the preceding
and that the preceding terms are apposed particulars:

(14) the prohibition of impulse, accident, range—the prohibition, in other
words, of freedom—

[James, *WOD*, II. 294]

Note by the way that the generalizing term replaces the particulars
and may include more than the enumerated particulars. In the next
example, which is from John Ruskin's *The Queen of the Air*, the apposi-

tion is of conditional clauses (the passage is discussed in a recent article by Frederick Kirchhoff[3]):

(15) [₁But if, for us also, as for the Greek, the sunrise means daily restoration to the sense of passionate gladness, and of perfect life]—[₂if it means the thrilling of new strength through every nerve,—the shedding over us of a better peace than the peace of night, in the power of the dawn,—and the purging of evil vision and fear by the baptism of its dew;] [₃if the sun itself is an influence, to us also, of spiritual good—and becomes thus in reality, not in imagination, to us also, a spiritual power,]—we may then soon over-pass the narrow limit of conception which kept that power impersonal, and rise with the Greek to the thought of an angel. . . .[4]

When we reach the second *if* clause, we must decide whether it is to be understood as a separate condition added to the first: as we read into it we may check for synonymous material, or fuller specification, and, finding it, conclude that it is not, but is instead an appositive. When we get to the third *if* clause, we must again ask if it constitutes a new, additional condition, and, on seeing that *influence of spiritual good* generalizes the *thrilling,* the *shedding,* and the *purging,* conclude that it also is not a new condition but merely gathers into itself the preceding two. It is quite possible, of course, that Ruskin does not expect us to consider these discriminations, nor even to notice the shift from human response to nature in the first two *if* clauses to the objective "influence" of the sun in the third, and that the intended effect is a blurring and fusing of object and response. We can perhaps say a bit more about the way this effect is achieved: the very act of deciding that the three conditions are in fact the same (i.e., appositive) may cause us to overlook the way in which the third clause is not quite the same.

In general, then, the reader can adopt a tactic of checking semantic relatedness between terms in a string: if the term following the first comma is synonymous with the initial term, or more specific or general, it is probably appositive to the initial term; if not, expect a conjunction and establish, tentatively, separate referential indices for each item. If one tries to apply such a strategy in the following passage, however, one may experience difficulties (the passage is part of Milton's list of devils manifested in secular mythology):

(16)   The rest were long to tell, though far renown'd,
        Th' Ionian Gods, of Javan's Issue held
        Gods, yet confest later than Heav'n and Earth
        Thir boasted Parents; Titan Heav'ns first born
        With his enormous brood, and birthright seis'd
        By younger Saturn, he from mightier Jove
        His own and Thea's Son like measure found;

[Milton, *PL*, I. 507–13]

Titan ... is possibly appositive to *the Ionian Gods* as a specification—but is Titan an Ionian God? Milton says the Ionian Gods had Heaven and Earth for parents, and Titan was Heaven's first born, and we may conclude that Milton is not drawing some arcane distinction between Ionian and Olympian Gods here.

There are two types of appositives, however, that will pose problems for a semantic inclusion tactic: the first is what might be called the replacing appositive: the appositive material is to be taken as an improvement on the initial formulation:

(17)   a proof of what—or of a part of what—

[James, *WOD*, I. 117]

(18)   a proof of their wisdom, their success, of the reality of what had happened—of what in fact, for the spirit of each, was still happening—

[James, *WOD*, II. 314]

Note that James in these two examples offsets these appositives heavily with dashes and some extra marking (*or, in fact*). He does not always do so, however: in the next example he teases the reader, who is uncertain whether to substitute 'musical' phrase for 'verbal' phrase:

(19)   the whole history of their house had the effect of some fine, florid voluminous phrase, say even a musical, that dropped first into

words, into notes, without sense, and then, hanging unfinished, into no words, no notes at all.[5]

This kind of double statement is typical of Faulkner as well:

(20) that day and himself and McCaslin juxtaposed, not against the wilderness but against the tamed land, the old wrong and shame itself, in repudiation and denial at least of the land and the wrong and the shame, even if he couldn't cure the wrong and eradicate the shame. . . .

[Faulkner, p. 721]

(Faulkner repeats the same appositive *land/shame and wrong* again later in the sentence.) The effect in these passages is to leave the reader uncertain whether one phrase is to replace the other ('the tamed land—which is to say really the shame and wrong [?slavery]') or to be equated with it on a higher, analogical level ('the tamed land—instance and symbol of the shame and wrong'). The latter option allows the two to be two and yet one. It is interesting, by the way, that James evidently repented of the playfulness of (19), since the New York Edition reads ". . . say even a musical, that dropped first into words and notes without sense and then, hanging unfinished, into no words nor any notes at all" (*WOD*, I. 4).

The notion of replacement introduces a certain slipperiness into the application of these categories. Even with the specifying and generalizing types, the final appositive has the last word—that is, it comes at the end of what often appears to be a process of getting it just right. With the replacing type, the final statement not only succeeds but supersedes the others—but this is perhaps a matter of degree: a writer may essentially develop his thinking about something through a string of appositives. We will examine some illustrations of this in Wordsworth in the next chapter.

The notion of higher or analogical identity brings us to the second problematic type of apposition. In its nature, it is a mix of coordination and apposition, since the terms are on one level referentially distinct, but their being apposed forces the reader to see them as identical—to perform, in most cases, some sort of inference. This sort of apposition may involve relatively obvious and 'local' inferences, as with the first set of examples to be cited where the inference in some sort of summation, usually a 'total impression':

(21) Can make a Heav'n of Hell, a Hell of Heav'n.

[Milton, *PL*, I. 255]

(22)   some glimps of joy, to have found thir chief
      Not in despair, to have found themselves not lost
      In loss it self;

[Milton, *PL*, I. 524–26]

(23) He seems to see them, endless, without order, empty, symbolical, bleak, skypointed not with ecstasy or passion but in adjuration, threat, and doom.

[Faulkner, *LA*, 426]

(24) She worked—and seemingly quite without design—upon the sympathy, the curiosity, the fancy of her associates. . . .

[James, *WOD*, I. 116]

(25) She exceeded, escaped measure, was surprising only because they were so far from great.

[James, *WOD*, I. 117]

(26) To feel the street, to feel the room, to feel the table-cloth and the centre-piece and the lamp, gave her a small, salutary sense at least of neither shirking nor lying.

[James, *WOD*, I. 4]

(27) The court was large and open, full of revelations, for our friend, of the habit of privacy, the peace of intervals, the dignity of distances and approaches;

[James, *AMB*, 145]

Typically the whole is an impression: different things are perceived as one or may be regarded as one in the context. Sometimes there is an explicit statement of the generalized whole, in which case we have a generalizing appositive:

(28) It is a kind of total grandeur at the end,
With every visible thing enlarged and yet
No more than a bed, a chair and moving nuns,
The immense theatre, the pillared porch,
The book and candle in your ambered room,

Total grandeur of a total edifice. . . .

[Stevens, *CP*, 510]

(29) It had in fact, as he was now aware, filled all the approaches, hovered in the court as he passed, hung on the staircase as he mounted, sounded in the grave rumble of the old bell, as little electric as possible, of which Chad, at the door, had pulled the ancient but neatly-kept tassel; it formed in short the clearest medium of its particular kind that he had ever breathed.

[James, *AMB*, 146]

Notice that the *in short* signals a generalizing statement to follow. The "summation" interpretation is as it were an easy inference: the harder ones arise when "outer" is juxtaposed to "inner," or the link is some sort of moral analogy which must be inferred: James's appositives are frequently of this nature. The following example from the beginning of *The Wings of the Dove* is typical of his appositional linking:

(30) Each time she turned in again, each time, in her impatience, she gave him up. . . .

[James, *WOD*, I. 3]

Her physical turning in, that is, is the 'outer' equivalent of her loss of patience. Faulkner also uses apposition to establish this sort of equivalence (here *it* refers to the land):

(31) Then suddenly he knew why he had never wanted to own any of it, arrest at least that much of what people called progress, measure his longevity at least against that much of its ultimate fate.

[Faulkner, p. 724]

Characteristic of this type of appositive is its direct thematic relevance—in context, the reader is not without guidance as to why the terms are apposed (and equated), though he must of course correctly apprehend the exact nature and scope of the identity.

In passages of narrative, we are rarely uncertain as to whether the apposition is based on complete identity or partial identity, since actions and things are obviously referentially distinct. Usually the higher unity is one of impression or significance embracing the distinguishably different things. In passages lacking this relation to a 'scene', we are on more uncertain ground. This is one source of difficulty with Wallace Stevens, as in the following examples:

(32) They are more than leaves that cover the barren rock

They bud the whitest eye, the pallidest sprout,
New senses in the engenderings of sense,
The desire to be at the end of distances,

The body quickened and the mind in root.

[Stevens, *CP*, 527]

(33) The rock is the habitation of the whole,
Its strength and measure, that which is near, point A
In a perspective that begins again

At B: the origin of the mango's rind.

[Stevens, *CP*, 528]

In "The Rock," which is a late but typical poem about metaphor and imagination, there is little or no 'scene' being described— rather, a mysterious entity or entities are said to be other things. A network of identification is set up, but no one term is more 'literal' or perspicuous than another. The concrete terms (*rock, leaves*) are in fact usually metaphors for something abstract—they do not give a referential anchor to things, so that the equivalences established are between metaphors, and the reader must judge in what respects the metaphors are equivalent without being able to check the things they refer to. (We will return to "The Rock" below.)

Note in this connection that in (III.22) Stevens 'cheats' on the apposition: *the bed, books,* etc. is written as an appositive but referred to by *these,* indicating they remain as separate entities. This is another source of abstractness in Stevens: the things or images are treated as 'mere instances' which could be multiplied indefinitely.

There is one type of participial that stands in an essentially appositional relation to a sentence. The so-called 'absolute' participial is one in which the Subject has not been deleted (or ellipsed) under coreference to a noun phrase in the main sentence—there is no noun phrase, that is, to which it is attached; the clause as a whole 'attaches' to the main clause. The 'attachment' is usually of an adverbial nature (cause and effect, temporal sequence) as with other participials, but Faulkner uses them as specifying appositives:

(34) [His house] was still kept for him by his dead wife's widowed niece and her children, and he was comfortable in it, his wants and needs and even the small trying harmless crochets of an old man looked after by blood at least related to the blood which he had elected out of all the earth to cherish.

[Faulkner, p. 722]

(35) He seemed to see the two of them—himself and the wilderness—as coevals, his own span as a hunter, a woodsman, not contemporary with his first breath but transmitted to him, assumed by him gladly, humbly, with joy and pride, from that old Major de Spain and that old Sam Fathers who had taught him to hunt, [₁the two spans running out together, not toward oblivion, nothingness, but into a dimension free of both time and space, where once more the untreed land warped and wrung to mathematical squares of rank cotton for the frantic old world people to turn into shells to shoot at one another, would find ample room for both—] [₂the names, the faces of the old men he had known and loved and for a little while outlived, moving again among the shades of tall unaxed trees and sightless brakes where the wild strong immortal game ran forever before the tireless belling immortal hounds, [₃falling and rising phoenix-like to the soundless guns.]]

[Faulkner, p. 724]

Here I take the first two appositive clauses as appositive to the main clause ("see the two of them as coevals"), but the second appositive clause could instead be regarded as appositive to the end of the first clause ("the untreed land would find ample room for both"). This could be diagrammed:

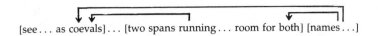

[see . . . as coevals] . . . [two spans running . . . room for both] [names . . .]

The final (Subjectless) participial either attaches to *wild strong immortal game* (falling and rising . . .) or is appositive to *moving again* . . ., in which case the men are also falling and rising phoenix-like—which is in fact the way I read this the first several times, although I would now say that the semantic link between immortal game and falling to the soundless guns is tighter. But of course the point is that the men and the wilderness are coevals and so, in the vision, both are eternally renewed.

2. DELAYED APPOSITION

When a writer uses a number of complex appositives, as Faulkner did in the passage just cited, the possibility of garden paths again arises. The appositives in the second stanza of (36) are not hard to link back to *an over-human god* since the nearer alternative is *we*, which is plural. In the third stanza, it is not too hard to see that *a constant fellow of destiny* is not appositive to *woe* . . . since *fellow* looks for a human referent, and Stevens does not otherwise engage in personification:

(36)   The fault lies with an over-human god,
       Who by sympathy has made himself a man
       And is not to be distinguished, when we cry

       Because we suffer, our oldest parent, peer
       Of the populace of the heart, the reddest lord,
       Who has gone before us in experience.

> If only he would not pity us so much,
> Weaken our fate, relieve us of woe both great
> And small, a constant fellow of destiny,
>
> A too, too human god, self-pity's kin
> And uncourageous genesis. . . .
>
> [Stevens, *CP*, 315]

Distinguished in the third line cited makes a slight problem for me: I tend to look for a complementing *from* phrase (something like *from us*) but eventually must give up the search. There is a mild pun here: *to be distinguished* can be read as a one-place predicate ("will not have distinction—i.e., greater dignity"). The next example, also from Stevens, is a little more difficult because *ruin* is semantically attracted to *misery*, but the appositive following clarifies the meaning of *afflatus* so that the phrase can be recognized as appositive to *it* (= grandeur)—again, reading ahead helps to solve the problem:

(37) Impatient for the grandeur that you need

> In so much misery; and yet finding it
> Only in misery, the afflatus of ruin,
> Profound poetry of the poor and of the dead. . . .
>
> [Stevens, *CP*, 509]

Part of the difficulty in this last example has to do with the relative semantic distance between *afflatus* and *grandeur*. The effect of 'distance' can readily be seen by reading down the following list of detached appositives taken from James's fiction. In the first two examples, the antecedent is repeated in the appositive phrase. In the third, *marks* and *tokens* are closely related, but in the fourth example (*principle/fruit*) and the fifth (*abruptness/policy*), the semantic distance increases and the coreference is a little harder to make out:

(38) They were mysteries of which her friends were conscious—those friends whose general explanation was to say that she was clever, . . .

> [James, *WOD*, I. 5]

(39) It was the name, above all, she would take in hand—the precious name she so liked and that. . . .

[James, *WOD*, I. 6]

(40) The pressure of want—whatever might be the case with the other force—was, however, presumably not active now, for the tokens of a chastened ease still abounded after all, many marks of a taste whose discriminations might perhaps have been called eccentric.

[James, *AMB*, 146]

(41) The principle I have just mentioned as operating had been, with the most newly disembarked of the two men, wholly instinctive—the fruit of a sharp sense that. . . .

[James, *AMB*, 17]

(42) the wisdom of the abruptness to which events had finally committed him, a policy that he was pleased to find not at all shaken as he now looked at his watch and wondered.

[James, *AMB*, 68]

Locating the antecedent of a detached appositive is frequently a source of difficulty in Faulkner. One very problematic appositive (*two threads* . . .) occurs in a passage from "The Bear" cited by Richard Ohmann:[6]

(43) the ledgers in which McCaslin recorded the slow outward trickle of food and supplies and equipment which returned each fall as cotton made and ginned and sold (two threads frail as truth and impalpable as equators yet cable-strong to bind for life them who made the cotton to the land their sweat fell on). . . .

[Faulkner, p. 290]

Ohmann identifies the antecedent of *two threads* . . . as *the trickle* and *the cotton*, but a little more precisely it would seem to be the outward trickle and the inward trickle—i.e., debits and credits. Here there really is no noun phrase referring to two things to which *two threads* is appositive (the trickle which returned is one thing)—the reader must construct one, much as he must with a sentential antecedent of a pronoun. As noted at the beginning of the chapter, this construction of an antecedent is not usually necessary and reflects an unusual looseness in Faulkner's use of appositives.

Another sort of difficulty, and for once not a garden path, occurs in the following passage where the 'semantic distance' between the appositive noun phrase (*the old bear* . . .) and its antecedent is great (as in [42]), and the linear distance from it is also great:

(44) It was as if the boy had already divined what his senses and intellect had not encompassed yet: that doomed wilderness whose edges were being constantly and punily gnawed at by men with ploughs and axes who feared it because it was wilderness, [men myriad and nameless even to one another in the land where the old bear had earned a name, and through which ran not even a mortal beast but an anachronism indominable and invincible out of an old, dead time,] [a phantom, epitome and apotheosis of the old, wild life which the little puny humans swarmed and hacked at in a fury of abhorrence and fear, like pygmies about the ankles of a drowsing elephant;]—[the old bear, solitary, indominable, and alone;]]. . . .

[Faulkner, p. 229]

Strictly speaking, *the old bear* . . . is appositive to *anachronism* . . . and to *phantom* . . ., but it may tend to float back to *that doomed wilderness,* gathering all of the previous material into itself as a kind of generalizing symbol. Faulkner encourages this identification by cross-linking bear and wilderness through the phrase *apotheosis of the old wild life.* We can diagram this cross-link with dashes:

that doomed wilderness. . . [phantom. . . of the old wild life . . .] [old bear. . .]

I will return to this fusional effect of complex apposition again shortly.

3. MULTIPLE APPOSITION

Suppose now we have two appositives at the end of a clause. If the main clause ends in a noun phrase, several connections are possible. We can diagram the possibilities as

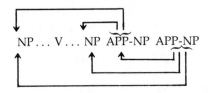

That is, both appositives could be coreferential to the same noun phrase (either Subject or final noun phrase), or the second could be appositive to something in the first, or the first could be appositive to the final noun phrase and the second appositive to the Subject noun phrase. In analyzing example (37) from Stevens, we have already made use of a tactic that takes two appositives occurring together to be coreferential. This is in general a fairly good strategy—when it fails, the passage becomes hard to perceive correctly. Consider, for example, the following stanzas from Stevens' "The Rock," which begin easily because the appositives are coreferential but end uneasily in that, I suspect, the last line is an elliptical rendering of "and a particular of being was/became that gross universe"—that is, the last four phrases are not all directly coreferential:

(45) As if nothingness contained a métier,
     A vital assumption, an impermanence
     In its permanent cold, an illusion so desired

     That the green leaves came and covered the high rock,
     That the lilacs came and bloomed, like a blindness cleaned,
     Exclaiming bright sight, as it was satisfied,

     In a birth of sight. The blooming and the muck
     Were being alive, an incessant being alive,
     A particular of being, that gross universe.

                                        [Stevens, CP, 526]

The next example, which consists of the lines immediately preceding (45), is also difficult because the appositives 'criss-cross': *an embrace* . . . (1) is not coreferential to *invention* but to *meeting* . . ., but *a theorem* . . . (2) does seem to be appositive to *invention:*

(46) The meeting at noon at the edge of the field seems like

An invention, [₁an embrace between one desperate clod
And another in a fantastic consciousness,
In a queer assertion of humanity:]

[₂A theorem proposed between the two—]
[₃Two figures in a nature of the sun,]
[₄In the sun's design of its own happiness]. . . .

[Stevens, *CP*, 525]

However, *fantastic consciousness* in (1) does seem roughly coreferential to *invention* and *theorem*—I will dash this coreference. Further, (3) *(two figures . . .)* appears to go back to *the meeting* . . ., but as (4) explicates *a nature of the sun*, this phrase links up to the 'fiction' set *(invention, theorem, fantastic consciousness)*. Diagramming the coreference, we have:

What we have then are two sets—event and the understanding of it—so cross-linked by apposition as to fuse fiction and reality: the lilacs of imagination do indeed cover the rock. This effect is similar to that of the final example in the previous chapter from Faulkner (30) and is one that Stevens and Faulkner strive for. Consider the stack of three appositives from "To An Old Philosopher":

(47) And you—it is you that speak it, without speech,
      [₁The loftiest syllables among loftiest things,]
      [₂The one invulnerable man among
      Crude captains], [₃the naked majesty, if you like,
      Of bird-nest arches and of rain-stained vaults.]

[Stevens, *CP*, 510]

The first appositive (1) is coreferential to *it* (= "the tragic accent of the scene"), the second (2) is appositive to *you*, and the third could be appositive to either *you* (he is the naked king) or *it* (the tragic accent of the scene):

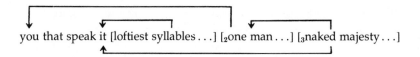

you that speak it [loftiest syllables . . .] [₂one man . . .] [₃naked majesty . . .]

The third appositive thus achieves a fusion: the old philosopher, as imagined by the poet, *is* the meaning of the scene, the poem beyond speech or the falsification of metaphor. Helen Vendler notes an ambiguous reference in the last lines of the poem, which contributes to the general fusional effect (these lines follow those cited in [28]):

(48) Total grandeur of a total edifice
      Chosen by an inquisitor of structures
      For himself. He stops upon *this threshold,*
      And if the design of all his words takes form
      And frame from thinking and is realized.

[Stevens, *CP*, 510–11]

She says, "we are no longer sure whether this is the threshold of heaven mentioned earlier in the poem or whether it is the threshold of the 'total edifice,' the construct of Santayana's life and work, now combined into a perfect whole, as one exemplifes the other"[7]—and, one might add, the threshold is also the end of the poem where Stevens stops, so that the poem is also *the edifice.*

The following passage from Faulkner's "The Bear" again gives

non-coreferential appositives, but this time the second is appositive to part of the preceding one:

(49) the big old bear with one trap-ruined foot that... had earned for
himself a name, a definite designation like a living man:—[the long
legend of corn-cribs broken down and rifled, of shoats and grown
pigs and even calves carried bodily into the woods and devoured,
and traps and deadfalls overthrown and dogs mangled and slain, and
shotgun and even rifle shots delivered at point-blank range yet with
no more effect than so many peas blown through a tube by a child]—
[a corridor of wreckage and destruction beginning back before the
boy was born, through which sped, not fast but rather with the ruthless and irresistible deliberation of a locomotive, the shaggy tremendous shape.]

[Faulkner, pp. 228–29]

The long legend is coreferential to *name*, and the *corridor* is a summarizing appositive to part of the preceding, but is linked loosely
to *legend* via *long:*

name...[long legend... broken down...] [corridor of wreckage...]

Again, the effect is to merge the historical events and results with
the interpretation of them recorded in verbal legend. It is interesting that the notion that reality and its expression are inseparable is
worked out through the same grammatical device in Faulkner and
in Stevens.

To say that it is done this way, of course, is not to say that it is
rightly done. In a series of very close readings of passages from
Stevens, Helen Vendler argues that the sort of blurring and
fusion of reference Stevens cultivates is not always esthetically
successful—sometimes they are evasions or false resolutions—and
she finds Stevens at his best when he controls or restricts his
virtuosity in this respect (see especially Chapter Seven of *On Extended Wings*). Her comments on his use of "marriage" as an image

of union without fusion of identity in the following lines form a kind of coda for this chapter:

(50)   Two things of opposite natures seem to depend
        On one another, as a man depends
        On a woman, day on night, the imagined

        On the real. This is the origin of change.
        Winter and spring, cold copulars, embrace
        And forth the particulars of rapture come.

        Music falls on the silence like a sense,
        A passion that we feel, not understand.
        Morning and afternoon are clasped together

        And North and South are an intrinsic couple
        And sun and rain a plural, like two lovers
        That walk away as one in the greenest body.

                                                    [Stevens, *CP*, 392]

She describes "a tentative and gradual merging of polarities, in which dependency becomes embrace, embrace becomes bringing-forth, and these partial or willed unions finally become necessary and intrinsic, as the opposites no longer consciously embrace but rather are clasped together and become a verbal identity in a dual noun—a couple, a plural" (*Wings*, p. 182).

We have reached in many of these last examples the limit of propositionally oriented reading. In fact, in describing cross-linking, we have gone beyond pure comprehension of scene and reconstruction of propositional content and into the area of imagery and associative nexes which constitute a distinct level of structure. It is interesting, however, that when writers press the devices of syntax (here, of apposition) to such extremes, processing becomes easier in terms of sets of 'images' than in terms of phrases and predicates: that is, rather than build from sentences and propositions to a larger sense of constructive intention, we may find it easier to grope toward the constructive intention by other means and then try to work out some sort of sentence and propositional structure which will approximate what one has already decided the passage must be saying. I do not mean to imply that the task of setting up clusters of images and inferring their relation is simple or easy—indeed, one could not do it without some knowledge of Stevens' (or Faulkner's) typical images for imagination and reality and a sense of the kinds of thematic oppositions likely to be operating. It happens that these passages are fusional in nature—that is, the cross-linking attempts to break down distinctions which the syntax postulates (but just barely). Given some familiarity with Stevens and Faulkner, one can suppose that they are trying to achieve the romantic symbol or apprehension of a wholeness beyond all distinctions. Another way of achieving this apprehension is to make propositional content so difficult to comprehend that the reader is virtually forced into following other structures, and the most radical way to do it is to write sentences that are ill-formed any way you parse them. In the next chapter we will examine claims made by critics that certain writers should not be read with the consciousness of sentence structure that we have been at so great pains to cultivate.

CHAPTER FIVE

Consciousness of Sentence Structure

I N this chapter, we will address a theme recurrent in literary criticism since Empson, namely, that one does not, or should not, always read certain authors in the way we have been describing. Rather, consciousness of clause and sentence structure should at times give way to other units or modes of perception. Such claims have been made for Faulkner and Spenser. Actually, different kinds and degrees of adjustment of our model have been suggested, and examination of these claims in the light of the model clarifies both the nature of the claims and some of the assumptions we have made.

1. SPENSER

In a very interesting chapter of his book *The Poetry of the Faerie Queene* (Princeton, 1966), Paul Alpers argues that one perhaps should read Spenser with less "consciousness of sentence structure" than other poets such as Marlowe, or, put the other way round, that Spenser does not expect or engage the reader's capacity for resisting the seductions of line structure and deciding between possible readings. The line, Alpers argues, is more a unit of perception and structure than in the work of certain other poets, the sentence less so. If a line appears functionally complete, take the line boundary as a clause or phrase boundary and you will rarely be significantly misled. This he calls the path of least resistance. There is enjambment in Spenser, but it is typically obligatory (i.e., between Subject and verb, or clearly transitive verb and Object), so that the reader cannot take the initial line to be complete. In cases where there is double syntax, the hovering element can generally be adequately read without enjambment—that is, it can be taken to be in construction with other words in the line containing it, though it may also go forward or back across line boundaries. Line ends are rarely the source of 'premature closure' of the type that requires reanalysis when we arrive at the next line. Hence, at the very least, the reader can rely on line boundaries as a clue to phrase and clause boundaries more in Spenser than in other poets. Among these other poets is certainly Milton, who enjambs endlessly and 'trickily', forcing an acute attention to syntactic structure and a distrust of line boundaries. For one quick illustration, consider these lines from Sonnet 23 ("Methought I saw...") (*mine* = my wife)

(1)   Mine as whom washt from spot of child-bed taint,
        Purification in the old Law did save,
        And such, as yet once more I trust to have
        Full sight of her in Heaven without restraint,
        Came vested all in white, pure as her mind:

                                    [Milton, Sonnet 23, 5–9]

Have at the end of the third line cited appears to complete the clause—he trusts to have his wife again, but the next line corrects the erroneous closure—there is no giving or taking in marriage in Heaven. Thus, as Stanley Fish demonstrates over and over in *Surprised by Sin*, the garden paths in Milton's writing lead again and again to error, some misapprehension which the reader must cast off.

Alpers goes farther, however, and claims that the line may give the right perceptual unit even though it is wrong or incomplete grammatically. Thus he points out that in the following lines:

(2)   Their frowning forheads with rough hornes yclad,
       And rusticke horror all a side doe lay

                                    [Spenser, *FQ*, I.vi. 11]

it serves the reader well to forget that the *forheads* of the first line
are coordinate with *rusticke horror* (they lay their *forheads* aside?—
this is what it says, grammatically), and this 'misperception' is
facilitated by the line division. Compare these lines from Donne,
where perceiving the coordination is critical:

(3)   Oh make thyself with holy mourning black,
       And red with blushing, as thou art with sin.
                                [Donne, "Holy Sonnet II," 11–12]

(4)   Oh! of thine only worthy blood,
       And my tears, make a heavenly lethean flood,
                                [Donne, "Holy Sonnet V," 10–11]

Similarly in Spenser a line boundary may cut an element free to
hover over various equally good possibilities:

(5)   She dolefull Lady, like a dreary Spright,
       Cald by strong charmes out of eternall night,
       Had deathes owne image figurd in her face,
                                    [Spenser, *FQ*, III.xii. 19]

(6)   Wherewith he grypt her gorge with so great paine,
       That soone to loose her wicked bands did her constraine.
                                    [Spenser, *FQ*, I.i. 19]

In (5), the participial in the middle line may be attached equally to
she dolefull Lady or *dreary Spright*—the difference is slight and the
effect is to fuse the two possible alternatives; in (6), the last line is
either a result clause or a relative clause (*that = so great paine*).
Neither analysis is a misperception. The syntax is permissive, Alpers says: "the independence of the lines means their separation
from each other, and . . . Spenser's verse keeps us from inspecting
the connection between the lines in a way that would make us treat

structural possibilities as alternative choices" (p. 86). For a final example, consider

(7)   And that new creature borne without her dew,
      Full of the makers guile, with vsage sly
      He taught to imitate that Lady trew,
      Whose semblance she did carrie vnder feigned hew.

[Spenser, *FQ*, I.i. 46]

With vsage sly can be grouped with *full of the makers guile* as a modifier of *that new creature*, or with *taught*, or with *imitate*—but of course Spenser is insisting on *the new creature* as a product of her maker, so all possibilities work.

If Alpers is right about how Spenser should be read, we must further modify our perceptual model, for these cases go beyond raising the weight we give to line division. The change would have to be made at the point where alternative readings are compared: what we need to do is soften the injunction: "choose the best" and tolerate multiple parsings. One could of course try to rank the alternatives, but Alpers suggests that this is not the proper spirit in which to read Spenser. Rather, one should simply take them all (provided they are congruent). This is more or less the attitude Empson advocates for 'hovering' clauses and phrases which he describes as giving "an interpenetrating and, as it were, fluid unity, in which phrases will go either with the sentence before or after and there is no break in the movement of the thought" (*Ambiguity*, p. 50), and again, in words cited by Alpers, "the renewal of energy gained from starting a new sentence is continually obtained here without the effect of repose given by letting a sentence stop" (p. 52). Such a mental process, where more than one propositional structure is entertained *and accepted*, has never been contemplated by psycholinguists, but there is nothing unthinkable about it.

Spenser's language differs from Milton's (among others) in a second way that appears to bear on Alpers' arguments: his sentences are strange and ungrammatical quite a bit more often, forcing the reader to choose the lesser of bad alternatives, as it were.

The process by which we select a best parsing is deprived of one of its primary grounds—choose the alternative that gives a grammatical parsing. There is first of all the vocabulary, strange even to Spenser's contemporaries: one cannot be sure whether a verb is transitive or not, for example, or whether it requires an animate Subject or Object, if one is not certain whether he has seen it before or whether it might have been differently used in Spenser's time. Many of the examples from Spenser cited in previous chapters are still slightly odd or 'off' sounding even when they have been correctly parsed (e.g., *To seeke her strayed Champion if she might attayne*) or require a rather special understanding of a key term (e.g., *That weaker sence it might haue rauisht quight*). Further, Spenser omits Subjects of subordinate clauses, so that the best parsing is ungrammatical:

(8)   but he againe
      Shooke him so hard, *that* forced him to speake.

[Spenser, *FQ*, I.i. 42]

(9)   The Geaunt strooke so maynly mercilesse,
      That could haue ouerthrowne a stony towre,

[Spenser, *FQ*, I.vii. 12]

(10) [the battle of Red Cross Knight and the dragon; *whom* = RCK]
      Whom so dismayd when that his foe beheld,
      He cast to suffer him no more respire,
      But gan his sturdie sterne about to weld,
      And him so strongly stroke, *that* to the ground him feld.

[Spenser, *FQ*, I.xi. 28]

In each of these, the italicized *that* could be either a relative pronoun or a marker of a result clause. The missing Subject in the subordinate clause makes us consider the relative pronoun interpretation, but one must in that case make up a cognate object as antecedent (shooke a shake, strooke a stroke, etc.); the presence of *so*, on the other hand, suggests that we have a result clause with a missing Subject. There is no right (grammatical) parsing. The problem is even worse when the *so* is not around to point to a result clause reading (Sugden notes that Spenser does use *that* as a result clause marker without *so*[1]):

(11) So as they trauelled, the drouping night. . . .
Vpon them fell, before her timely howre;
That forced them to seeke some couert bowre. . . .

[Spenser, *FQ*, IV.v. 32]

(12) With wrathfull hand I slew her innocent;
That after soone I dearely did lament.

[Spenser, *FQ*, II.iv. 29]

Sugden (p. 58) reads these *that*s as relative pronouns with sentential antecedents ("the unusually early night-fall"; "my wrathful slaying of her"), but if a result reading is possible earlier, it is so here, though (11) would still be ungrammatical. Subjects are missing from coordinate clauses in the next examples, but the Subject of the first clause is not the missing Subject of the later ones (as it would have to be to be grammatical even, I believe, in Early Modern English). I note the reading I prefer:

(13)   Her humblenesse low,
In so ritch weedes and seeming glorious show,
Did so much enmove his stout heroicke heart,
And said, 'Deare dame, your suddein ouerthrow. . . .

[Spenser, *FQ*, I.ii. 21]

(14) Much did his words the gentle Ladie quell,
And turn'd aside for shame to heare, what he did tell.

[Spenser, *FQ*, V.iii. 16]

(15) [*it* = women's faire aspect]
Yet could it not sterne Artegall retaine,
Nor hold from suite of his avowed quest,
Which he had vndertane to Gloriane;
But left his loue, albe her strong request,
Faire Britomart, in languor and vnrest,
And he rode him selfe uppon his first intent:

[Spenser, *FQ*, V.viii. 3]

These examples are not difficult as the previous set because there is no alternative parsing to be weighed—we interpret them essentially as we would if there were pronouns present, looking back for the likeliest individual to function as Subject when the Subject of the first clause proves to be inappropriate (*humbleness said* is bad; *his words turn'd* (her) *aside* is bad, (*turn'd,* if coordinate to *did quell,* would be *turn*); *it left . . . and rode him selfe* is definitely bad). Nonetheless, the better reading is ungrammatical. Finally, in the next two examples, Objects have been ungrammatically deleted (again I indicate my preference along with the obvious function):

(16) (Her) [= Ate] false Duessa who full well did know
      (To be most fit to trouble noble knights,
      Which hunt for honor, raised from below,
      Out of the dwellings of the damned sprights. . . .

[Spenser, *FQ,* IV.i. 19]

(17) The patron of true Holinesse,
      Foule Errour doth defeate;
      Hypocrisie (him) to entrappe,
      Doth to his home entreate.

[Spenser, *FQ,* Argument to I.i]

In these, again, one eventually works out what they have to mean, but one's confidence that the best reading is grammatical is shaken, and one is less ready to prefer sentence structure to line division. The general procedure of reading by parsing is further challenged by the various irregular and highly unusual placement of phrases outside of subordinate clauses discussed in Chapter II and again exemplified in (10). When reading (10), we again work out what the lines have to mean, but without any confidence that the inferred parsing is supported by grammaticality.

Such are some of the consequences of writing—in Jonson's somewhat severe words—"no language," but there are others which can be seen by considering Milton. We have seen numerous examples of Milton's fondness for multiply coordinate structures (S

V O, V O, V O, etc.). These are as rare in Spenser as they are common in Milton, and the reason would seem to lie partly in their running across several lines and partly in the 'contract' between poet and reader that they will parse if the reader is sufficiently conscious of syntactic structure. Milton can lead his reader through more complex syntactic thickets than Spenser because he rarely leaves him with only a choice between garden paths.

2. WORDSWORTH

Alpers suggests that the Romantics loved Spenser because he does allow one to follow the path of least resistance: instead of an active, decisive speaking voice sustaining sentence structure against the blandishments of line and rhyme, we have a "peculiarly passive sensibility," which is mirrored in the reader's diminished consciousness of sentence structure (p. 75). It is interesting to apply these notions to a Romantic poet, and I will do so to Wordsworth, who, as much as any Romantic, affected 'the Miltonic'. Even when he is most obviously echoing Milton, however, as in the beginning of *The Prelude,* there is a decidedly un-Miltonic looseness of syntactic structure. For one thing, the sentences often trail appositives or other phrases which are quite long, leaving the reader uncertain whether they initiate a new clause or not:

(18) Sometimes it suits me better to invent
　　A tale from my own heart, more near akin
　　To my own passions and habitual thoughts;
　　Some variegated story, in the main
　　Lofty, but the unsubstantial structure melts
　　Before the very sun that brightens it,
　　Mist into air dissolving! Then a wish,
　　My last and favourite aspiration, mounts
　　With yearning toward some philosophic song
　　Of Truth that cherishes our daily life;
　　With meditations passionate from deep
　　Recesses in man's heart, immortal verse
　　Thoughtfully fitted to the Orphean lyre;
　　　　　　　　　　[Wordsworth, *Prel.* I. 221–33]

The punctuation adds to the difficulty—one would expect the semicolon after *Lofty* rather than after *thoughts* (the 1805 version has only a comma after *thoughts*). The parallelism of *with yearning* and *with meditations passionate* suggests that they are appositive, though they are semantically alike only on one point (passion) and not on another (articulation). Alternatively, *meditations passionate* could, on semantic grounds, be appositive to *philosophic song* (they are both articulated), but this violates the definition of apposition, which applies only to like structures: here *with meditations passionate* is a prepositional phrase and cannot be appositive to the noun phrase *philosophic song*. Also, the relation of *immortal verse* to the preceding is a little uncertain: plainly it is coreferential to *philosophic song*, but is it in addition appositive to *meditations passionate*, or is there an ellipsed second *toward* ("mounts with meditations passionate toward immortal verse")? The syntax here is not so much permissive as it is indeterminate, and deciding all the questions just raised does not make the sense of the passage much clearer. In Wordsworth we may stop working out complete syntactic structures, not because it cannot be done, as sometimes in Spenser, but because it is distracting and irrelevant to do so—there are more direct ways to get the import of the passage. We realize the extent to which we have been able to relax syntactic analysis and hypothesis testing when we encounter a passage that does require attention to syntax:

(19)   But from this awful burthen I full soon
    235 Take refuge and beguile myself with trust
          That mellower years will bring a riper mind
          And clearer insight. Thus my days are past
          In contradiction; with no skill to part
          Vague longing, haply bred by want of power,
    240 From paramount impulse not to be withstood,
          A timorous capacity from prudence,
          From circumspection, infinite delay.
                            [Wordsworth, *Prel.* I. 234–42]

It is certainly not easy to "part" the contradiction here. The double enjambment contributes to the problem: line 240 must not be taken as a modifier of *want of power* or of *vague longing* in the previous line ("a vague longing which is from paramount impulse...") but must be related to *part* at the end of the preceding line ("part longing from impulse..."). Even when Wordsworth warns us with *contradiction*, we take him to mean something vague like "self-deception" or "confusion" and are unprepared to work out the tight syntax of *'part* a from b, c from d, from e, f'. The whole passage is really quite clever—we have been so lured into his frame of mind that we share his inability.

One of Wordsworth's characteristic practices that most undermines reliance on parsing is his ellipsis of semantically rather empty main verbs. Consider the following two cases:

(20)　　[I] listen to the grave reports
　　　　Of dire enchantments faced and overcome
　　　　By the strong mind, and tales of warlike feats,
　　　　Where spear encountered spear, and sword with sword
　　　　Fought, as if conscious of the blazonry
　　　　That the shield bore, so glorious was the strife;
　　　　Whence inspiration for a song that winds
　　　　Through everchanging scenes of votive quest
　　　　Wrongs to redress, harmonious tribute paid
　　　　To patient courage and unblemished truth,
　　　　To firm devotion, zeal unquenchable,
　　　　And Christian meekness hallowing faithful loves.
　　　　　　　　　　　　　　　　　[Wordsworth, *Prel.* I. 174–85]

The easiest way to get the material following *whence* into a clause is to suppose an ellipsed main verb *comes* or *came*, which is largely redundant, given *whence*, but grammatically unusual to omit. One can force the material into a clause without assuming ellipsis if one takes *paid* as the main verb ("whence inspiration... paid harmonious tribute to patient courage..."), but the tenses jar somewhat: why is the relative clause (a song *that winds* ...) present tense if the "main verb" is past tense? The reading so derived is also irrelevant—

a high price to pay for its grammaticality. The next case involves an ellipsed *be:*

(21)   Thanks to both,
      And their congenial powers, that, while they join
      In breaking up a long-continued frost,
      Bring with them vernal promises, the hope
      Of active days urged on by flying hours,—
      Days of sweet leisure, taxed with patient thought
      Abstruse, nor wanting punctual service high,
      Matins and vespers of harmonious verse!

                                        [Wordsworth, *Prel.* I. 38–45]

One may continue to expect the main clause right up until the exclamation mark, and then one realizes the first line should be read "Thanks *be* to both. . . ." Again, the ellipsis is a bit unusual, but it is better to lower one's expectation that the text will be a succession of clauses than to exhaust oneself waiting for a verb that never actually comes. Another problem in this passage is whether *days of sweet leisure* is appositive to the promised *active days.* At first, the contrast of *active/leisure* suggests that they are not coreferential, but as the modifiers *taxed* and *punctual service* accumulate, we begin to think the leisure could be pretty active. No quick decision is possible here: the situation is like that described by Stanley Fish with *fiend/spot.* In this case, we do construct two entities and ponder the question of their possible identity.

Wordsworth's use of appositives exemplified here does not quite fall under any of the categories delineated in the preceding chapter. As these appositives unfold, they seem to transform the initial formulation so that a possible underlying unity is discovered, which is equivalent to the realization that the two phrases are appositive after all. The effect is to redefine our understanding of the initial term, as here *active* is transformed so that it is compatible with *leisure* and then the opposition is recast in terms of *ritual service,* which is neither work nor play but something transcending both. This particular clash and resolution is absent in the 1805 version, which reads:

the hope
Of active days, of dignity and thought,
Of prowess in an honourable field
Pure passions, virtue, knowledge, and delight
The holy life of music and of verse.

[11. 41–45]

There is a similar effect in the following lines from *The Prelude* where the initial clash of *domineering instinct* and *fluent receptacle* is so great that one at first resists seeing them as appositives but then begins to think that they may be appositive after all as the overtones of passivity in *fluent receptacle* become even more overt in the next *that* clause (which may be appositive to the preceding clause, there being a link via the notion of self-sufficiency):

(22) Nor did the inexperience of my youth
      Preclude conviction, that a spirit strong
      In hope, and trained to noble aspirations,
      A spirit thoroughly faithful to itself,
      Is for Society's unreasoning herd
      A domineering instinct, serves at once
      For way and guide, a fluent receptacle
      That gathers up each petty straggling rill
      And vein of water, glad to be rolled on
      In safe obedience; that a mind, whose rest
      Is where it ought to be, in self-restraint,
      In circumspection and simplicity,
      Falls rarely in entire discomfiture
      Below its aim, or meets with, from without,
      A treachery that foils it or defeats;

[Wordsworth, *Prel.* X. 164–78]

The passage is remarkable in the way it modulates insensibly from flirtation with the "Great Man" into stoicism (and, in the lines following, into a kind of Kantian moral consciousness). The changing philosophic stance is paralleled by shifts in the way that the first stance is viewed through the succession of appositives and equivalences: *instinct—way and guide—fluent receptacle,* the *way and guide* forming a kind of bridge from the activity of *domineering in-*

stinct to the passivity of *receptacle* (which may be qualified in obscure ways by *fluent*). I am not sure whether Wordsworth considers the moral philosophies to be exactly the same or not: the *direction* of the thought away from political involvement is important, not distinctions of moral philosophies. Our initial understanding of *domineering instinct* is so modified by its identification with *fluent receptacle* that we are prepared for a further redefinition in the direction of even greater (political) passivity. The intent of the passages seems to be just the opposite of distinction, namely, to find a common ground underlying these stances without wrestling them into strict identity. It is interesting that the *way and guide* and *fluent receptacle* are not in the 1805 version—it is as if Wordsworth tried to assist the reader in the imaginative progression from one stance to the other. The 1805 version reads:

> A Spirit thoroughly faithful to itself,
> Unquenchable, unsleeping, undismay'd,
> Was as an instinct among Men, a stream
> That gather'd up each petty straggling rill
> And vein of water, glad to be roll'd on
> In safe obedience, that a mind whose rest
> Was where it ought to be. . . .

[11. 148–54]

These passages suggest a possibility we have not yet considered, namely, that the reader may stop parsing into well-formed sentences or propositions and stop specifying the reference of nouns and pronouns exactly. What then would the units of perception be? Wordsworth provides three kinds of structural clues. First, 'positive' things go together and 'negative' things go together in opposition to the positive things (notice how in the 1850 edition Wordsworth helps the reader to identify *each petty straggling rill* as the mob by adding *Society's unreasoning herd*). Hence, when the good things and bad things are mixed, it is hard to part them, as in example (19)—the alertness to syntactic distinction and opposition has been lulled to sleep. Second, parallel phrases (e.g., the *that*-clauses and the *with* phrases of [18]) go together. With both of these clues, 'going together' may not be exactly apposition nor coordination, just association. Third, there is usually a strong rhetorical pointing to the initiation of a significantly new train of thought which to a considerable degree substitutes for sharp clause boundaries. One must attend to the beginnings of sentences which sustain a pattern (*sometimes. . . sometimes. . . .; then. . . now. . .*), mark a reversal (*nor . . .*) or other shift (*therefore, thus . . .*), or break off with an interjection (*Oh! . . .*) or other emphatic construction (*How oft . . .!*). Finally, structural clues aside, the reader who is interpreting successfully will become attuned not only to the sorts of distinctions and points Wordsworth wants to make, but the sorts that he does not want to make and will not expect the reader to make.

Obviously this sort of handling of syntax has its limitations and dangers. One limitation is that the ability to draw sharp, quick distinctions and oppositions syntactically is lost. On the whole, this is not a major loss for Wordsworth, for he does not court the critical, analytic involvement of the reader that Milton or Donne does, but rather an involvement sympathetic to the exploration of feelings nearly too deep for words. One danger is that the reader will simply lose track of more and more things until he finally bogs down. I will cite two passages from *The Excursion* which illustrate the mind-numbing possibilities of Wordsworth's verse when the subject or the sense require alertness to sentence structure:

(23) Happy is he who lives to understand,
    Not human nature only, but explores
    All natures,—to the end that he may find
    The law that governs each; and where begins
    The union, the partition where, that makes
    Kind and degree, among all visible Beings;
    The constitutions, powers, and faculties,
    Which they inherit,—cannot step beyond,—
    And cannot fall beneath; that do assign
    To every class its station and its office,

> Through all the mighty commonwealth of things;
> Up from the creeping plant to sovereign Man.
>
> [Wordsworth, *Excur.* IV. 332–43]

One's grip on syntax begins to loosen in the first two lines: where is the rest of the Object of *understand?* It is also hard to decide what *the constitutions, powers, and faculties* is appositive to (*kind and degree? union and partition? law that governs?*), or whether it is perhaps a further Object of *find.* It is hard to decide on a referent for *that* when we aren't sure how many candidates there are. The passage continues:

(24)   Such converse, if directed by a meek,
      Sincere, and humble spirit, teaches love:
      For knowledge is delight; and such delight
      Breeds love: yet, suited as it rather is
      To thought and to the climbing intellect,
      It teaches less to love, than to adore;
      If that be not indeed the highest love!

> [Wordsworth, *Excur.* IV. 343–49]

It is not too clear what *such converse* refers to (exploring all natures?), and the *it* of the last few lines might be either *converse* or *delight.* On this last point, the exact reference could be said not to matter, since delight and converse should be one, but in the earlier ones a system of knowledge is being articulated, and here the obscure reference is fatal. By the end of the passage the weary reader may have shifted from 'doesn't matter' to 'don't care'. The attempt at parallelism is made (*such converse, such delight* in [24]; *that governs, that makes, that do assign* in [23]—these modify different noun phrases, however), but it doesn't adequately organize the passage.

In the next example, the reader is suddenly called upon to resolve grammatical ambiguities when he is scarcely alert:

(25)   Strains of power
      Were they, to seize and occupy the sense;
      But to a higher mark than song can reach
      Rose this pure eloquence. And, when the stream

Which overflowed the soul was passed away,
30   A consciousness remained that it had left,
Deposited upon the silent shore
Of memory, images and precious thoughts,
That shall not die, and cannot be destroyed.
                                        [Wordsworth, *Excur.* VII. 25–33]

The trouble begins here with *that it had left,* which could be a
relative clause ("a consciousness which it had left") or a noun
phrase complement ("consciousness of its leaving"). The line end
and enjambed next line containing the oddly dangled participial
deposited . . . support closing off the clause at the end of line 30, and
memory, images, and precious thoughts appear to belong together in
the same line, but eventually one realizes that they do not belong
together—rather, *images and precious thoughts* is the delayed Object
of *left,* which is then conclusively identified as a complement
clause. We thus reconstruct "a consciousness remained that the
stream had left images and precious thoughts that shall not die and
cannot be destroyed deposited upon the silent shore of memory."
To parse this correctly, we must enjamb across two line ends pursuing the sentence structure, and, while Milton trains us to do this,
Wordsworth does not. And we must parse it correctly: it is just
plain wrong to take *that it had left* as a complete clause either relative or complementing. As a complete clause, the relative interpretation is better; about the time one adopts that reading, one discov-
ers the missing Object and must revert to the complement clause
interpretation. I do not see how Wordsworth's customary rhetorical speaking voice could guide us through these lines—he is simply
writing verse the reader does not expect him to write. Consciousness of sentence structure and the habit of rejecting garden paths
are not things you can turn on and off.

3. FAULKNER

With the exception of the last example and (19), the complexities
we find in Wordsworth could be found in prose: the line is not the

unit of perception that it is in Spenser. Indeed, some of the same looseness of sentence structure can be found in Faulkner, and when reading Faulkner, one has the same experience of losing the thread in certain passages. Robert Zoellner has discussed some of the looseness of the prose in *Absalom, Absalom!*—the difficulty of locating referents of noun phrases, of deciding whether they are trailing appositives to the preceding sentences or Subjects of a verb to come; the large and complex chunks of modifying and parenthetical material separating Subjects from their verbs; the fragments and incomplete clauses—and has put forth the claim that Alpers made for Spenser: it frequently doesn't matter which reading one takes.[2] Here is part of Zoellner's first example:

(26) It was a summer of wistaria. The twilight was full of it and of the smell of his father's cigar as they sat on the front gallery after supper until it would be time for Quentin to start, while in the deep shaggy lawn below the veranda the fireflies blew and drifted in soft random—the odor, the scent, which five months later Mr Compson's letter would carry up from Mississippi and over the long iron New England snow and into Quentin's sitting-room at Harvard.

[Faulkner, *ABS*, 31]

The odor, the scent . . . is, as Zoellner notes, a trailing appositive, and it presents the additional difficulty of determining the referent: is it cigar smoke only, or is wistaria there too? (Note that an inference is needed to get the wistaria: twilight full of wistaria → smell of wistaria.) Obviously even the attempt to choose between alternatives is misguided, since the odor evokes the whole atmosphere of the evening and the place. Unfortunately, Zoellner also confuses the question of consciousness of sentence structure by making virtually contradictory claims about the way the reader should read. At first, he says, "Faulkner demands that the reader maintain the maximum possible consciousness of the *whole* extended sentence—the sentence-continuum—from beginning to end. In this case, the syntactical ambiguity of 'the odor, the scent' jars the reader out of his habitual casualness and forces him, if he hopes to maintain a sense of logical continuity, to keep the entire word-pattern in the vivid forefront of consciousness" (pp. 487–88), but later he argues that Faulkner is out to break down conventional, logical categorization and to present primary experience as an unsorted whole: "Faulkner will have no hierarchy of sentences or sequences of impressions; he aims at the total impression and the total sentence" (p. 489). (How does one maintain logical continuity while abandoning logical categorization?) I must confess I find the notion of total sentence intriguing, but I do not see how we can avoid the fact that it is with perception as with love: "the will is infinite and the execution confined.... the desire is boundless and the act a slave to limit." The possibility latent in Zoellner's qualification "if he hopes to maintain his sense of logical continuity" is real, I think, for many readers—they surrender that hope (or desire). They must certainly surrender it in a 'sentence', also cited by Zoellner, which appears a few lines farther on:

(27) That Sunday morning in June with the bells ringing peaceful and peremptory and a little cacophonous—the denominations in concord though not in tune—and the ladies and children, and house negroes to carry the parasols and flywhisks, and even a few men (the ladies moving in hoops among the miniature broadcloth of little boys and the pantalettes of little girls, in the skirts of the time when ladies did not walk but floated) when the other men sitting with their feet on the railing of the Holston House gallery looked up, and there the stranger was.

[Faulkner, *ABS*, 31]

Read it as often as you like; you will not find a main verb before the *when*. Clearly Zoellner is right that one should surrender to the impression being evoked here. The incantatory *and ... and ... and ...* is a reliable indication in Faulkner that such surrender is in order. The case is much more advanced in Faulkner than in Wordsworth, just as the grammatical irregularities are more numerous. The parallel with Wordsworth can be carried one step further: what replaces syntax and punctuation is a highly rhetorical voice making heavy use of parallelism and the good words/bad words opposition. One reason both writers are said to exhibit intensely moral consciousnesses is that they require the reader to make active use of moral categorizations in perception—which is to say, they activate the moral consciousness of the reader. Also, when both rhetorical and syntactic structures break down, passages dissolve into "things" and "events" loosely associated but indeterminately related. There is one fairly reliable clue that one is not reading for sentences: upon reaching a period, one asks himself "what did that sentence say?" and cannot exactly answer. Usually one can say a good bit specifying what the sentence is *about*—i.e., the feeling evoked by the things and the tone of the passage—one is simply not prepared to specify what is predicated of what. Readers who are dissatisfied until they can arrive at a well-formed propositional structure frequently find Faulkner somewhat vexing in the way Conrad Aiken describes: "It is annoying, at the end of a sentence, to find that one does not know in the least what was the subject of the verb that dangles *in vacuo*—it is distracting to have to go back and sort out the meaning, track down the structure from clause to clause, then only to find that after all it doesn't much matter, and that the obscurity was perhaps neither subtle nor important."[3] As Aiken sees it, consciousness of sentence structure is exactly the wrong thing to bring to Faulkner:

> And to the extent that one *is* annoyed and distracted, and *does* thus go back and work it out, it may be at once added that Mr. Faulkner has defeated his own ends. One has had, of course, to emerge from the stream, and to step away from it, in order to properly see it; and as Mr. Faulkner works precisely by a process of *immersion*, of hypnotizing his reader into *remaining immersed* in his stream, this occasional blunder produces irritation and failure. [p. 137]

Aiken does not say very must about how one perceives in a state of hypnotized immersion, and he is plainly uncomfortable about an unqualified commitment to irrationalism, but other critics have developed this way of defending Faulkner, and we will return to this question in the next chapter.

One might suppose, and in fact I did at one time suppose, that the ultimate signal to abandon sentence structuring is the suppression of punctuation. In fact, however, the unpunctuated stretches of interior monologue (and remembered speech) in Faulkner are rarely harder to parse into sentences than the punctuated sections and sometimes easier. It is as if the author, having taken away the clues of punctuation, more strictly honors the other signals of structure and less often constructs elaborate structures (most commonly, Faulkner omits periods but leaves commas and colons in). Anthony Burgess pointed out that this is so in Joyce as well (*Joysprick*, Chapter Four), noting that one can punctuate the passages fairly confidently, and one can also do so with Faulkner. Consider this passage from *The Sound and the Fury:*

(28) Women are like that they dont acquire knowledge of people we are for that they are just born with a practical fertility of suspicion that makes a crop every so often and usually right they have an affinity for evil for supplying whatever the evil lacks in itself for drawing it about them instinctively as you do bedclothing in slumber fertilising the mind for it until the evil has served its purpose whether it ever existed or no. . . .

[Faulkner, *SF*, Vintage, 115]

It is interesting to notice how the structural signals take over: the nominative case pronouns mark the beginnings of new sentences; the appositive *for* phrases are marked by repetition of the *for; fertilising* obviously marks the beginning of a participial parallel to *drawing*, and so on. Clause boundaries are not always quite so evident, but they can always be made out (that is, we do not have overlapping syntax):

(29) Country people poor things they never saw an auto before lots of them honk the horn Candace so *She wouldn't look at me* they'll get out of the way *wouldn't look at me* your father wouldn't like it if you were to injure one of them I'll declare your father will simply have to get an auto now. . . .

[Faulkner, *SF*, Vintage, 113]

The italics, for once, are Faulkner's and mark a train of thought interrupting the remembered speaking. One may perceive *lots of them* as the Subject of *honk* at first, but the *they'll* could not be coreferential to the Subject of *honk*—one eventually infers that *Candace* is present and addressed as *you* and is driving.

It is perhaps a bit misleading to refer to the clues we take advantage of here as wholly structural. The nominative forms *we* and *they* in (28) are helpful, but they don't eliminate all uncertainties. The first lines of (28) might be divided:

> they dont acquire knowledge of people we are/ for that they are just born. . .

Making the division here, however, obscures the opposition of *we* and *they* that plainly is part of the burden of the passage (cf.:

> they dont acquire knowledge of people/ we are for that/ they are just born . . .

These passages become easier to read as we catch the voice of the speaker with its phrasing, diction and tone. *I'll declare*, for example, always initiates, never interrupts or terminates, a sentence, often introduces something hyperbolical, and so on. Faulkner makes us read more with our ears by taking away some of the clues of the eye, but he certainly does not force us to stop parsing the text into sentences.

4. JAMES

James is an interesting contrast to Faulkner because they have certain points of similarity, particularly the practice of interrupting sentences with lengthy and complex modifiers and parentheticals which render the basic process of parsing difficult. Again, critics have tried to specify the attitude toward syntax that the reader develops, or should develop. Clearly the paramount difference between James and Faulkner is that James always writes grammatical sentences—one can rely on that, however difficult it may be in a given instance to put the sentence together. Jane Tompkins describes a sense of resolution one experiences as one wins through to a complete sentence in James. Citing the following sentence from "The Beast in the Jungle,"

(30) Then it was, just at the turn, as he afterwards made it out to himself, that, everything else failing, she herself decided to take up the case and, as it were, save the situation.

she says, "In James's sentence, the effort of holding the mind in suspense while each of the intervening modifications is gathered in, intensifies the force of the outcome and produces, in the end, a sense that not only the 'situation,' but the sentence itself has been 'saved' "[4]—a little bit later, she adds in an elegant imitation of the master's syntax (though not his diction): "The hard-won syntactic resolutions, delayed by frustrating qualifications, share, by virtue of their intensity and the sense they afford of welcome relief, the orgasmic nature of the story's conclusion" (p. 191). Plainly the sense of completion, not to say release, that she describes is available only to those who are conscious, even acutely conscious, of sentence structure. Further, as she implies, garden paths and other misperceptions are rarely fruitful—they are diversions from the main event—and in James it generally matters very much which is the best reading (e.g., whether *the warning* refers to Strether's note or to Chad's reply in [11] of Chapter III). Notice, however, that the element of choice between alternatives is not involved in reading James as much, say, as in reading Milton. There is no path of least resistance: one must struggle to put the sentence together at all. Further, one's satisfaction in having assembled a sentence is sometimes diminished by an uneasiness about what qualifications have been made to the main thought. Indeed, I think Tompkins' account of the sense of syntactic resolution needs to be tempered with some remarks of Stephen Booth's on "the lure of an unfinished syntactic unit" in Shakespeare's *Sonnets:*

As long as the syntax marches along without interruption, a reader will follow it across mires of conflicting meanings and impressions toward the clarification that the incompleteness of a syntactical unit allows him to assume will follow. As long as the syntactical unit is incomplete, the reader's understanding can be incomplete or even uncertain without disturbing him. He assumes that the completion of one will complete the other. In the sonnets the completion of a syntactical unit will often neither disappoint the reader nor straighten out the preceding conflicts.[5]

Problems of reference and coreference in James have also been said to heighten the reader's consciousness of sentence structure. Seymour Chatman, for example, quotes and extends Vernon Lee's early (1923) comment that James forces his readers to be "intellectuals" by constructing mazes of coreference: "[his reader] must remember what the pronoun stands for . . . the Reader will have to be, spontaneously, at full cock of attention, a person accustomed to bear things in mind, to carry on a meaning from sentence to sentence, to think in abbreviations; in other words he will have to be an intellectual, as distinguished from an impulsive or *imageful* person."[6] Chatman quite properly extends this observation to putting together coreferring definite noun phrases (pp. 85–86) and to supplying ellipsed material (pp. 100–101). The necessity of solving these problems, Chatman says, weeds out the lazy and inattentive reader: only those willing to adopt an "analytic stance" can survive. The solutions involved with reference and coreference differ in one important respect from those with phrase and clause structure, namely, one frequently attains only relative certainty, particularly in the case of ellipsed material. Uncertainties are perhaps never totally dispelled, and R. W. Short's remarks are at least as faithful to my experience of the text as Tompkins' or Chatman's: "The finality, the crystallization, that ordinary sentence order and signs defining relationship bestow upon the prose has been skilfully foregone in favor of other values. In these peculiar sentences, facts remain tentative, intentions fluid, and conclusions evanescent."[7] To be sure, the questions that Short says are unanswered are those of comprehension rather than sentence perception, but I think his comments are a salutary reminder that even the alert "intellectual" reader often experiences an incomplete grasp and qualified certainty.

5. STEVENS

Stevens demands attention to sentence structure and logical form while at the same time pressing them, and the readers, beyond their limits. The reader must learn to read resolutely across line and even stanza boundaries in pursuit of the sentence. Stevens enjambs as heavily as Milton, and even splits auxiliaries and main verbs across a line boundary—which is most uncommon even in Milton. Notice, for example, how one misses the point in the following lines from "The Sense of the Sleight-of-Hand Man" (cited in full in Chapter III [5]) if one lets the *as if . . .* dangle loosely:

(31)   So bluish clouds
    Occurred above the empty house and the leaves
    Of the rhododendrons rattled their gold,
    As if someone lived there.

[Stevens, *CP*, 222]

That is, the appearances create a sense of "presence" which is false (the house is empty). Similarly, somewhat later in the poem there is a fairly obscure *it* which must be identified—it is wrong to read the phrase loosely as "so it goes":

(32) To think of a dove with an eye of grenadine
    And pines that are cornets, so it occurs,
    And a little island full of geese and stars:

The referent for *it* is essentially (falsifying) poetizing—*one's grand flights,* etc.—of the first line and the 'occurrences' of (32). The point is perhaps made in the sharpest way by the disagreement between Helen Vendler and Frank Doggett about the reference of the last word in "The Man on The Dump" (again note Stevens's use of definite noun phrases). The last line is "Where was it one first heard of the truth? The the" (*CP*, 203). Vendler holds that the last *the* refers to the self (oneself), citing lines from another poem, while Doggett identifies the referent as "reality." As we have seen, in some passages of Romantic poetry these alternatives need not be distinguished, but here much turns on what referent one identifies for *the*.[8]

However, as Helen Vendler, struggling against annoyance, shows in her introductory chapter of *On Extended Wings,* Stevens frequently aims at collapsing distinctions he has set up, and we have already seen many examples of this in the foregoing chapters. Stevens' method is essentially dialectical in that an excess of syntax and logic lead to their transcendence. At least, they do when they are successful—when they are not, they collapse into confusion, surfeiting in their own too much. To read Stevens, one must parse and parse, and when one loses the thread, return and pick it up. Even this may not save one, but it is the only way to get beyond the fairly vague sense of the poems that is the besetting vice of Stevens criticism.

We have thus considered four modifications of our model of reading. The first is really an adjustment within the model giving greater weight to line boundaries as a clue to perception: one still parses into well-formed propositional structures and selects the best reading on the basis of grammaticality. The second is a further adjustment for coping with ungrammatical texts: one continues to aim for the best propositional content, but without sentence structure as a guide. The third modification, taking two propositional structures for the same stretch of text, is a more radical modification or departure from 'ordinary' reading, and the fourth is so radical a departure one might want to call it something else, for in it well-formed propositional structures are not consistently constructed, though pieces of them may be assembled: one reads rather by associating things into clusters or aggregates held together by feeling and related to other clusters by a current of feeling. This last sort of perception is present, I think, even when one is reading for well-formed propositions—it merely comes to have greater prominence as a primary way of perceiving with texts that obscure or elude parsing into sentences. Alliteration and other figures of sound, for example, may lead us to associate words together in a way that facilitates parsing, as in Milton's *place . . . prison . . . portion* (Chapter II [53]), or may take a quasi-independent role in organizing the perception of the passage, as Alpers argues they do in Spenser, and Booth in Shakespeare. Readers must adjust the degree of their reliance on parsing as a way of apprehending for each text, and it appears that the appropriate mode of reading may vary from writer to writer and even over particular stretches of the same writer's work. And surely the value readers place on the experiences provided by one sort of text or another depends on the sorts of mental operations that give them pleasure: some readers find what I may loosely call romantic texts vague, unclear, decadent, and unsatisfying, preferring the cool, sharp edges of a writer who forces decisions and repays the effort of making them; others find those texts dry and cold. We need not, and should not, stop with a cursory *de gustibus*, however, for a number of critics have tried to specify the particular effects and values of these diverse styles, and their methods of finding and describing values in syntax deserve closer examination—this will be the subject of the final chapter. Before that, however, in the next chapter we will extend our model of reading into areas having to do not with the structure of individual sentences as much as with the integration of sentences into their contexts.

CHAPTER SIX

Integration into Context

H ERBERT Clark among others has pointed out that language processing involves more than perception of propositional structure and identification of reference and that sentences are not processed in isolation but in relation to contexts. We have in fact described ways that context enters into perception (via the notion of theme in Chapter One) and comprehension of reference, but context is even more important in regard to another aspect of processing: information constructed from the text is not merely displayed before the mind; rather, it is linked or integrated into previous information. Although there appear to be a number of different types of integration signaled by different constructions, the general notion emerges clearly from an example discussed by J. D. Bransford and M. K. Johnson:

(1)   Watching a Peace March from the Fortieth Floor
The view was breathtaking. From the window one could see the crowd below. Everything looked extremely small from such a distance, but the colorful costumes could still be seen. Everyone seemed to be moving in one direction in an orderly fashion and there seemed to be little children as well as adults. The landing was gentle, and luckily the atmosphere was such that no special suits had to be worn. At first there was a great deal of activity. Later, when the speeches started, the crowd quieted down. The man with the television camera

took many shots of the setting and the crowd. Everyone was very friendly and seemed glad when the music started.[1]

It is a little hard to see what the sentence beginning *The landing . . .* is doing in this narrative. One may imagine various circumstances that would create bridges linking the sentence to the context (A police helicopter landing? A march to the airport?), but the sentence requires more than the usual amount of work. If, however, the passage is retitled "A Space Trip to an Inhabited Planet," the *landing* sentence fits in easily, although the sequence of words is exactly the same, because our view of things and expectations of what might be specified are greatly altered. Notice that the second part of the sentence, "and luckily the atmosphere was such that no special suits had to be worn," does not present a reference problem so much as a relevance problem. Given the assumption induced by the first title, the observation seems either overwhelmingly banal or sardonic (one recalls peace demonstrations at which the atmosphere required a mask if not a suit). The passage illustrates two points in a particularly dramatic way: we may find the relevance of a piece of information by altering our conception of what the passage as a whole is about, and, more generally, we do not comprehend by adding each completed sentence to the pile of ones previously processed; rather, we view each new sentence in relation to the set of expectations and possibilities arising from the previous ones. As Bransford and Johnson put it, "The meaning of an input cannot be determined independently of the context into which an individual is trying to assimilate it" (p. 414).

This paragraph is in one respect misleadingly simplified and dramatic, however: rarely does one encounter a sentence that so resists integration into its context. Also, one may often settle for a degree of integration less than that potentially attainable—settle, that is, with little sense of incomprehension or confusion. We are leaving behind now the areas where it is clear whether or not one has processed successfully, where one either has a well-formed propositional structure or not, has either assigned reference or failed to. Comprehension of a text in its full coherence is perhaps an ideal which each reading approximates. Nonetheless, it is possible to examine various constructions as we have in previous chapters, noting how they may cue, or baffle, integrative strategies, and discover thereby how the passages and our processes work upon each other.

1 . ANTICIPATING NEGATIVES

Perhaps the first point about a negative is that it negates an expectation. Although something is said not to be the case, it might have been: to comprehend it, then, we must see the expectation that is negated as a plausible one, an outgrowth of possibilities inherent in the world at that point. It should not take the reader wholly by surprise: it must be expectable. When no context is available, we must create one. This is simple enough most of the time, to be sure: Ian Watt points out that the mention in the first lines of *The Ambassadors* that ". . . Waymarsh was not to arrive . . ." suggests an expectation in the character's mind that he was to arrive.[2] At times James can describe in considerable detail what sort of expected behavior, response, or feeling a character did not experience (as in the opening paragraphs of *The Ambassadors*)— such description characterizes in terms of what is possible or imaginable for the character.

Having cancelled a certain possibility, a writer may then go on to specify which alternative possibility was in fact actualized. This gives the basic *'not x but y'* pattern that James, Faulkner, and Stevens (among others) are fond of. The processing of such a sequence may vary depending on how many alternatives there are in the context. A *not x* term announces that a certain range of possibilities is under consideration: in addition, it may, if there are only two possibilities likely (*x* and *y*), effectively communicate *y*, so that the *but y* part is redundant. Herbert Clark discusses what he calls a 'conversion' strategy for processing negative terms which would convert the negative into its 'opposite' (e.g., *not even* →

"odd" in the context of numerical reasoning). Clark notes that such a strategy can involve a certain amount of cheating unless the context helps by narrowing down the range of relevant 'opposites' (e.g., "over" is not certain to be the opposite of *not under* unless the situation allows of only the two conditions).[3] Sentences in literature, however, are usually context rich, and we will assume that comprehending a *not x* term can involve projecting a set of possible *y* terms. If the context allows one to narrow the set, one may be relatively able to guess the *but y* before reading it and hence read it with a sense of recognition or of reassurance that one is relatively 'inside' the world of the work. One feels like an insider in that the particular term, while often not totally predictable, is far from a surprise: one can play a game of anticipating at least the sort of word that must come next, and admire the author's 'solution' to the puzzle he has set up. Suppose, for example, that one is reading through the *Collected Poems of Wallace Stevens* and reads the first words of the last title "Not Ideas About the Thing But ____ " —if the rest of the title comes as a surprise, one has been turning the pages too quickly.* This point is difficult to illustrate without citation of extensive stretches of texts, but can perhaps be grasped from two passages from Faulkner's "The Bear" where some of the *but y*'s are even more predictable with more context:

(2) [he is riding into the uncultivated wilderness in a wagon] while the wilderness closed behind his entrance as it had opened momentarily to accept him, opening before his advancement as it closed behind his progress, no fixed path the wagon followed but a channel nonexistent ten yards ahead of it and ceasing to exist ten yards after it had passed, the wagon progressing not by its own volition but by attrition of their intact yet fluid circumambience, drowsing, earless, almost lightless.
[Faulkner, p. 231]

(3) There was always a bottle present, so that it would seem to him that those fine fierce instants of heart and brain and courage and wiliness and speed were concentrated and distilled into that brown liquor

*The Thing Itself"

> which not women, not boys and children, but only hunters drank, drinking not of the blood they spilled but some condensation of the wild immortal spirit, drinking it moderately, humbly even, not with the pagan's base and baseless hope of acquiring thereby the virtues of cunning and strength and speed but in salute to them.
>
> [Faulkner, p. 228]

Note in (3) that the penultimate "not with the pagan's base and baseless hope, etc." involves less tension than the preceding cases because we know that it is going to come out roughly equivalent to *moderately, even humbly.* We may not always try to guess the positive term when we get the negative first, but I think we do when the context lets us.

Because of this strategy of constructing a set of opposites or antitheses, the *not x but y* sequence lends itself to drawing distinctions in a rather overt sort of way that suggests that the distinction drawn is of considerable thematic relevance, as indeed it is in the next example from Faulkner, speaking of the wilderness:

(4) There was some of it left, although now it was two hundred miles from Jefferson when once it had been thirty. He had watched it, not being conquered, destroyed, so much as retreating since its purpose was served now. . . .

> [Faulkner, p. 713]

Faulkner does like to use the construction to set up oppositions or to extend and articulate oppositions already established, so that the *but y* part rarely catches one up short—one has usually a pretty good idea of where things are going by the time one gets to it, though the *salute* in (3) is a nice little touch. This is much less the case with Stevens, for example, mainly because his poems are more elliptical, the alternatives less constrained by any fictive scene or argument. Section VI of "Credences of Summer", for example, begins with this construction, but there has been no mention of rocks, breaking, mountains, or hermits:

(5) The rock cannot be broken. It is the truth.
     It rises from land and sea and covers them.

> It is a mountain half way green and then,
> The other immeasurable half, such rock
> As placid air becomes. But it is not
> A hermit's truth nor symbol in hermitage.
> It is the visible rock, the audible,
> The brilliant mercy of a sure repose,
> On this present ground, the vividest repose.

> [Stevens, *CP*, 375]

It is hard to see how "it is not a hermit's truth" is an alternative that springs to mind out of the preceding reflections. The most recently mentioned "immeasurable half" of the rock suggests something immaterial, or at least unlike the usual rock. *Hermit's truth* suggests something visionary and private, and of course we pick up "symbolic" in the next phrase. We can gain confirmation that these are the relevant attributes conveyed by *hermit's truth* from the positive terms which replace it (*visible, audible,* etc.), taking advantage of the antithetic nature of the construction. This procedure reverses the usual one for the *not x but y* sequence: instead of guessing *y* on the basis of *not x*, we read forward to *y* for help in grasping the import of *x*, which then may suggest to us how *x* is a possible outgrowth of what precedes it ("though it is the ground of being, it is manifest and sensuously apprehended, not inferred or sensed at the margin of perception"). Familiarity with Stevens's characteristic themes and images may help one pick out the attributes of the terms likely to be opposed, but one would have to be of uncanny penetration to be able to predict what sort of thing would follow the *not,* much less the particular image. Other sections in Stevens's longer poems require this reversed processing, as for example the section from "Notes Toward A Supreme Fiction" (*CP*, 399) beginning with four *not x*'s followed by four *y*'s—one has to get to those *y*'s before being very confident of the meaning of the *x*'s. Even when Stevens uses the sequence to summarize a section, so that the reason for the *not x* is fairly clear, the *y* is not totally predictable:

(6)   The man
     In that old coat, those sagging pantaloons,

> It is of him, ephebe, to make, to confect
> The final elegance, not to console
> Nor sanctify, but plainly to propound.
>
> [Stevens, *CP*, 389]

(7)   Then Ozymandias said the spouse, the bride
>   Is never naked. A fictive covering
>   Weaves always glistening from the heart and mind.
>
> [Stevens, *CP*, 396]

The sense of completion afforded by these lines seems in part a result of their guessability: one knows one has understood, and has gotten a bit ahead of the game, much as one can derive some satisfaction and sense of finality from guessing the last word in a heroic couplet. There are times, too, when the sense of resolution may occur without full comprehension of the relation of the 'maxim' to its context. This I believe is the case with the lines often quoted out of context:

(8)   Perhaps,
>   The man-hero is not the exceptional monster,
>   But he that of repetition is most master.
>
> [Stevens, *CP*, 406]

Reading these lines in context, we have a sense of at last understanding what the alternatives in the passage are—or at least of being able to organize it in terms of alternatives. My point here is rather like Stephen Booth's point about the couplets in many of Shakespeare's sonnets: by place, form, and convention, they proclaim closure, summary, comment, or other finality, and the reader may be satisfied without being able to say why.

2. ADDITIVE CONJUNCTS

Coordinating two clauses suggests that they have something in common or belong together or are about the same thing. Hence when we read a coordinate sentence, we will try to infer some common topic or link if one is not obvious in the context. Further, attaching an additive conjunct like *too, also, neither/either, nor,* or *as well* to the second clause (*x, and y too*) heightens this sense of relatedness and indeed more strongly insists that some portion of *y* is the same as *x*, some portion different: either the Subjects are the same and what is predicated of them differs, or the Subjects are different and what is predicated is the same:[4]

> John killed a bear and Bill killed one too.
> John killed a bear and (he) skinned it too.

(Even the 'different' parts, by the way, must belong to the same set of related possibilities:

? John killed a bull and cut off its ears too.
OK John cut off the tail of the bull and cut off its ears too.

The second is better because we group the two different actions as parts of some sort of 'bull-fighting ritual'.)

In a number of publications Herbert Clark and Susan Haviland have advanced what they call the Given/New Strategy of comprehension, which in general involves distinguishing the Given information in a clause (that which is already in memory from previous clauses) from that which is New. The purpose of this sorting is to integrate the New information into memory at the point where the Given is stored.[5] They have studied various constructions which mark the distribution of Given and New information, among them sentences with the additive conjuncts *too* and *not . . . either.* As one would expect, they found that where the Given part of the second clause is a repetition of material in the first, this sorting is made fairly easily, but when the Given information is expressed in a form different from that in which it originally appeared or is only an inference from previous material, the second clause is comprehended more slowly because of the extra time required to match it or link it via inference to its earlier expression. That is, sequences like (b) were comprehended more slowly than (a):

a) Fred was right about the new rules. He was right about the old ones too.
b) Fred wasn't wrong about the new rules. He was right about the old ones too.

The (b) sequence requires a little more time because we must convert *right* to *not wrong* in the second sentence of (b) (or vice-versa) in order to recognize it as part of the information already given in the first sentence. It would seem that this is another example of the evils of elegant variation—variation in the way the Given information is expressed is especially evil since it interferes with the sorting out of the second clause for comprehension. Haviland and Clark found, by the way, that substituting synonymous expressions does not impede comprehension (e.g., *correct* for *right* in the example given)—it is the extra inference involved in getting from *right* (or *correct*) back to *not wrong* that takes the time. This model gains support from, and provides an explanation for, the difficulties we may encounter in Milton's use of *nor* as a (negative) additive conjunct.

In Milton's use generally, *nor* varies in force between "and not" and "and not . . . either," where the second formulation captures the tighter degree of integration into context just discussed. Most of the time he uses *nor* to signal this tighter integration (but cf. *PL* I, 396–401). Such *nor*-clauses can be split into a part which is the Given (the same as a part of the previous clause) and a part which contrasts the New alternative to the previous one:

(9)   The hasty multitude
         Admiring enter'd, and the work some praise
         And some the Architect: his hand was known
         In Heav'n by many a Towred structure high,
         Where Scepter'd Angels held thir residence,
         And sat as Princes, whom the supreme King
         Exalted to such power, and gave to rule,
         Each in his Hierarchie, the Orders bright.
         Nor was his name unheard or unador'd
         In ancient Greece; and in Ausonian land
         Men call'd him Mulciber. . . .

                                        [Milton, *PL*, I. 730–40]

Here the Given in the *nor*-clause is "his name was not unheard nor unador'd"—to recognize it as equivalent to "his hand was known" involves several steps: we must avoid identifying the second *his* as the *supreme King,* reaching instead back to the earlier *his* (parallelism may help); then we must convert *his name* to *his hand* (that is to say, recognize the essential identity). It remains to match *nor . . . unheard or unador'd* with *known.* Note that these are not strictly equivalent in degree because of the conversational principle that converts "not un-ADJ" sequences to "slightly to moderately ADJ".[6] If we match by converting the double negative term to "heard and adored" (and hence "known"), we distort the meaning somewhat, missing the qualification contained in the "slightly to moderately." The point is like that made in regard to the appositives from Ruskin (15) in Chapter IV: in our rush to match the equivalent terms we may ignore subtle differences. (If we converted in the other direction, by the way, [*known* → "not unknown"] we would not distort the meaning of the second term.) This is, for Milton, a fairly simple example in that the terms at least match up fairly well as syntactic units. The next examples break down that syntactic correspondence in various ways:

(10)   After these appear'd
        A crew who under Names of old Renown,
        Osiris, Isis, Orus and their Train
        With monstrous shapes and sorceries abus'd
        Fanatic Egypt and her Priests, to seek
        Thir wandring Gods disguis'd in brutish forms
        Rather then human. Nor did Israel scape
        Th' infection when thir borrow'd Gold compos'd
        The Calf in Oreb:

                                        [Milton, *PL,* I. 476–84]

The Given in the second clause is "not scape the infection." Notice that *the infection* has no corresponding noun phrase in the first clause, nor does *(e)scape* have a corresponding verb, and the differing terms (*Egypt* and *Israel*) have different syntactic functions in the two clauses (Direct Object and Subject, respectively). Here, with the lack of syntactic parallel, it might be easier to split the second

clause into Given/New by finding the clearly New, assuming the
rest is somehow Given. We have not fully comprehended, however, until we have linked the Given in the second clause to material in the first. Here we can do so in general terms ('beast
idolatry'), but Merritt Hughes gives a more particular link to the
god Apis in his note to these lines. The syntax gives even less help
in the next example:

(11)   Anon they move
        In perfect Phalanx to the Dorian mood
        Of Flutes and soft Recorders; such as rais'd
        To hight of noblest temper Hero's old
        Arming to Battel, and in stead of rage
        Deliberate valour breath'd, firm and unmov'd
        With dread of death to flight or foul retreat,
        Nor wanting power to mitigate and swage
        With solemn touches, troubl'd thoughts, and chase
        Anguish and doubt and fear and sorrow and pain
        From mortal or immortal minds.

                                        [Milton, *PL*, I. 549-59]

Here the Given material is "not wanting power to," and again no
exactly paralleling phrases are to be found in the first clause. Rather, they must be inferred (if it raised them, then it must have had
power to raise them; again, a double negative conversion is
required—*not wanting* = "having"). Even the tactic suggested for
the previous example of splitting by finding the New information
doesn't work too well here, because the New information must be
in some sort of alternation with the information of the previous
clause. The opposition of Egypt/Israel was easy to spot, but the
opposition here—(power to) rouse/soothe—requires pretty complete processing of the clauses to discover. Also, of course, the
modifying material (*instead of rage* . . .) intervening between the first
clause and the second makes one search further to see what material the second clause is juxtaposed to. We see in this example, as in
the previous one, that the very process of matching the second
clause to the first may involve considerable reinterpretation of the

first clause, or, to put it another way, the second clause highlights things in the first clause.

In the next example, the Given information is most easily expressed as an inference which matches with an inference from the first clause:

(12) Though of thir Names in heav'nly Records now
      Be no memorial, blotted out and ras'd
      By thir Rebellion, from the Books of Life.
      Nor had they yet among the Sons of Eve
      Got them new Names. . . .

                                        [Milton, *PL*, I. 361-65]

For the statement of the Given, we may take the inference from "not yet have got new names" to "not now have ( ) names." From the first clause we can extract a proposition matching this "not now have ( ) names"—where the blanks are filled in with the alternating information (*original*/*new*). The last example I will cite is like (9) in that it is not immediately clear what the second clause is conjoined to:

(13)   They heard, and were abasht, and up they sprung
          Upon the wing, as when men wont to watch
          On duty, sleeping found by whom they dread,
          Rouse and bestir themselves ere well awake.
          Nor did they not perceave the evil plight
          In which they were, or the fierce pains not feel;
                                        [Milton, *PL*, I. 331-36]

Should the *nor*-clause be matched against the simile, or against the clause preceding the simile? The period after *awake* allows this second possibility. We can check for portions that establish a Given in the *nor* clause or that alternate with the New. It is hard on a quick scan to determine whether *they* refers to the watchmen or the fallen angels lying on the lake of fire, but it would presumably be Given information in either case. Perhaps the first point to come into focus is *the evil plight*—if watchmen are found sleeping by those whom they dread, then they too are in an evil plight—and we can infer that, rousing, they do not perceive it, sleepily. What then is the alternating New information? Perhaps a little surprisingly, we are left with *they* (pronouns are rarely New—what makes *they* New here is that it is a shift of reference to the other "they"). That is, *they* refers not to the watchmen but to the fallen angels. According to this analysis, *they* should be read with contrastive stress, and, if it is so read, the lines are much easier to comprehend (and vice-versa). Perhaps one thing that makes it hard to imagine a contrastive stress on *they* is that it is in the third position in the line, which is generally filled with an unstressed syllable. Imagining oneself 'hearing' the line, in other words, will not in this case make it easier to comprehend.

3 . EPIC SIMILES

The Given/New strategy can perhaps be extended to a construction that Haviland and Clark did not discuss, namely, to epic similes. In Milton and Spenser, these typically have the form of a fairly extended description of some scene or event (y) which is likened to the matter at hand (x). Some of the individuals and properties in y correspond to individuals and properties already described for x (i.e., their descriptions repeat in terms appropriate to y information already given for x), and some of the properties are New and can be added to our 'knowledge' of x. If indeed we are left with substantial chunks of information in y that cannot be attached to x either as corresponding terms to individuals in x or as New properties of those individuals, we will scratch our heads and say that we don't know what the simile is doing in its context.

Since comprehending an extended simile involves splitting up the simile in terms of Given/New information by matching corresponding terms in x and y, considerations like those discussed in the previous section arise. A simile (y) which allows alignment of corresponding parts is a little quicker to split than one which does not (*ceteris paribus*, as always). In the second canto of *The Faerie*

Queene, for example, there is a simile attached to the description of a battle between the Red Cross Knight and Sans Foi which begins

(14) As when two rams stird with ambitious pride,
      Fight for the rule of the rich fleeced flocke,
      Their horned fronts so fierce on either side
      Do meete. . . .

[Spenser, *FQ*, I.ii. 16]

It is easy to establish a point-by-point correspondence between the figures and events in the scene and those in the simile, and hence it is clear what the New material is in y and where it is to be attached in x. In this particular case, Spenser explicitly points up the application:

(15) Do meete, that with the terrour of the shocke
      Astonied both, stand sencelesse as a blocke,
      Forgetfull of the hanging victory:
      So stood these twaine, vnmoued as a rocke,
      Both staring fierce, and holding idely
      The broken reliques of their former cruelty.

[Spenser, *FQ*, I.ii. 16]

(A few points remain uncertain: does Spenser mean the horns to parallel the spears? If so, are they broken too? Is there anything in x [the battle of the knights] corresponding to "rule of the rich fleeced flocke"?) This is about as straightforward as a simile can be. Somewhat less aligned is the simile (stanza 21) attached to the description of Errour's vomit (stanza 20) of the first canto of the *Faerie Queene:*

(16) Therewith she spewd out of her filthy maw
      A floud of poyson horrible and blacke,
      Full of great lumpes of flesh and gobbets raw,
      Which stunck so vildly, that it forst him slacke
      His grasping hold, and from her turne him backe:
      Her vomit full of bookes and papers was,
      With loathly frogs and toades, which eyes did lacke,

And creeping sought way in the weedy gras:
Her filthy parbreake all the place defiled has.

(21)

As when old father Nilus gins to swell
With timely pride aboue the Aegyptian vale,
His fattie waues do fertile slime outwell,
And ouerflow each plaine and lowly dale:
But when his later spring gins to auale,
Huge heapes of mudd he leaues, wherein there breed
Ten thousand kindes of creatures, partly male
And partly female of his fruitfull seed;
Such vgly monstrous shapes elswhere may no man reed.

[Spenser, *FQ*, I.i. 20–21]

The first outwelling fluid (*the fertile slime*) does not correspond to
her vomit; rather, it is the mud left behind that does, suggesting
that Errour's products arise from some sort of remnant of natural
fertility. Note that when there is an 'application', as here, it merely
underlines the main ostensible point or points of similitude (here
the ugliness and monstrosity of the offspring)—it does not exhaus-
tively enumerate them.

The facilitating power of alignment can perhaps be grasped in
the following contrasting pair from Milton:

(17)   his form had not yet lost
    All her Original brightness, nor appear'd
    Less than Arch Angel ruind, and th' excess
    Of Glory obscur'd: As when the Sun new ris'n
    Looks through the Horizontal misty Air
    Shorn of his Beams, or from behind the Moon
    In dim Eclips disastrous twilight sheds
    On half the Nations, and with fear of change
    Perplexes Monarchs. Dark'n'd so, yet shon
    Above them all th' Arch Angel:

[Milton, *PL*, I. 591–600]

(18) Yet to thir Generals Voyce they soon obeyd
    Innumerable. As when the potent Rod

Of Amrams Son in Egypts evill day
Wav'd round the Coast, up call'd a pitchy cloud
Of Locusts, warping on the Eastern Wind,
That ore the Realm of impious Pharoah hung
Like Night, and darken'd all the Land of Nile:
So numberless were those bad Angels seen
Hovering on wing under the Cope of Hell
'Twixt upper, nether, and surrounding Fires;

[Milton, *PL*, I. 337–46]

In (17), which is in fact a double simile, *Satan* and *the sun* obviously align (*brightness* is a bit of extra help), so that whatever is predicated of the sun in either simile is to be carried over to Satan. In (18), however, we have been focusing on the fallen angels and we must read through several lines before we find the corresponding term (*locusts*). Then we may build backwards toward finding the term in *x* that does correspond to *the potent Rod* (a footnote identifying Amram's son as Moses may be helpful): Moses' calling up the locusts, then, corresponds to Satan's calling up the fallen angels from the burning lake. The corresponding terms do not exactly leap out, but once aligned, they give the interesting pairing: Moses/Satan. It is easy to take a shortcut here via *thir Generals Voyce* to mismatch the fallen angels (led by Satan) to the children of Israel (led by Amram's son) and thus to miss the diminishing force of the simile.

Sometimes a property in *y* may not be explicitly mentioned but can be inferred. Usually, however, if a writer wants this property to be noticed, he will mention it. Thus there is an unmentioned Given property of diluvial mud in (16)—Spenser himself points this out in his 'application' of the simile:

(19) The same so sore annoyed has the knight,
      That welnigh choked with the deadly stinke,
      His forces faile, ne can no longer fight.

[Spenser, *FQ*, I.i. 22]

Similarly in the wonderfully complex Vallambrosa simile in *Paradise Lost*, a New property of *y* to be carried over to *x* is left momentarily to be inferred:

(20)   till on the Beach
    Of that inflamed Sea, he stood and call'd
    His Legions, Angel Forms, who lay intrans't
    Thick as Autumnal Leaves that strow the Brooks
    In Vallambrosa, where th' Etrurian shades
    High overarch't imbowr; or scatterd sedge
    Afloat, when with fierce Winds Orion arm'd
    Hath vext the Red-Sea Coast, whose waves orethrew
    Busiris and his Memphian Chivalry,
    While with perfidious hatred they pursu'd
    The Sojourners of Goshen, who beheld
    From the safe shore thir floating Carkases
    And broken Chariot Wheels, so thick bestrown
    Abject and lost lay these, covering the Flood,
    Under amazement of thir hideous change.
                                    [Milton, *PL*, I. 299–313]

Abject and *lost* are explicitly mentioned in the 'application': they can be inferred from the imagined events and scene of Pharoah's shattered army, but they have not been explicitly predicated of it in the simile. This simile is hard to process for another reason. It is overtly a double, actually a triple, simile, and we do not get the basis (i.e., the Given points of correspondence) of the third simile (the bodies floating on the Red Sea) for six lines—it is true that there is simply a lot of information coming at the reader, but I think it would be easier to assimilate if the basis of the third simile were aligned with the other two and presented earlier. Not only is New information easier to process once we have identified the Given (and hence know to process the New as New), but here we are not even sure we should be processing the material as a simile until we get to the Given.

Once we have identified the Given and New information in y, we face the second great part of comprehending the simile, which is determining in what sense the New properties in y apply in x. In most cases they only apply analogously: we are juxtaposing situations and events from different areas of experience, and the New attributes of y that we want to attach in x may require translation into the domain of x. Some of these New attributes may be more in the nature of connotations or associations that outright properties, as is perhaps the case in the sun/Satan simile (17), which associates considerable magnificence and power with Satan. Similarly, the matching of Satan and Moses in (18) as performers of mighty acts enhances Satan's stature. Perhaps we should suppose that all the properties of the corresponding term in y can be attached to the one in x and further analyzed as time and information allow. Even if they never receive a satisfactory analysis, they remain attached and can link in associative networks, such as those clustering around Galileo's telescope in *Paradise Lost* and the "cloud of gnats" similes in Book I of *The Faerie Queene*. Similes may be integrated into their contexts to different degrees and in different ways even within a single work.

4. CONDITIONALS

Integration thus far has been largely 'factual'—statements presumed true are integrated into the world we imagine to exist—though similes may require adjustment so that the analogous term is added to the matter at hand. Now, however, we add a difficulty: how does one process information that is offered as only possibly true (or probably false) in the world? I will make a basic assumption here, namely, that we try to assess the truth value in the fictive world as soon as possible. Reasoning from possible facts appears to be quite difficult, and many critics have noted that we tend to take material so reasoned from, elaborated, or qualified as true. In practical terms, the truth of y depends on the truth of x in '*if* x, *then* y' (though technically we should not assume y is false if x is false, we tend to do so), so that a decision on the truth of y can be spared if one can decide the truth of x. In cases where the truth of x is obscure, we may go to y for help, treating *if* as a full biconditional ("if and only if").

Language has devices for assisting the Reader/Hearer in this process by marking the clauses that are unlikely to be true (i.e., are counter-factual). Some confusion exists over this marking, however, which means that readers may not always be able to rely on it. The most common markings of the antecedent (x) clause for counter-factuality are the use of a past tense where a present would otherwise be expected (or *had,* where a past tense would be expected) or the use of *were (to)* (or *were to have,* where a past tense would be expected). In addition, the consequent (y) is marked with *should* or *would.* These marks are usually sufficient to identify a clause as counter-factual—in terms of processing, to screen it out of the truth determination process, giving it the value 'false'. Consider this illustration from Wallace Stevens:

(21)   So that if one went to the moon,
       Or anywhere beyond, to a different element,
       One would be drowned in the air of difference,
       Incapable of belief, in the difference.

                                        [Stevens, *CP,* 258]

The preceding lines are in the present tense, so the past tense of *went* marks the antecedent as counter-factual, as does the *would* in the consequent (the material in the antecedent, of course, also makes the clause pretty improbable).[7] When a writer chooses not to use counter-factual forms, he forces us to determine the truth value—he leaves it open, as it were, and hence, as Helen Vendler observes of Stevens, moves the material in the direction of (possible) truth. One thing we do know about counter-factuals is that readers do draw the inference 'x is false' and may even think they have read it.[8]

The more complex processing occurs when a sentence passes the counter-factual screening and must be assessed for truth in the fictive world (contextual frame). The following example poses a genuinely open possibility in the antecedent, though the consequent suggests that we perhaps should refer the antecedent to the bin for 'unlikely-to-be-answered questions' rather than the bin for 'hold-for-further-confirmation surmises':

(22) If there is inarticulateness behind it, articulateness is nullified by the immobility of the face itself; if hope or yearning, neither hope nor yearning show.

[Faulkner, LA, 324]

This passage is very difficult to read as written—it is much easier if we are guided by the parallelism with *hope or yearning* and remove the *in-* in *inarticulateness* ("if there is articulateness behind it, articulateness is nullified . . ."), but the alternation between the negative and positive forms seems deliberate and appears in the other editions I have checked. The best I can paraphrase is something like "If one supposes inarticulateness behind it, that merely reflects the way that articulateness is nullified . . ."). We can conclude from her behavior that the consequent (articulateness is nullified . . .) is true, hence probably also the antecedent, or at least it is effectively true. Henry James makes this assessing of the antecedent difficult by using antecedents which are, in our knowledge, already pretty well established as true:

(23) he would have sketched to himself his impression of her as "Well, she's more thoroughly civilized—!" If "More thoroughly than *whom?*" would not have been for him a sequel to this remark, that was just by reason of his deep consciousness of the bearing of his comparison.

[James, AMB, 21]

(24) That fact bloomed for him, in the firelight and lamplight that glowed their welcome through the London fog, as the flower of her difference; just as her difference itself—part of which was her striking him as older in a degree for which no mere couple of months could account—was the fruit of their intimate relation. If she was different it was because they had chosen together that she should be. . . .

[James, WOD, II. 313–14]

(25) Each time she turned in again, each time, in her impatience, she gave him up, it was to sound to a deeper depth, while she tasted the faint flat emanation of things, the failure of fortune and of honour. If she continued to wait it was really in a manner that she might n't add the

shame of fear, of individual, of personal collapse, to all the other shames.

[James, *WOD*, I, 3–4]

In (23) it appears that we should assume he did not continue, since the quotation is broken off; in (25) it seems she did continue, since there is no mention of her leaving; in (24) there seems little doubt that she is different. We thus experience a slight double-take: why is there any uncertainty about it, and, if there is, how am I, the reader, to resolve it? I find that in these cases, I check the consequent clause and, finding it giving a reason or purpose for the antecedent, resume my initial assumption that the antecedent is true. It seems that James is using *if* as an odd sort of concessive conjunct ("if x is so [and though somewhat unexpected, it does seem to be so], then it is less unexpected when we consider y"). The following examples are harder to process because the consequent does not help to decide the truth of the antecedent:

(26) If, however, he had suppressed the matter by leaving Victoria he would at once suppress now, in turn, whatever else suited.

[James, *WOD*, II. 297]

(27) If she saw more things than her fine face in the dull glass of her father's lodgings she might have seen that after all she was not herself a fact in the collapse.

[James, *WOD*, I. 5–6]

Indeed, we do not know whether she did see farther in (27), and, as one suspects from the consequent, we are not going to find out very soon. One of James' numerous unusual demands on the reader is that he be prepared to field the whole range of possibility that clauses with *if* may serve up, taking his clues where he can get them and tolerating a considerable amount of unresolved uncertainty.

What we might call the conditional simile ('x *as if* y') is a favorite construction of several of our authors and is, as Wayne Booth suggests, in some respects the modern equivalent of the epic simile.[9] Our interest in it here is that the *y* is typically, though not always, counter-factual (and is not as reliably marked with counterfactual forms—see Quirk et al., p. 755). James's uses are typical in this regard. Seymour Chatman cites three from the first chapter of *The Ambassadors:*

(28) She paused while our friend took in these things, and it was as if a good deal of talk had already passed.

[James, *AMB*, 19]

(29) It was almost as if she had been in possession and received him as a guest.

[James, *AMB*, 19–20]

(30) It was as if this personage [the lady in the glass cage] had seen herself instantly superseded.

[James, *AMB*, 20]

Strether has exchanged only a few sentences with Maria, they are at a hotel, and the woman in the cage is presumably wholly indifferent to Strether's esteem or loss of it. It seems to me obvious that these are all counter-factual, and it is important that we code them as such, and I am astonished at Chatman's comment: "he [Strether] needs to conjecture, and the instrument of conjecture is *as if*. It is a safe instrument, since no one—neither Strether nor his interpreter—is necessarily comitted [sic] to it as the exact state of things."[10] We should all be committed to it as not the exact state of things.

The point is important, for the construction can be used to introduce a possible conjecture as it frequently does in Faulkner. Wayne Booth calls attention to two pages in *Light in August* which present the impressions and surmises of the minister Hightower of his two visitors, of which the following is a sample:

(31) They enter not with diffidence, but with something puppetlike about them, as if they were operated by clumsy springwork. The woman appears to be the more assured, or at least the more conscious, of the two of them. It is as though, for all her frozen and mechanically

moved inertia, she had come for some definite purpose or at least with some vague hope. But he sees at once that the man is in something like coma, as though oblivious and utterly indifferent to his whereabouts, and yet withal a quality latent and explosive, paradoxically rapt and alert at the same time.

[Faulkner, *LA*, 323]

Clearly all but the first of the conjectures are of possible reasons for the behavior of the visitors, not known, or perhaps to be known with certainty, but distinctly possible. Somewhat the same sort of possibility exists for the boy's intuition in the passage cited as (IV.44).

This construction, with the possible truth of *y*, is common in passages relating feelings and impressions where one wants to stress the subjectivity of the experiencing consciousness and suggest that the possible cause or explanation has some truth because of the truth of one's impression or feeling (i.e., one supposes, loosely, '*y* can account for x; I feel/observe x; hence y'— good old Affirming the Consequent, one of your most deeply rooted logical fallacies). Here is an example noted by Helen Vendler from Stevens:

(32) And we feel, in a way apart, for a moment, as if
      There was a bright scienza outside of ourselves,

      A gaiety that is being, not merely knowing,
      The will to be and to be total in belief,
      Provoking a laughter, an agreement, by surprise.

[Stevens, *CP*, 248]

If we feel that way, perhaps in a sense it is so—one would not want to rule it out by using *were* in place of *was*. It is possible that the final *as if* of "To An Old Philosopher" that so puzzles Vendler is to be taken as a (possible) explanation of the preceding fact:

(33)   He stops upon this threshold,
      As if the design of all his words takes form
      And frame from thinking and is realized.

[Stevens, *CP*, 511]

'He stops, and it may be because the world for him finally becomes fully actual'—perhaps, though since it is his final moment, we will not know.

Thus Stevens and Faulkner can use this construction to suggest possibilities the truth value of which we may never be able to assess. They are nonetheless not terribly hard to process. This I think is a reflection of the basic principle that the problem is *reasoning from* an uncertain premise: these *if*-clauses have no consequents (or consequences in processing). According to the principles sketched here, the next *if*-clauses should be quite hard to read through:

(34) But it was she and not the sea we heard.

> For she was the maker of the song she sang.
> The ever-hooded, tragic-gestured sea
> Was merely a place by which she walked to sing.
> Whose spirit is this? we said, because we knew
> It was the spirit that we sought and knew
> That we should ask this often as she sang.
>
> If it was only the dark voice of the sea
> That rose, or even colored by many waves;
> If it was only the outer voice of sky
> And cloud, of the sunken coral water-walled,
> However clear, it would have been deep air,
> The heaving speech of air, a summer sound
> Repeated in a summer without end
> And sound alone. But it was more than that. . . .
>
> [Stevens, *CP*, 129]

I have given the context which seems on the face of it to make it likely that the *if*-clauses are going to be rejected as false. They are not clearly counter-factual, however, and we must consider whether in fact they may be abandoning the earlier affirmation that it was she and not the sea we heard. Scanning to the consequent does not help much—one gets some confirmation for the counter-factual interpretation, since we might suppose that as song, it is not merely sound but has intelligible words attached (hence consequent appears false, hence also antecedent). We are nonetheless happy for the reassurance of *But it was more than that* that we have guessed right—he has not abandoned the earlier affirmation. The more we need and fasten on this reassurance, the less we will be able to make sense of what comes next:

> More even than her voice, and ours, among
> The meaningless plungings of water and the wind,
> Theatrical distances, bronze shadows heaped
> On high horizons, mountainous atmospheres
> Of sky and sea.

[Stevens, CP, 129]

If, as I have suggested, we concentrate on her song and its properties as song, it is a bit shocking to realize that we are not talking just about her song but about 'that which rose', which, it appears, includes a mixture of the intelligible and the unintelligible. If this explanation of the difficulty of these lines is correct, then they should be easier to read with *were* substituted for *was* in the two crucial instances, since we would then not have to worry about the truth of the *if*-clause.

5. *AT LEAST*

Words such as *even, only, just, merely, at least* and so on make reference to expectations by means of what is sometimes called 'scales of degree of strength': *only x*, for example, means "x and not y", where y is understood as some point further on on the relevant scale of degree of strength.[11] *Only* also conveys the notion that y might well be expected under the circumstances. The x over which these words operate is usually to the right of the word, and there are certain interesting problems involved in specifying exactly what portion of the material to the right is the x (these problems have received much attention from linguists). One practical way to make these decisions as one reads is to formulate the expectation that would arise from one item or another being taken as x and then check the expectation against those compatible with the context. In a sentence such as

> Jean only sells paintings to museums.

the x could be taken as *paintings* or as *museums* or as *sells*, and we would have as the 'not y' terms ". . . not prints," ". . . not private collectors," ". . . not donates," respectively, where the context would help select the correct x. This is an interesting case where a problem of perception (what does the word operate over—i.e., what is x?) may be decided by a tour through comprehension.

The phrase *at least* is particularly interesting because it can have scope (i.e., have its x) to the left or to the right. Some writers honor a convention of punctuation on this point that if *at least* has scope to the left, it is to be set off with commas as a kind of parenthetic afterthought. James, for example, appears to be observing this convention in the following examples:

(35) He *had* announced himself—six months before; had written out at least that Chad wasn't to be surprised should he see him some day turn up.

[James, *AMB*, 68]

(36) To feel the street, to feel the room, to feel the table-cloth and the centre-piece and the lamp, gave her a small, salutary sense, at least, of neither shirking nor lying.

[James, *WOD*, I. 4]

In (35), the scope of *at least* taken to the right gives 'at least that Chad wasn't to be surprised etc.' The general formula for *at least* is roughly '*at least x if not (y)*'. Applied here we get 'if not (that he was seeking Chad out)', which is certainly consistent with what we know in context. Trying scope to the left, however, gives us a puzzling 'at least written out, if not ( ).' In (36), however, it does have scope to the left, since we get 'at least gave her a small salutary sense if not (a greater comfort or conviction). . . .'

Faulkner, however, appears not to observe the convention and even to seek the ambiguities that result. There are two passages with ambiguous *at least*s cited in Chapter IV (20 and 31). The first contains the sequence:

in repudiation and denial at least of the land and the wrong and the shame

Taking scope to the left, we get 'in at least repudiation and denial if not (?some more positive coming-to-terms-with)'; taking it to the right we get 'in repudiation and denial of at least the land and the wrong and the shame if not (? the people and the good)'. This latter expectation has little support in the context, and indeed the passage removes any uncertainty by continuing "even if he couldn't cure the wrong and eradicate the shame...."—so the scope does go to the left despite the absence of commas. In the second instance in Chapter IV, however, Faulkner is in no haste to resolve uncertainties:

(IV.31)
> Then suddenly he knew why he had never wanted to own any of it, arrest at least that much of what people called progress, measure his longevity at least against that much of its ultimate fate.

Taking the first *at least* first, we get with scope to the left

'at least arrest if not(?reverse) that much of what people called progress'

which works well here, taking *that much . . .* as the amount of land he would own and presumably save from 'taming'. The alternative, with scope to the right, is

'arrest that much at least of what people called progress if not (?the whole process of exploitation)'

and this is fine in context also. The next phrase is presumably appositive and repeats the pattern:

'measure at least his longevity if not (??that of his heirs or, his strength) against...'

'measure his longevity against at least that much of its ultimate fate if not (the full working out of its destiny)'

Again, both of these are possible. I must admit that I had to think a bit to come up with the alternative marked with two question marks, but Faulkner so strongly insists on parallelism here that I was spurred to find it. As in the examples discussed in Chapter V, Faulkner seems to court the ambiguity (note that punctuation or rephrasing could remove it) and to intend for us not to try to choose between the alternatives.

There are a number of other words and constructions we could examine that induce a splitting into Given/New and matching to context. I will touch on one discussed by Seymour Chatman, namely, the pseudo-cleft (or *wh*-cleft) construction which James is fond of. He cites as typical the following example from the first chapter of *The Ambassadors*:

(37) What had come as straight to him as a ball in a well-played game—
    and caught moreover not less neatly—was just the air, in the person
    of his friend, of having seen and chosen, the air of achieved posses-
    sion of these vague qualities and quantities that figured to him, collec-
    tively, as the advantage snatched from lucky chances.

                                                              [James, *AMB*, 20–21]

He observes that the pseudo-cleft conveys

    the hint that it was predictable that something should indeed come to
    him, and that our part is rather to note its arrival than to be surprised
    by its content. It is as if James were saying, 'You are, of course, dear
    and so knowledgeable reader, correctly anticipating that Strether, this
    sensitive instrument, would 'catch' something, make some inference
    about Maria; what in fact *had* come as straight to him as a ball . . . was . . .'
    The cleft construction presupposes a reader capable, ready, indeed,
    eager, to make such predictions.

                                                        [*Later Style*, pp. 67–68]

In terms of our model, the material between *what* and the copula is Given information, the focus of attention, in fact. With James, however, the material in that slot may be only implicitly present in the matter preceding, and indeed he often uses the pseudo-cleft to make a little leap forward, redefining something that has been latent or struggling toward expression in what preceded it. This passage, for example, comes at the end of an examination of impressions and reflections that had come to Strether. Chatman misses the mark on two counts here: there is nothing 'Jamesian' in the assumption of Givenness set up by this construction, and one does not have to derive one's expectations from general axioms (the 'sensitivity of Strether' etc.) but from relatively immediate context (and inferences based on it)—as, indeed, is always the case with such constructions. Chatman's account of his response is sensitive enough—it is his explanation of it that is defective. This is a particularly clear illustration of the usefulness of a model of processing in placing particular observations in perspective.

The integrative processes we have discussed are of a somewhat different and, if you will, higher order than those studied in previous chapters in three general respects. For one thing, they are tied less to syntax than to strategies for perception of propositional structure and comprehension of reference. Clearly they do involve linear precedence, or priority in time, but they do not involve grammatical relations crucially. I did suggest that grammatical parallelism would facilitate matching, but it does so mainly because it gives linear parallelism (if Subjects correspond to Subjects, then first things correspond to first things, and so on). Further, the terms of matching and analysis are not intrinsically syntactic units. Given/New contrasts can be established between parts of words or phrases. Still, it does appear that a clause is easier to integrate into a context if the units in the clause correspond fairly directly to the terms of the context, which suggests that the context is not stored in an entirely form-neutral way at the time the next clause is integrated into it. These are interesting speculations which await further investigation.

A second point of difference is that processing on this level may be more a matter of preference and degree than processing on the levels discussed earlier. We do have to decide, for example, whether the fallen angels perceived their plight or not in (13)—that is part of the propositional structure of the sentence—but we may decline to decide whether the simile means to attach the property 'dreaded by those he rouses' to Satan or not. Haviland and Clark decided to leave it up to their subjects to decide when they felt that they had comprehended the sentences adequately. Their results then mean that the subjects took longer to comprehend to their own satisfaction the indirectly related sentences than they did for the directly related ones, suggesting that they were monitoring their processing for successful linking up of the sentence to its context. So it appears that we have some means of gauging our performance here.

The third difference is suggested by the fact that while processing on this level may be more or less difficult for reasons we have discussed, it is not made difficult by the generation of garden paths. These processes do not seem to lead one into error. It appears that these strategies are more concerned with the processing of information—in the cases at hand, of anticipating and storing it—than they are with the content of the information. Hence they do not ever produce misconstructed content—the typical product of their malfunctioning is a blurred or muddled sense of what exactly has been said, what contrasted, or compared with what, not a definite mistake. But the fact that they have to do with process—with the way the text is sized up and taken in—rather than content does not diminish their aesthetic importance. In fact, we could probably explain more about why certain people enjoy certain styles along the lines indicated here than along those of previous chapters. In the next and final chapter, we will see how values other than pleasure have been ascribed to certain complexities of processing.

CHAPTER SEVEN

Some Values of Complex Processing

 $\mathbf{I}$ N this chapter we address a second major topic in literary criticism that has remained on the periphery of earlier chapters, namely, the aesthetic effect, function, or value of ambiguity and difficulty. There are, very broadly, two basic ways that expressive value has been ascribed to difficult writing. The first is the method of Empson, which has been used primarily for poetry and which works at a level of close or fine detail. The second method applies at a higher level of generality and to notably mannered writers (such as James and Faulkner). We will begin with the first 'school' and with an examination of Empson's practice in *Seven Types of Ambiguity* since it has been a model for 'close reading' for several decades. Empson discusses a number of passages involving parsing difficulties, pronominal reference, and ellipsis, including the following lines from "The Waste Land", some of which were cited in (III.35):

(1)   In vials of ivory and coloured glass
       Unstoppered, lurked her strange synthetic perfumes,
       Unguent, powdered, or liquid—troubled, confused
       And drowned the sense in odours; stirred by the air
       That freshened from the window, these ascended
       In fattening the prolonged candleflames.

In regard to the third line he says, "after *powdered* and the two similar words have acted as adjectives, it gives a sense of swooning or squinting, or the *stirring* of things seen through heat convection currents, to think of *troubled* and *confused* as verbs" (p. 78). The experience of the reader, that is, directly enacts the thing being described. Empson further notes that *these* could have *perfumes, sense,* and/or *odours* as antecedent, observing as the effect, "there is a curious heightening of the sense of texture from all this dalliance; a suspension of all need for active decision" (p. 78). The language here is uncannily reminiscent of Chapter Five: Empson appears to be saying that the reader begins to give up active structuring of the sentences and to surrender to a flow of impressions, thus experiencing a kind of passivity and lassitude in processing which here reflects the theme of debilitating sensuality.

Perceptual uncertainty is again the source of the effect described in the next passage, which is also from T. S. Eliot:

(2)   Webster was much possessed by death
      And saw the skull beneath the skin;
      And breastless creatures underground
      Leaned backward with a lipless grin.

Empson points out that the last two lines could be taken as an independent clause ("meanwhile they leaned...") or as coordinate to *skull* ("saw the skull beneath the skin and saw creatures that were leaned backward...."), concluding that "The verse, whose point is the knowledge of what is beyond knowledge, is made much more eerie by this slight doubt" (p. 79).

Since Empson's method is essentially that of pointing out a correlation between processing and the theme or point of the passage, it will fail to convince if either term is inaccurately described. Some of his comments on a passage from Samuel Johnson's "The Vanity of Human Wishes" are based on difficulties that seem to me to be unreal:

(3)   What murdered Wentworth, and what exiled Hyde,
        By kings protected, and to kings allied?
        What but their wish indulged in courts to shine,
        And power too great to keep, or to resign?

Empson first considers whether *power* is coordinate to *wish* or to *shine* (this second possibility seems forced to me, as it would require assumption of an ellipsed *for* "wish to shine and [for] power..."). He then asks what the last line might mean in terms of unexpressed causality (why could it not be kept or resigned?). He concludes, "the line, I think, conveys by its knotted complexity, by the sense that there are grammatical depths the casual reader has not plumbed, some such ideas of fatal involution as these I have been elaborating" (pp. 69–70). Here one must register a demurral: the last line is not *grammatically* knotted, and in fact I experience little difficulty with respect to the "unexpressed causality," which I trace to a general maxim,

> The greater one's power is, the more difficult it can be to retain or resign.

One may of course ask why this maxim is true, but one does not have to ask, or run over traditional beliefs about power, any more than one must think up a large portion of elementary economics to comprehend the maxim,

> When supply exceeds demand, prices fall.

This example illustrates the usefulness of a model of processing which is able to predict difficulties: it provides a kind of independent check on whether a putative difficulty is a real one. This is a point we have touched on before in regard to ellipsis of logical subjects with participials (Chapter III), the 'two spots or one' argument between Fish and Rader (Chapters IV and V), and ellipsis of various things in James (Chapter V). In all of these cases, an adequate model of processing can set certain limits to the subjectivity of the critic.

There is perhaps no parallel check on 'the point' of a passage, though error and fudging are possible here also. One might, for example, quibble slightly about the notion that "knowledge of what is beyond knowledge" is the point of (2). In general, Empson's method is most convincing when the point is pretty directly the propositional content of the passage, as it was in the first part of example (1) and as it is, for that matter, in the passage from *Paradise Lost* describing the entry of the devils into Pandemonium (Chapter II [41]) or (19) of Chapter V from *The Prelude* on the inability to distinguish. Stephen Booth uses Empson's method heavily: the following comment on the slippery syntax of "Sonnet 33" is representative: "Each violation of the reader's confidence in his expectations about a syntactical pattern evokes a miniature experience for the reader that mirrors the experience of betrayed expectations which is the subject of the poem. . . ."[1] The method is less convincing when the point is more remote from propositional content and approaches vacuity when the point is something imagined but not said. Paul Alpers is following Empson's procedure when he cites the following lines from Marlowe:

(4) Home when he came, he seem'd not to be there,
     But like exiled aire thrust from his sphere,
     Set in a forren place, and straight from thence,
     Alcides like, by mightie violence,
     He would have chac'd away the swelling maine,
     That him from her unjustly did detaine.

and comments, "The lines are rather hard to get into focus. . . . But the very active sentence structuring here demanded of us is turned to poetic use: the concentrated effort we give to these lines supports the sense of heroic expenditure of strength in those that follow."[2] I agree that the lines are hard to get into focus: the main question is whether *set in a forren place* is another complement of *seem'd* ("He seem'd not there to be but . . . set in a forren place") or attaches to *aire* parallel to *thrust* ("aire thrust from his sphere, set in a forren place"). *Set in a forren place* is not too good semantically as a modifier of *aire* because it calls for a physical object more strongly than *thrust from his sphere* does. The extra energy and resolution come when we reject this latter possibility, resisting the temptation to attach *set . . .* to the immediately preceding phrase, and skip back over to *he* instead. Alper's statement of 'the point', however, seems wrong to me: there is no "heroic expenditure of strength" here, only a fairly grandiose (and unacted) desire to sweep the ocean aside.

There is, by the way, another possibility here based on an emendation of *aire* to *heir* suggested by L. C. Martin.[3] This textual crux is worth a bit of our attention even though it requires an excursus because it raises the question of why one would choose an apparently ungrammatical reading over a grammatical one. *Aire* has the textual authority but was a common Elizabethan spelling for *heir*. Reading "heir," however, poses the difficulty that one would expect *an* in front of it—i.e., *heir*, unlike *air*, is a count noun requiring an article in the singular. Actually, the reader familiar with Elizabethan poetry might know that *a(n)* was frequently omitted following *like, as,* and *then,*[4] but the absence of *an* is a reason not to read *heir* for the modern reader. Millar McClure rejects the emendation (or modernization) to *heir* because he says the line makes sense with *air*.[5] True enough, but the whole construction makes more sense with *heir*, which accounts for *exiled* (one exiles heirs but expels air), *set in a forren place*, which can now attach to *heir* (linking up to *exiled*), and the water which separates the exile from his proper sphere (the English characteristically think of exile in terms of leaving the island). The general point is that the sort of thing textual critics and editors do is simply a specialized version of what the reader must do in deciding between two readings: the decision is an interpretive act.[6]

There are other variations in the way *the point* is defined. In a recent "Note on Ruskin's Mythography" Frederick Kirchhoff argues that Ruskin's style in *The Queen of the Air* touched on in

Chapter IV is designed to evoke in the reader the "mythic consciousness" which Ruskin desires to recover. In *Surprised by Sin,* for another example, Stanley Fish argues that the general point is the fallibility of human understanding, and that this is enacted by the reader as he misperceives. Fish employs similar arguments in *Self-Consuming Artifacts.* It might be argued that we have shifted from aesthetic value to didactic value, but the common ground is that one is arguing that the language "does what it says," or leads the reader through a process that replicates or enacts the meaning of the passage.

Difficulties in Faulkner and James do not lend themselves to this sort of treatment, and the expressive function of complexity has been judged instead according to an odd canon of verisimilitude: the language of a passage is effective if it conveys "consciousness" of one sort or another. The following statements are fairly typical:

> In his most characteristic writing, [he] is trying to render the transcendent life of the mind, the crowded composite of associative and analytical consciousness which expands the vibrant moment into the reaches of all time, simultaneously observing, remembering, interpreting, and modifying the object of its awareness. To this end the sentence as a rhetorical unit (however strained) is made to hold diverse yet related elements in a sort of saturated solution, which is perhaps the nearest that language as the instrument of fiction can come to the instantaneous complexities of consciousness itself.
>
> [Warren Beck[7]]

> Not only is the reader forced to hold two or more possible sense resolutions in the forefront of his consciousness as he moves along, but distinctions of time and space merge, qualitative differentiations are erased, and the neat compartmentalized autonomy of the conventional sentence is done away with. [He] simply presents a mass of experience in a lump, *now,* as it enters the consciousness.
>
> [Robert Zoellner[8]]

> He designs a sentence whose very structure simulates the process of the mind, the manner in which we apprehend or perceive an idea. The dash and colon connect distinct ideas with an ease and fluency

that belie the discreteness of the statements—they contribute an air of reality to the character's mental process.

[Barry Menikoff[9]]

But because [his] parentheses break into his sentences unpredictably, they seem the product not so much of measured deliberation as of uncontrolled impulse. . . . Because [his] qualifications do not seem the result of any planned dislocation of syntax, they lend his prose an air of immediacy at the same time that they extend its analytic function.

[Jane Tompkins[10]]

I have tried to trick the reader by quoting out of context and replacing the authors' names by *he* as indicated: the first two citations are describing Faulkner, the second two James. The similarity of the passages is a bit unsettling, since the experiences provided by these authors are so diverse, suggesting that some further analysis is in order. One can with effort discriminate between the passages on James and those on Faulkner: those on Faulkner describe experience only partly ordered or conceptualized, while those on James describe the process of conceptualization. Such differentiation seems to go in the right direction, and our question becomes, "What is the basis for it in the language, or, how can it be clarified by analysis of the difficulties peculiar to each style?"

In an important sense, the passages cited are describing illusions, in that the reader's direct experience is entirely verbal, yet the critics describe senses of pre-verbal or coming-to-be-verbal experience. Certain passages in James are so overt in this regard as almost to call attention to their artifice, as for example the following:

(5)   . . . many marks of a taste whose discriminations might perhaps have been called eccentric. He guessed at intense little preferences and sharp little exclusions, a deep suspicion of the vulgar and a personal view of the right. The general result of this was something for which he had no name on the spot quite ready, but something he would have come nearest to naming in speaking of it as the air of supreme respectability, the consciousness, small, still, reserved, but none the less distinct and diffused, of private honour. The air of supreme

respectability—that was a strange blank wall for his adventure to have brought him to break his nose against. It had in fact, as he was now aware, filled all the approaches. . . .

[James, *AMB*, 146]

The Jamesian consciousness does not simply and quickly name things and impressions—it struggles through the process of defining and articulating its initial impressions. Once the impression has been named properly, however, the name becomes a reality one can break his nose against and a point of departure for further meditation. The pronouns in this passage are typical: they are at first vague in reference ("the general result of *this*," "*it*") and then highly specific ("*that* was a strange blank wall," "*it* had filled . . ."). Not all impressions receive this lavish articulation: the hedged *might perhaps have been called eccentric* is an 'easy' naming that is not the stimulus to thinking the next item is. It is perhaps worth stressing that this use of appositives to define and specify is not inherent in the construction. Stevens, for example, uses them in his early manner to underscore the arbitrariness of the 'names' for reality, though, as Helen Vendler argues, he uses them in his later manner more in the fashion of James to sharpen a formulation.[11]

In James, this process of groping toward articulation does not (usually) create the impression of a fumbling or inarticulate mind but rather of an acute and exacting one. What then is the source of the difficulty? As Tompkins' remarks suggest, the difficulties arise (for the reader) from the parenthetical and qualifying material which might be said to be the product of a hyper-acute consciousness—one which deflects and obstructs the development of its own thinking toward its chosen goal, or, if you prefer, enriches and qualifies it even before it is fully there to be qualified.

There is an important difference between the remarks of Menikoff and those of Tompkins, however, that returns us to the central point of artifice. Menikoff attributes the impression created by the style to the character, but Tompkins attributes it to the narrative voice—it is a mode of speaking, not thinking. Tompkins at the end of the passage says the interruptions "do not seem the result of any planned dislocation of syntax," by which she seems to mean they are not patently 'rhetorical' in the tradition of the high style (not, for example, produced by inversions of normal order). The interruptions do nonetheless regularly fall in certain unusual places in James' late style. In the late style, and only there, the 'qualifications' occur very heavily between auxiliary and main verbs, and between nouns and prepositional complements (there are illustrations of both in [5]). Now, interruptions at these points produce special perceptual problems for the reader (as I have shown in Chapter Two), but these points are not what one might call natural joints in *thoughts*. That is an admittedly unsupportable statement, but it does seem to me that one does not hesitate or ponder over what verb to use after a modal or what complement to add to a noun *as one thinks*—the concept is already there. Tompkins is right, I believe, to emphasize the voice speaking: the effect is of a voice that knows what it is going to say. The qualifying thought is an 'extra' qualifying what in many cases has not yet been said (or processed by the reader) but is already in the narrator's mind calling forth the qualification. Similarly, the speaker presumably knows the referents of nouns and pronouns, however much effort the reader must expend to figure them out. This is why readers sometimes feel teased or pestered by James, wanting him to get to the point which he knows and is withholding from us. Likewise, James frequently splits an idiomatic string which is only clearly recognizable as an idiom when the last word is read:

(6)   He pulled himself then at last together. . . .

[James, *AMB*, 67]

Again, the speaker cannot be uncertain of what is to follow. Thus the difficulty of perception experienced by the reader is not precisely that experienced by the speaking consciousness: the effort we experience does, however, tend to be projected onto the character as his effort to bring a complex impression to full articulation.

Similarly, Ian Watt gives as a function of the abundance of negatives in the opening of *The Ambassadors* that "it enacts Strether's
tendency to hesitation and qualification."[12] The abundance does
not enact anything—the reader does, and the hesitation, in particular, is surely more his than Strether's: Strether is never more sure
of his plans and intentions than at this point in the novel. It is not
so much that James "designs sentences whose very structure simu-
lates the process of the mind, the manner in which we apprehend
or perceive an idea," as that he designs sentences whose structures
trigger processes which simulate (but do not mirror) this "process
of the mind."

The difficulties with Faulkner are not the result of parenthesis
and qualification interrupting the sentences at strange points. R.
W. Short established that the source of difficulty in James is not the
length of sentence,[13] but length is certainly a factor in Faulkner,
and the chief sources of length are relative, participial, and adverbial clauses: phrase and clauses sprout modifiers, and these
modifiers have modifiers, at every turn. When a Subject noun
phrase becomes weighted with appositives, participials, and relative clauses, it is simply hard to hold in the mind as a unit while
processing the other parts. In general, the primary source of confusion is the profusion of things and properties which may overload
the reader's capacity for sorting out—Beck's "saturated solution"
metaphor is not bad and is certainly better than Zoellner's
metaphor of the "mass in a lump." The appositives, for example,
add to and extend the initial phrase rather than narrowing or
specifying it more exactly as they do in James. The effect in Faulkner is a sense of great richness, each thing a plenum bearing relations to other things even more diverse and numerous than the
teller can pack in. The relative and adverbial clauses tie each thing
and event into so many other events and relations that the current
function in the sentence recedes in importance and is lost. Conrad
Aiken described this quality of fullness in relation to the speaking
voice:

> Overelaborate they certainly are, baroque and involuted in the extreme, these sentences: trailing clauses, one after another, shadowily in apposition, or perhaps not even with so much connection as that; parenthesis after parenthesis, the parenthesis itself often containing one or more parentheses.... It is as if Mr. Faulkner, in a sort of hurried despair, has decided to try to tell us everything, absolutely everything, every last origin or course or quality or qualification, and every possible future or permutation as well, in one terrifically concentrated effort: each sentence to be, as it were, a microcosm.
>
> [Aiken, p. 137]

Warren Beck and more recent critics tend to accept the illusion and to speak of Faulkner's sentences as presenting "consciousness" directly. Thus Aiken's "terrifically concentrated effort" of telling becomes Beck's heightened, "crowded, composite consciousness" and Zoellner's "total consciousness."

As noted in the previous chapter, Aiken sketched a defense of Faulkner's style in terms of the hypnotic immersion that it promotes in the reader. This theme has been expanded by other critics, notably Walter Slatoff. Slatoff is not quite ready to say flatly that Faulkner induces a hypnotic trance or dream state, but he does argue that Faulkner's "presentation," which thwarts the usual categories and processes of rational thought, has positive value insofar as it frees "the emotional life from the trammels of critical thinking."[14] Indeed, he argues that Faulkner's style is a means of containing and articulating, but not logically resolving, a great deal of ambivalence and uncertainty about the human condition: there is resolution and release of an emotional kind, but the reader is often unable to say exactly what has been resolved. I believe this is a just assessment: a minor example is the lovely passage cited at the end of Chapter Four of the vision of the eternally renewing hunt, and a larger example would be Chapter Twenty of *Light in August*, which contains numerous sentences still largely uninterpretable for me, but does afford this sort of emotional release in the final image.

A curious result of this line of thinking is that the claim of verisimilitude falls out: if the value of the language is the experience it gives the reader, then it really does not matter whether it represents consciousness "like it really is." The reader may never experience a moment of consciousness like it except when reading more Faulkner—indeed, in a strict sense, he won't—but the value of the experience of reading Faulkner can simply be taken to be the value one places *on that experience*. And the same can be said of all the authors we read.

Toward a Specification of Response

L ET the last question of the Introduction be the first of the conclusion: what sorts of principles guide, or should guide, readers and critics in reading literary texts? The first four chapters sketched a rather narrow view of reading—as narrow, explicit, and coherent, in fact, as I could make it—and later two chapter considered ways that it might be modified to deal with certain texts. In its narrowest and simplest, this model of reading holds that readers process texts into the best propositional structure which renders a texv grammatical (according to the reader's knowledge). The reader's experiences of pursuing garden paths, making premature closures, and losing the thread constitute evidence that he is reading for sentence and propositional structure according to the strategies we have outlined. Assuming the operation of these strategies, we have been able to predict experiences of difficulty and misperception with some success, though, as we have seen, semantic, referential, and structural strategies work together in complex ways. This model presumably characterizes the way readers approach most texts and the way they might approach literary texts as well.

Consider now the reader who opens a text in Early Modern English. The spellings are unfamiliar, impeding word recognition; the punctuation is different and, therefore, sometimes misleading as a clue to sentence structure; the words themselves may have different grammatical and semantic properties, so that one is never sure whether the word one thinks one recognizes will function just as it does in Modern English; finally, the rules of syntax may be different, so that structural clues he customarily depends on may be absent. When he begins reading the text, he does not know the extent to which his knowledge and assumptions—and the strategies based on them—will serve him, and he must read with a certain tentativeness, making do with a conditional certainty. In effect, he analogizes: "if these words are words I know, and this text works according to rules I know, then this means '...'." One will have to settle sometimes for a near match, as in readings we have considered correct in previous chapters ("to seek if she might attain her strayed champion"; "when they had hunted through (the labyrinth) by tract(?)"; "her swollen heart seemed to bereave her speech"). There is a strain involved for the reader in all of this—Spenser and Milton (and Shakespeare) *are* hard to read, probably impossible to read with our accustomed certainty that we have got the sentence right. At this point, the reader must either begin to adapt his customary strategies to the text or try to make out some sort of meaning without much regard for sentence structure. One can hack up a complex structure into simple chunks which are not wildly off base, as, for example, when one interprets *Her swollen hart her speach seemd to bereaue* as "she was sad, so she stopped talking, or, she choked up" (this was offered me as a paraphrase by a graduate student). But it is not on target either, since the *seemed* gets lost and turns out to be crucial (she is a hypocrite). To be sure, perhaps Spenser wants the reader to mistake the show of feeling for true feeling just as his somewhat dim hero does, but he is also trying to train the reader to see through hypocrisy.

One value of the extended analysis we have conducted is that it becomes possible to specify some of the adjustments the reader needs to make to get the sentence structure of these particular writers. When reading Spenser, one will have to process a lot of *which when* constructions, Subjectless subordinate clauses, and Object + to + verb sequences—with all of these, I have suggested, he may extend strategies he already has for other constructions by analogy, as it were. He will also find it useful to rely fairly heavily on line ends as indicators of what can be grouped with what, and it will serve him well to reduce reliance on serial-ordering strategies for identifying Subjects and Objects in favor of semantic (and thematic) strategies. The last adjustment is also useful for Milton, but line ends must be virtually disregarded as a clue to syntactic grouping. Some strategy for putting split coordinate elements back together will be useful—the one suggested is based on checking for shared semantic features. He will also have to process a goodly number of detached and strayed participials and relative clauses, and it will help to devalue his usual assumption that the noun phrase to the immediate left is the head to which the participial must be attached or which the relative clause modifies. When reading James, one will have to cope with parenthetical material spreading the main sentence elements. With Faulkner, one had better reduce his reliance on the canonical order strategy, since the S V A O order is common, and be wary of apparently transitive verbs. With Stevens, one must struggle to interpret each appositive and not let a string of them dissolve into a blur. These are practical suggestions: even when students do not find my suggested adjustment the best one for them, they do find that description of the sources of difficulty and some practice in coping with the constructions as types do make their reading easier, better, and more satisfying. One cannot, after all, experience most of the effects described in the previous chapter if he has given up trying to specify reference, attachment, and syntactic structure generally.

The model of reading sketched here does seem to furnish the beginning of a predictive and normative specification of response of the type Fish desires. In fact, it is a restriction of the more general notion of response that he presents: ''The category of response includes any and all of the activities provoked by a string of words: the projection of syntactical and/or lexical probabilities;

their subsequent occurrence or non-occurrence; attitudes toward persons, or things, or ideas referred to; the reversal or questioning of those attitudes; and much more" (*Self-Consuming Artifacts,* p. 388). It is the *any* that is the problem rather than the *all.* I have tried to distinguish between questions the reader must ask from those he may, and we can also distinguish assumptions he is likely to make from those that he may. It is a plain fact that not all readers find all of Fish's 'difficult' passages as difficult as he says they are. Ralph Rader picks out some vulnerable examples which, he says, the mind's "meaning-oriented direction-finder" guides one through,[1] and one might put the matter the other way as well: if a putative difficulty does not follow from an axiom of processing theory, one should be cautious about claiming that the reader will experience it. Fish claims that a *that*-clause at the beginning of a sentence will generally be taken to be factive (i.e., as if *the fact* had been ellipsed before *that*), but this does not follow from any principle of processing or fact of grammar: many verbs and adjectival predicates take non-factive *that*-clause Subjects, and an initial *that*-clause need not even be a Subject. The reasonable procedure is to look ahead to the governing predicate, at which point assignment of the clause as the Subject will settle the matter of its factivity. Obviously this methodological point will gain in force as the theory of language processing is developed.

The point of Rader's "meaning-oriented direction-finder" is in part that Fish's 'method' is too responsive to *any* response: it does not sort out responses, nor give any primacy to the processes of reconstructing propositional content. Rader is trying to defend the objectivity of structure in the text: we are not free to impose any grouping of words and elements that we find interesting nor do we attempt to exercise such freedom when we read. We are 'oriented' or direct ourselves when we read toward the construction of propositional content, and this orientation shapes and constrains our apprehension of the text. It may clarify the issues to distinguish between the goals or questions to be answered and the means of answering them. Some of the questions we try to answer as we read are those having to do with propositional content and reference. The very terms of these questions involve some apprehension of phrases, and hence reading cannot avoid positing and identifying some syntactic units. As we have seen, however, there are many ways of getting answers to these questions. The answers may not involve syntactic solutions and may be the incidental byproduct of some process of interpretation or inference. Interpretation has also its units and patterns of analysis (e.g., 'image' clusters and oppositions) which may or may not coincide with syntactic units and patterns. We need to know more about comprehension and interpretation and how they can interact with perception before we can decide the question of the primacy of perception of propositional structure. But from where we are now, we can at least see a little more clearly the outlines of a model of reading.

INDEX OF PASSAGES CITED

(Page references, when given, are to the editions cited in the Note on the Texts, p. xiii. The numbers following the colon refer to the chapter number and example number in this volume.)

BIBLIOGRAPHY

Abbott, E. A. *A Shakespearian Grammar* (1870; rpt. New York: Dover Publications Inc., 1966).

Aiken, Conrad. "William Faulkner: The Novel as Form," in *William Faulkner: Three Decades of Criticism*, Frederick J. Hoffman and Olga W. Vickery, eds. (East Lansing: Michigan State University Press, 1960), pp. 135–41.

Alpers, Paul. *The Poetry of The Faerie Queene* (Princeton: Princeton University Press, 1967).

Beck, Warren. "William Faulkner's Style," in *William Faulkner: Three Decades of Criticism*, Frederick J. Hoffman and Olga W. Vickery, eds. (East Lansing: Michigan State University Press, 1960, pp. 142–55.

Beckett, Samuel. *The Unnameable* (New York: Grove Press, 1970).

Bever, Thomas G. "The Cognitive Basis for Linguistic Structures," in *Cognition and the Development of Language*, John R. Hayes, ed. (New York: Wiley and Sons, 1970), pp. 279–362.

———, J. M. Carroll, and R. Hurtig. "Analogy," in *An Integrated Theory of Linguistic Ability*, T. G. Bever, J. J. Katz, and D. T. Langendoen, eds. (New York: Thomas Y. Crowell, 1976), pp. 149–82.

Bolinger, Dwight. *Aspects of Language,* 2nd ed. (New York: Harcourt, Brace, Jovanovich, 1975).

———. "Pronouns and Repeated Nouns," 1977. Available from the Indiana University Linguistics Club.

Booth, Stephen. *An Essay on Shakespeare's Sonnets* (New Haven: Yale University Press, 1969).

Booth, Wayne C. *The Rhetoric of Fiction* (Chicago: University of Chicago Press, 1961).

Bransford, J. D. and M. K. Johnson. "Considerations of Some Problems of Comprehension," in *Visual Information Processing*, W. G. Chase, ed. (New York: Academic Press, 1973), pp. 383–438.

Burgess, Anthony. *Joysprick* (London: André Deutsch, 1973).

Cairns, Helen S. and Charles E. Cairns. *Psycholinguistics* (New York: Holt, Rinehart and Winston, 1976).

Carroll, John M. and Michael K. Tanenhaus. "Functional Clauses Are the Primary Units of Sentence Perception." 1976. Available from the Indiana University Linguistics Club.

192

Chafe, Wallace L. "Givenness, Contrastiveness, Definiteness, Subjects, Topics, and Point of View," in *Subject and Topic,* Charles N. Li, ed. (New York: Academic Press, 1976), pp. 25–55.

Charniak, Eugene. "Context and the Reference Problem," in *Natural Language Processing,* Randall Rustin, ed. (New York: Algorithmics Press, 1973), pp. 311–30.

Chatman, Seymour. "Milton's Participial Style," *Publications of the Modern Language Association* 83 (Oct. 1968), 1386–99.

———. *The Later Style of Henry James* (Oxford: Blackwell, 1972).

Chomsky, Noam. *Aspects of the Theory of Syntax* (Cambridge, Mass.: MIT Press, 1965).

Clark, Herbert H. "Semantics and Comprehension," in *Current Trends in Linguistics,* Vol. 12, Part 3, Thomas A. Sebeok, ed. (The Hague: Mouton, 1974), pp. 1291–1498.

———. "Inferences in Comprehension," in *Basic Processes in Reading— Perception and Comprehension,* D. LaBerge and S. J. Samuels, eds., (Hillsdale, New Jersey: Lawrence Erlbaum Associates, 1977).

——— and Eve V. Clark. *Psychology and Language* (New York: Harcourt, Brace, Jovanovich, 1977).

——— and Susan E. Haviland. "Psychological Processes as Linguistic Explanation," *Explaining Linguistic Phenomena,* David Cohen, ed. (Washington, D.C.: Hemisphere Publishing Corporation, 1974), pp. 91–124.

———. "Comprehension and the Given-New Contract," in *Discourse Production and Comprehension,* Roy Freedle, ed. (Norwood, N.J.: Ablex Publishing Corporation, 1977), pp. 1–40.

Culler, Jonathan. *Structuralist Poetics* (Ithaca: Cornell University Press, 1975).

Dillon, George L. "Inversions and Deletions in English Poetry," *Language and Style* 8 (Summer, 1975): 220–37.

———. "Clause, Pause, and Punctuation in Poetry," *Linguistics* 169 (1976): 5–20.

———. "Kames and Kiparsky on Syntactic Boundaries," *Language and Style* 10 (Winter, 1977): 16–22.

———. *Introduction to Contemporary Linguistic Semantics* (Englewood Cliffs: Prentice-Hall, Inc., 1977).

——— and Frederick Kirchhoff. "On the Form and Function of Free Indirect Style," *Poetics and the Theory of Literature* 1 (1976): 431–40.

Emma, Ronald. *Milton's Syntax* (The Hague: Mouton, 1964).

Empson, William. *Seven Types of Ambiguity* (1930; New York: New Directions, n.d.).

Enkvist, Nils Erik. *Linguistic Stylistics* (The Hague: Mouton, 1973).

Fillenbaum, Samuel. "On Coping with Ordered and Unordered Conjunctive Sentences," *Journal of Experimental Psychology* 87 (1971): 93–98.

———. "Memory for Counterfactual Conditionals," *Journal of Experimental Psychology* 102 (1974): 44–49.

———. "Pragmatic Normalization: Further Results for Some Conjunctive and Disjunctive Sentences," *Journal of Experimental Psychology* 102 (1974): 574–78.

Fish, Stanley E. *Surprised by Sin* (Berkeley: University of California Press, 1971).

———. *Self-Consuming Artifacts* (Berkeley: University of California Press, 1972).

———. "What is Stylistics and Why are They Saying Such Terrible Things About It?" in *Approaches to Poetics*, Seymour Chatman (New York: Columbia University Press, 1973), pp. 109–52.

———. "Facts and Fictions: A Reply to Ralph Rader," *Critical Inquiry* 1 (June, 1975): 883–91.

———. "Interpreting the *Variorum*," *Critical Inquiry* 2 (Spring, 1976): 465–86.

Fodor, J. A., T. G. Bever, and M. F. Garrett. *The Psychology of Language* (New York: McGraw-Hill Book Company, 1974).

Fowler, Henry W. *A Dictionary of Modern English Usage* (Oxford University Press, n.d.).

Fowler, Roger. "Style and the Concept of Deep Structure," *Journal of Literary Semantics* 1 (1972): 5–24.

Freedle, Roy O. "Language Users as Fallible Information-Processors: Implications for Measuring and Modeling Comprehension," in *Language Comprehension and the Acquisition of Knowledge*, ed. Roy O. Freedle and John B. Carroll (Washington, D.C.: V. H. Winston and Sons, 1972), pp. 169–210.

Garvey, Catherine, Alfonso Caramazza, and Jack Yates. "Factors Influencing Assignment of Pronoun Antecedents," *Cognition* 3 (1974/5): 227–44.

Gibson, Elaine and Harry Levin, *The Psychology of Reading* (Cambridge, Mass.: MIT Press, 1975).

Goodman, Kenneth S. "Psycholinguistic Universals in the Reading Process," in *Psycholinguistics and Reading*, Frank Smith, ed. (New York: Holt, Rinehart, and Winston, 1973), pp. 21–27.

Grosu, Alexander. *The Strategic Content of Island Constraints*. Ohio State Working Papers in Linguistics, no. 13 (Columbus, Ohio: Ohio State Department of Linguistics, 1972).

Halliday, M. A. K. and Ruqaiya Hasan. *Cohesion in English* (London: Longmans, 1976).

Haviland, Susan and Herbert H. Clark. "What's New? Acquiring New Information as a Process in Comprehension," *Journal of Verbal Learning and Verbal Behavior* 13 (1974): 512–21.

Hill, Archibald A. *Constituent and Pattern in Poetry* (Austin: University of Texas Press, 1976).

Hirsch, E. D. Jr. *The Aims of Interpretation* (Chicago: University of Chicago Press, 1976).

Hollander, John. "'Sense Variously Drawn Out': Some Observations on English Enjambment," in *Literary Theory and Structure: Essays in Honor of William K. Wimsatt*, Frank Brady, John Palmer, and Martin Price, eds. (New Haven: Yale University Press, 1973), pp. 201–25.

Holmes, V. M. and I. J. Watson. "The Role of Surface Order and Surface Deletion in Sentence Perception," *Quarterly Journal of Experimental Psychology* 28 (1976): 55–65.

Kantor, Robert N. "Discourse Connection and Demonstratives," paper presented at the Winter 1976 Meeting of the Linguistic Society of America (Philadelphia).

Kimball, John. "Seven Principles of Surface Structure Parsing in Natural Language," *Cognition* 2 (1973), 15–48.

Kirchhoff, Frederick. "A Note on Ruskin's Mythography," *Victorian Newsletter*, 50 (Fall, 1976): 24–27.

Kuno, Susumo. "Three Perspectives in the Functional Approach to Syntax," in *Papers from the Parasession on Functionalism*, Robin E. Grossman, L. James San, and Timothy J. Vance, eds. (Chicago: University of Chicago Department of Linguistics/CLS, 1975), pp. 276–336.

Lakoff, George. "The Role of Deduction in Grammar," in *Studies in Linguistic Semantics*, Charles J. Fillmore and D. Terence Langendoen, eds. (New York: Holt, Rinehart and Winston, Inc., 1971), pp. 63–72.

——— and Henry Thompson. "Dative Questions in Cognitive Grammar," in *Papers from the Parasession on Functionalism*, Robin E. Grossman, L. James San, and Timothy J. Vance, eds. (Chicago: University of Chicago Department of Linguistics/CLS, 1975), pp. 337–50.

Langacker, Ronald W. and Patricia Munro. "Passives and Their Meaning," *Language* 51 (1975): 789–830.

Langendoen, D. Terence and Thomas G. Bever. "Can a Not Unhappy Person Be Called a Not Sad One?" in *An Integrated Theory of Linguistic Ability*, Thomas G. Bever, Jerrold J. Katz, and D. Terence Langendoen, eds. (New York: Thomas Y. Crowell, 1976), pp. 239–260.

Langendoen, D. Terence, Nancy Kalish-Landon, and John Dore. "Dative Questions: A Study in the Relation of Acceptability to Grammaticality of an English Sentence Type," in Bever, Katz, and Langendoen, pp. 195–224.

Lee, Vernon. *The Handling of Words* (London, 1923).

Menikoff, Barry. "Punctuation and Point of View in the Late Style of Henry James," *Style* 4 (1970): 29–47.

Miller, George A. "The Magical Number Seven Plus or Minus Two: Some Limits on our Capacity for Processing Information," *Psychological Review* 63 (1956): 81–97.

Newstead, E. Stephen. "Semantic Constraints and Sentence Perception," *British Journal of Psychology* 67 (March, 1976): 165–74.

Ohmann, Richard. "Generative Grammar and the Concept of Literary Style," in *Contemporary Essays on Style,* Glen A. Love and Michael Payne, eds. (Glenview, Ill.: Scott, Foresman, 1969), pp. 133–48.

———. "Literature as Sentences," in Love and Payne, pp. 149–56.

Olson, David R. "Language and Thought: Aspects of a Cognitive Theory of Semantics," *Psychological Review* 77 (1970): 257–73.

———. "Language Use for Communicating, Instructing, and Thinking," in *Language Comprehension and the Acquisition of Knowledge,* Roy O. Freedle and John B. Carroll, eds. (Washington, D.C.: V. H. Winston and Sons, 1972), pp. 139–68.

Osgood, Charles E. "Where Do Sentences Come From?" in *Semantics: An Interdisciplinary Reader,* Danny Steinberg and Leon Jakobovits, eds. (Cambridge: Cambridge University Press, 1971), pp. 497–529.

Partridge, A. C. *Tudor to Augustan English* (London: André Deutsch, 1969).

Quirk, Randolph, Sidney Greenbaum, Geoffrey Leech, and Jan Svartvik, *A Grammar of Contemporary English* (London: Longmans, 1972).

Rader, Ralph. "Fact, Theory, and Literary Explanation," *Critical Inquiry* 1 (Dec. 1974): 245–72.

———. "The Concept of Genre and Eighteenth-Century Studies," in *New Approaches to Eighteenth-Century Literature: Selected Papers from the English Institute* (New York: Columbia University Press, 1974).

Richards, I. A. *Practical Criticism* (1929; Harcourt, Brace and World, Inc., n.d.).

Rieger, Charles J. "Conceptual Memory and Inference," in *Conceptual Information Processing,* Roger C. Schank, ed. (New York: North-Holland/American Elsevier, 1975), pp. 157–288.

Ross, John Robert. Constraints on Variables in Syntax, (Dissertation, MIT, 1967; available from the Indiana University Linguistics Club).

Short, R. W. "The Sentence Structure of Henry James," *American Literature* 18 (1946): 71–88.

Slatoff, Walter. "The Edge of Order: The Pattern of Faulkner's Rhetoric," *Twentieth Century Literature* 3 (Oct. 1957), 107–27.

Smith, Frank. *Psycholinguistics and Reading* (New York: Holt, Rinehart, and Winston, 1973).

Springston, Frederick J. Some Cognitive Aspects of Presupposed Coreferential Anaphora (Dissertation, Stanford University, 1975).

Sugden, Herbert W. *The Grammar of Spenser's Faerie Queene* (Linguistic Society of America, University of Pennsylvania, 1936).

Thorndyke, Perry W. "The Role of Inference in Discourse Comprehension," *Journal of Verbal Learning and Verbal Behavior* 15 (1976): 437–46.

Tompkins, Jane P. "'The Beast in the Jungle': An Analysis of James's Late Style," *Modern Fiction Studies* 16 (1970): 185–91.

Vendler, Helen H. *On Extended Wings* (Cambridge, Mass.: Harvard University Press, 1969).

Watt, Ian. "The First Paragraph of *The Ambassadors:* An Explication," in *Contemporary Essays on Style,* Glen A. Love and Michael Payne, eds. (Glenview, Ill.: Scott, Foresman and Company, 1969), pp. 266–92.

Wilks, Yorick. "Preference Semantics," in *Formal Semantics of Natural Language,* Edward L. Keenan, ed. (Cambridge: Cambridge University Press, 1975), pp. 329–48.

Winograd, Terry. *Understanding Natural Language* (New York: Academic Press, 1972).

Woods, William A. "An Experimental Parsing System for Transition Network Grammars," In *Natural Language Processing,* Randall Rustin, ed. (New York: Algorithmics Press, 1973), pp. 111–54.

Zoellner, Robert H. "Faulkner's Prose Style in *Absalom, Absalom!,*" *American Literature* 30 (1959), 427–50.

NOTES

INTRODUCTION

1. Richard Ohmann, "Literature as Sentences," in *Contemporary Essays on Style*, Glen A. Love and Michael Payne, eds. (Glenview, Ill.: Scott, Foresman and Company, 1969), p. 157.

2. Roger Fowler, "Style and the Concept of Deep Structure," *Journal of Literary Semantics* 1 (1972): 5–24.

3. Stanley Fish, "What is Stylistics and Why are They Saying Such Terrible Things About It?" in *Approaches to Poetics*, Seymour Chatman, ed. (New York: Columbia University Press, 1973), pp. 109–52.

4. Noam Chomsky, *Aspects of the Theory of Syntax* (Cambridge, Mass.: MIT Press, 1965), p. 9; the eminent grammarian referred to is Charles J. Fillmore, and his confession is in "Subjects, Speakers, and Roles," in *Semantics of Natural Language*, Donald Davidson and Gilbert Harmon, eds. (Dordrecht: D. Reidel Publishing Company, 1972), pp. 1–24.

5. Jerry A. Fodor, Thomas G. Bever, and Michael F. Garrett, *The Psychology of Language* (New York: McGraw Hill Book Company, 1974), p. 6; Helen S. Cairns and Charles E. Cairns, *Psycholinguistics* (New York: Holt, Rinehart and Winston, 1976), pp. 150–56.

6. Charles Rieger lists and discusses sixteen types of inferences in his "Conceptual Memory and Inference," in *Conceptual Information Processing*, Roger C. Schank, ed. (New York: North-Holland/American Elsevier, 1975), pp. 157–288.

7. Perry W. Thorndyke, "The Role of Inference in Discourse Comprehension," *Journal of Verbal Learning and Verbal Behavior* 15 (1976): 437–46. Herbert Clark has advanced this view in numerous publications (see Bibliography and the brief discussion in Herbert H. Clark and Eve V. Clark, *Psychology and Language* [New York: Harcourt, Brace, Jovanovich, Inc., 1977], pp. 95–98, 161–64). They use the term 'Global Representation' where I will use 'contextual frame'.

8. J. D. Bransford and M. K. Johnson, "Considerations of Some Problems of Comprehension," in *Visual Information Processing*, W. G. Chase, ed. (New York: Academic Press, 1973), p. 400.

9. See the discussion in Elaine Gibson and Harry Levin's *The Psychology of Reading* (Cambridge, Mass.: MIT Press, 1975), pp. 476–77 et passim; Kenneth S. Goodman, "Psycholinguistic Universals in the Reading Process," in *Psycholinguistics and Reading*, Frank Smith, ed. (New York: Holt,

Rinehart, and Winston, Inc., 1973), pp. 21-27; also Frank Smith, "Decoding: The Great Fallacy," in his *Psycholinguistics and Reading,* pp. 70-83.

10. For a summary of the features of this convention, see George Dillon and Frederick Kirchhoff, "On the Form and Function of Indirect Free Style," *Poetics and the Theory of Literature* 1 (1976): 431-40.

11. Samuel Fillenbaum, "Pragmatic Normalization: Further Results for Some Conjunctive and Disjunctive Sentences," *Journal of Experimental Psychology* 102 (1974): 574-78.

12. See Clark and Clark, pp. 121-28, or George L. Dillon, *Introduction to Contemporary Linguistic Semantics* (Englewood Cliffs, N.J.: Prentice-Hall, Inc., 1977), pp. 108-15. E. D. Hirsch, Jr. stresses perception of irony as an interpretative act in his *The Aims of Interpretation* (Chicago: University of Chicago Press, 1976), pp. 23-24.

13. William Empson, *Seven Types of Ambiguity* (1930; New York: New Directions, n.d.), pp. 209-10.

14. Thomas G. Bever, "The Cognitive Basis for Linguistic Structures," in *Cognition and the Development of Language,* John R. Hayes, ed. (New York: John Wiley and Sons, 1970), p. 296.

15. One of the more recent and sophisticated treatments of this point is by E. Stephen Newstead, "Semantic Constraints and Sentence Perception," *British Journal of Psychology* 67 (March, 1976): 165-74.

16. Terry Winograd, *Understanding Natural Language* (New York: Academic Press, 1972), pp. 22-23; John Kimball, "Seven Principles of Surface Structure Parsing in Natural Language," *Cognition* 2 (1973): 15-48. I do not mean to endorse Kimball's model as a model of processing, however.

17. D. Terence Langendoen, Nancy Kalish-Landon, and John Dore, "Dative Questions: A Study in the Relation of Acceptability to Grammaticality of an English Sentence Type," in *An Integrated Theory of Linguistic Ability,* Thomas G. Bever, Jerrold J. Katz, and D. Terence Langendoen, eds. (New York: Thomas Y. Crowell Company, 1976), pp. 195-223; George Lakoff and Henry Thompson, "Dative Questions in Cognitive Grammar," in *Papers from the Parasession on Functionalism,* Robin E. Grossman, L. James San, and Timothy J. Vance, eds. (Chicago: Department of Linguistics/CLS, University of Chicago, 1975), pp. 337-50.

18. See the speculations on the relative costliness of semantic vs. syntactic screening in William A. Woods's "An Experimental Parsing System for Transition Network Grammars," in *Natural Language Processing,* Randall Rustin, ed. (New York: Algorithmics Press, 1973), pp. 144-45.

19. Nils Erik Enkvist, *Linguistic Stylistics* (The Hague: Mouton, 1973), p. 42.

20. Stanley E. Fish, *Surprised by Sin* (1967; Berkeley: University of Cal-

ifornia Press, 1971); Walter Slatoff, "The Edge of Order: The Pattern of Faulkner's Rhetoric," *Twentieth Century Literature* 3 (Oct. 1957): 107–27.

21. Stanley E. Fish, *Self-Consuming Artifacts: The Experience of Seventeenth-Century Literature* (Berkeley: University of California Press, 1972), p. 398.

1. PHRASES AND THEIR FUNCTIONS

1. Most of the evidence for the phrase as a unit of processing summarized in Herbert and Eve Clark's *Psychology and Language* (New York: Harcourt, Brace, Jovanovich, Inc., 1977), pp. 50–57, is based on heard sentences, but there is also much good evidence for it as a unit of reading reviewed in Elaine Gibson and Harry Levin's *The Psychology of Reading* (Cambridge, Mass.: MIT Press, 1975), pp. 363–66, 382–84.

2. I will use these terms rather than Bever's Actor-Action-Goal since, as Alexander Grosu points out, when non-action verbs are involved (e.g., *hear*) the point is to get logical Subject and logical Object right, Actor (or Agent) not being in question (*The Strategic Content of Island Constraints*, Ohio State Working Papers in Linguistics, no. 13 [Ohio State University: Department of Linguistics], 1972, p. 62). That is, logical Subject and logical Object are more general notions, and particular predicates characterize their logical Subjects and Objects in particular ways (i.e., as Agent, Experiencer, Patient, etc.).

3. John Robert Ross, "Constraints on Variables in Syntax," (Dissertation, MIT, 1967) (available from Indiana University Linguistics Club), pp. 89ff.

4. See for example John Hollander's paper "Sense Variously Drawn Out': Some Observations on English Enjambment," in *Literary Theory and Structure: Essays in Honor of William K. Wimsatt*, Frank Brady, John Palmer, and Martin Price, eds. (New Haven: Yale University Press, 1973), pp. 201–25.

5. On the expectation of pause as it affects perception, see George L Dillon, "Clause, Pause, and Punctuation in Poetry," *Linguistics* 169 (1976): 5–20. For a model of 'normal' relation of syntactic boundaries to caesura and dieresis, see Dillon, "Kames and Kiparsky on Syntactic Boundaries," *Language and Style* 10 (Winter, 1977): 16–22. See Clark and Clark (pp. 51–52) for a report of research on phrase/line alignment.

6. George Dillon, "Inversions and Deletions in English Poetry," *Language and Style* 8 (Summer, 1975): 223–24.

7. Paul Alpers, *The Poetry of The Faerie Queene* (Princeton: Princeton University Press, 1967), p. 73.

8. Note that the notion of 'expectable' is broader than what Susumo Kuno in various publications calls 'predictable'. I am not claiming that the writer's mention of the noun phrase is in any sense predictable from context. Kuno refers to certain themes as 'unpredictable' that I would call expectable. See Herbert H. Clark, "Inferences in Comprehension," in *Basic Processes in Reading*, D. LaBerge and S. J. Samuels, eds. (Hillsdale, N.J.: Lawrence Erlbaum Assoc., 1977).

9. The motive for this inversion is often to get the verb, which is bisyllabic and stressed on the final syllable, into line-final position. This is discussed in "Inversions and Deletions" (p. 232).

10. The obscure reference of *it* in the second parenthetical of (60) adds to the difficulty. It might refer to *reflexion* in the main sentence, or *sacrifice* in the parenthetical immediately preceding.

11. George A. Miller, "The Magical Number Seven Plus or Minus Two: Some Limits on Our Capacity for Processing Information," *Psychological Review* 63 (1956): pp. 81–97.

12. Ronald Emma in *Milton's Syntax* (The Hague: Mouton, 1964), p. 145, found many examples of the S O V order in Milton's poetry, but none in his samples of Milton's prose.

2. CLAUSE BOUNDARIES

1. See J. A. Fodor, T. G. Bever, and M. F. Garrett, *The Psychology of Language* (New York: McGraw-Hill Book Company, 1974), pp. 329–44; Helen S. Cairns and Charles E. Cairns, *Psycholinguistics: A Cognitive View of Language* (New York: Holt, Rinehart, and Winston, 1976), pp. 161–66; John M. Carroll and Michael K. Tanenhaus, "Functional Clauses Are the Primary Units of Sentence Perception," 1976 (available from the Indiana University Linguistics Club).

2. Stephen Booth, *An Essay on Shakespeare's Sonnets* (New Haven: Yale University Press, 1969), pp. 55–56.

3. John Robert Ross, Constraints on Variables in Syntax (Dissertation, MIT, 1967) (available from the Indiana University Linguistics Club) p. 70. Herbert W. Sugden notes this preposing over a relative in his *The Grammar of Spenser's Faerie Queene* (Linguistic Society of America, University of Pennsylvania, 1936), p. 51.

4. A. C. Partridge notes that a relative pronoun Object of an infinitive was often placed before the *to* in literary language of the sixteenth century (citing Spenser), but this seems part of the larger tendency to place Objects there, relative or not: *Tudor to Augustan English* (London: André Deutsch,

1969), p. 171. Sugden says the relative pronoun always precedes the *to* in Spenser (*The Grammar of Spenser's Faerie Queene*, p. 51).

5. Edwin Greenlaw, Charles Grosvenor Osgood, Frederick Morgan Padelford, and Ray Heffner, eds. *The Works of Edmund Spenser* (Baltimore: The Johns Hopkins Press, 1938), VI. p. 482.

6. Spenser and Milton tend, for example, to use a semicolon (when a comma is also possible) at line ends and in line-medial (caesural) position. Rhyme and stress patterns are other obvious reasons for inversion.

3. REFERENCE, COREFERENCE, AND ATTACHMENT
I: PRONOUNS AND PARTICIPIALS

1. Another difference is that we can delay identifying reference for some time without jamming perception. This point is interestingly discussed by Charles Rieger in his "Conceptual Memory and Inference" in *Conceptual Information Processing*, Roger C. Schank, ed. (New York/ Amsterdam: American Elsevier/North Holland, 1975), p. 273, and by Eugene Charniak in "Context and the Reference Problem," in *Natural Language Processing*, Randall Rustin, ed. (New York: Algorithmics Press, 1973), pp. 311–30.

2. T. G. Bever, John M. Carroll, and R. Hurtig, "Analogy," in *An Integrated Theory of Linguistic Ability*, T. G. Bever, J. J. Katz, and D. T. Langendoen, eds. (New York: Thomas Y. Crowell, 1976), pp. 149–82.

3. Herbert Sugden, *The Grammar of Spenser's Faerie Queene* (Philadelphia: Linguistic Society of America/University of Pennsylvania, 1936), p. 30.

4. Seymour Chatman, *The Later Style of Henry James* (Oxford: Blackwell, 1972), p. 85. The shift from *the same secret principle* to *this principle* illustrates the phenomenon of 'modifier-shedding' noted by Charles E. Osgood in his "Where Do Sentences Come From," in *Semantics: An Interdisciplinary Reader*, Danny Steinberg and Leon Jakobovits, eds. (Cambridge: Cambridge University Press, 1971), pp. 512–14.

5. Jonathan Culler holds that the inferred relation of the meditative persona to the scene is governed by conventions of specifically literary interpretation: "The fictional situation of discourse must be constructed so as to have a thematic function," (*Structuralist Poetics* [Ithaca, New York: Cornell University Press, 1975], p. 167). Some of his observations are quite suggestive, as is his largely unsuccessful attempt to use interpretive categories to solve problems of comprehending reference in a notably elliptical poem by John Ashberry.

6. I. A. Richards, *Practical Criticism* (1929; New York: Harcourt, Brace and World, Inc., n.d.), pp. 161–62.

7. *Selections from the Poetical Works of Edmund Spenser*, S. K. Heninger, Jr., ed. (Boston: Houghton Mifflin Company, 1970), p. 322.

8. Catherine Garvey, Alfonso Caramazza, and Jack Yates, "Factors Influencing Assignment of Pronoun Antecedents," *Cognition* 3 (1974/5): 227–43. They identify four additional factors that influence the identification of the pronoun in strings of the form:

$$NP_1 \text{ verbed } NP_2 \text{ because PRONOUN} \ldots$$

(1) Active-Passive:

(i) John recognised Michael because he ...
(ii) Michael was recognised by John because he ...

Passive sharply raised the identification of *Michael* as the antecedent. This seems to reflect increased weight being given to a general strategy for Subject pronouns: "Assume the theme of the second clause is the same as the first." Apparently one assumes that if passive has been applied to move *Michael* into theme position, the maneuver means to set up 'constant theme'. This strategy may account for part of the difficulty of example (11) in the text.

(2) Positive-Negative:

(i) The soldiers feared the natives because they ...
(ii) The soldiers did not fear the natives because they ...

The natives were less often taken to be the antecedents in the negative sentences (though they were in the majority of cases even in the negatives).

(3) Some inherent property of the verb assigning either NP_1 or NP_2 as the main causative force in the event (and thus setting it up as the antecedent of the pronoun):

(i) John telephoned Harry because he ...
    argued with
(ii) John praised Harry because he ...
    admired

They found verbs in (i) biased the pronoun strongly toward *John*, in (ii) toward *Harry*.

(4) Congruent/Noncongruent (i.e., likelier event in terms of status and roles)

(i) The father praised his son because he ...
(ii) The son praised his father because he ...

The incongruence in some cases destroyed the inherent bias imposed by the verb: here the strong bias in favor of *his son* in (i) disappears.

To this list of factors we might add the effect of grammatical parallelism which Frederick Springston found (Some Cognitive Aspects of Presupposed Coreferential Anaphora, Ph.D. Dissertation, Stanford University, 1975) in his Experiments 7 and 8. The weakness of both of these studies is that they eliminate context, placing the subjects in an unusual situation where they seem to be groping for clues or making maximal use of structural clues. Springston further simplifies by having only one correct antecedent—a choice between possible ones or of no antecedent at all never confronts his subjects.

M. A. K. Halliday and Ruqaiya Hasan also discuss these points in their *Cohesion in English* (London: Longman, 1976), pp. 310–12. Also, Terry Winograd lists 'weights' attached to various possible antecedents in his sub-program SMIT (*Understanding Natural Language*, pp. 158–62).

9. T. G. Bever, "The Cognitive Basis of Linguistic Structures," in *Cognition and the Development of Language*, John R. Hayes, ed. (New York: John Wiley and Sons, 1970), p. 320.

10. William Faulkner, *The Sound and the Fury* (New York: Vintage Books, n.d.), p. 16.

11. Susumo Kuno, "Three Perspectives in the Functional Approach to Syntax," in *Papers from the Parasession on Functionalism*, Robin E. Grossman, L. James San, and Timothy J. Vance, eds. (Chicago: University of Chicago Department of Linguistics/CLS, 1975), pp. 276–336. Dwight Bolinger, in "Pronouns and Repeated Nouns" (1977; available from the Indiana University Linguistics Club) fundamentally agrees with this position [which he attributes to Gilles S. Delisle].

12. For a summary of the conventions of free indirect style and discussion of their function, see Dillon and Kirchhoff, "On the Form and Function of Free Indirect Style," *Poetics and the Theory of Literature* 1 (1976): 431–40.

13. Robert H. Zoellner, "Faulkner's Prose Style in *Absalom, Absalom!*," *American Literature* 30 (1959): 495.

14. Stanley Fish, "What is Stylistics and Why Are They Saying Such Terrible Things About It?" in *Approaches to Poetics*, Seymour Chatman, ed. (New York: Columbia University Press, 1973), p. 120.

15. Seymour Chatman, "Milton's Participial Style," *Publications of the Modern Language Association*, 83 (Oct. 1968): 1386–99.

16. Ronald W. Langacker and Patricia Munro, "Passives and Their Meaning," *Language* 51 (1975): 789–830.

17. The "brainwashing" term is Fowler's: Roger Fowler, "Style and the Concept of Deep Structure," *Journal of Literary Semantics* 1 (1972): 18.

18. A recent study by V. M. Holmes and I. J. Watson suggests that readers do not reconstruct Logical Subjects which have been omitted in passives. ("The Role of Surface Order and Surface Deletion in Sentence Perception," *Quarterly Journal of Experimental Psychology* 28 [1976]: 55–65.) They found that passives with omitted Logical Subjects were comprehended *more quickly* than sentences with purely adjectival predicates (i.e., A faster than B:

A. All three of my friends were invited.
B. All three of my friends were hungry.)

and that comprehension time did not differ between passives with relatively predictable logical Subjects and those with unpredictable ones (*She knew that the shelves had been ruined*—Subject is more unpredictable), suggesting that readers are not attempting to specify the omitted logical Subjects. Holmes and Watson do not, however, rule out the possibility that readers may try to specify omitted logical Subjects in meaningful contexts.

Surely context does lead one to size things up in certain ways. One person who read (I.46) out of context:

As when the potent Rod
Of Amrams son in Egypts evill day
Wav'd round the Coast, up call'd a pitchy cloud. . . .

told me she had specified the Subject of *wav'd* as "the ocean" (from *Coast*). Being told that Amram's son was Moses, however, she produced a different picture with a different specification of the Waver.

4. REFERENCE, COREFERENCE, AND ATTACHMENT
II: APPOSITION

1. Ralph Rader, "Fact, Theory, and Literary Explanation," *Critical Inquiry* 1 (Dec. 1974): 266.
2. Stanley Fish, *Surprised by Sin* (Berkeley: University of California Press, 1971), p. 27.
3. Frederick Kirchhoff, "A Note on Ruskin's Mythography," *Victorian Newsletter* 50 (Fall, 1976): 24–27.
4. *The Works of John Ruskin,* Sir Edward Tyes Cook and Alexander Dundas Oglivy Wedderburn, eds. (London: George Allen, 1903–12), XIX. 302–303.
5. Henry James, *The Wings of the Dove* (Dell, 1958), p. 20.
6. Richard Ohmann, "Generative Grammar and the Concept of Literary

Style," in *Contemporary Essays on Style,* Glen Love and Michael Payne, eds. (Glenview: Scott, Foresman, 1969), p. 141.

7. Helen H. Vendler, *On Extended Wings* (Cambridge, Mass.: Harvard University Press, 1969), p. 34.

5. CONSCIOUSNESS OF SENTENCE STRUCTURE

1. Herbert Sugden, *The Grammar of Spenser's Faerie Queene* (Baltimore: Linguistic Society of America/University of Pennsylvania, 1936), p. 213.

2. Robert Zoellner, "Faulkner's Prose Style in *Absalom, Absalom!*" *American Literature* 30 (1959): 501.

3. Conrad Aiken, "William Faulkner: The Novel as Form," in *William Faulkner, Three Decades of Criticism,* Frederick J. Hoffman and Olga W. Vickery, eds. (East Lansing: Michigan State University Press, 1960), p. 137.

4. Jane P. Tompkins,"'The Beast in the Jungle': An Analysis of James's Late Style," *Modern Fiction Studies* 16 (1970): 190.

5. Stephen Booth, *An Essay on Shakespeare's Sonnets* (New Haven: Yale University Press, 1969), pp. 151–52.

6. Vernon Lee, *The Handling of Words* (London, 1923), p. 244; cited in Seymour Chatman, *The Later Style of Henry James* (Oxford: Blackwell, 1972), p. 58.

7. R. W. Short, "The Sentence Structure of Henry James," *American Literature* 18 (1946): 73–74.

8. For what it is worth, I agree with Doggett on the referent of *the.* If it is reasonable to draw on other poems, I would prefer to cite the last line of "The Motive for Metaphor" ("The vital, arrogant, fatal, dominant X"—*CP,* 288) as a parallel. Taking "reality" as the referent does not make the last line affirmative, however, since it simply says, "Where was it one first heard of the truth? The notion of a reality beyond fictive distortion?" which in the context may mean, "How did it come about that I set out in pursuit of a possibly unreal ideal, which may be only a projection of the self?" See *On Extended Wings,* p. 19 and note.

6. INTEGRATION AND CONTEXT

1. J. D. Bransford and M. K. Johnson, "Considerations of Some Problems of Comprehension," in *Visual Information Processing,* W. G. Chase, ed. (New York: Academic Press, 1973), p. 412.

2. Ian Watt, "The First Paragraph of *The Ambassadors:* An Explication," in *Contemporary Essays on Style,* Glen A. Love and Michael Payne, eds. (Glenview: Scott, Foresman and Company, 1969), pp. 273–74.

3. Herbert H. Clark, "Semantics and Comprehension," in *Current Trends in Linguistics*, Vol. 12 (Part 3) T. A. Sebeok, eds. (The Hague: Mouton, 1974), pp. 1305–08.

4. George Lakoff, "The Role of Deduction in Grammar," in *Studies in Linguistic Semantics*, Charles J. Fillmore and D. Terence Langendoen, eds. (New York: Holt, Rinehart and Winston, Inc., 1971), pp. 63–77. Lakoff credits Georgia Green with some of these observations.

5. Herbert H. Clark and Susan E. Haviland, "Psychological Processes as Linguistic Explanation," in *Explaining Linguistic Phenomena*, David Cohen, ed. (Washington, D.C.: Hemisphere Publishing Corporation, 1974), p. 105: see also Susan Haviland and Herbert Clark, "What's New? Acquiring New Information as a Process in Comprehension," *Journal of Verbal Learning and Verbal Behavior* 13 (1974): 512–21; and also the brief discussion in Clark and Clark, pp. 91–98, and the references therein cited.

6. D. Terence Langendoen and Thomas G. Bever, "Can a Not Unhappy Person Be Called a Not Sad One?" in *An Integrated Theory of Linguistic Ability*, T. G. Bever, J. J. Katz, and D. Terence Langendoen, eds. (New York: Thomas Y. Crowell, 1976), pp. 239–60.

7. Helen Vendler seems to feel there is something improper or colloquial about using simple past to mark a counter-factual, as here (see *On Extended Wings*, p. 29).

8. Samuel Fillenbaum, "Memory for Counterfactual Conditionals," *Journal of Experimental Psychology* 102 (1974): 44–49.

9. Wayne C. Booth, *The Rhetoric of Fiction* (Chicago: University of Chicago Press, 1961), p. 184.

10. Seymour Chatman, *The Later Style of Henry James* (Oxford: Basil Blackwell, 1972), p. 73.

11. See George Dillon, *Introduction to Contemporary Semantics* (Englewood Cliffs: Prentice-Hall, Inc., 1977), pp. 105–07.

7. SOME VALUES OF COMPLEX PROCESSING

1. Stephen Booth, *An Essay on Shakespeare's Sonnets* (New Haven: Yale University Press, 1969), p. 55.

2. Paul Alpers, *The Poetry of the Faerie Queene* (Princeton: Princeton University Press, 1966), pp. 81–82.

3. L. C. Martin, ed. *Marlowe's Poems* (London, 1931).

4. E. A. Abbott, *A Shakespearian Grammar* (1870; rpt. New York: Dover Publications, Inc., 1966), p. 59.

5. Christopher Marlowe, *The Poems*, Millar McClure, ed. (Methuen and Company, 1968), p. 32.

6. Stanley Fish has stressed this point in his "Interpreting the *Variorum*," *Critical Inquiry* 2:3 (Spring, 1976): 465–86. Note that I am here invoking the notion that the reading is to be preferred which yields the greatest semantic density or number of 'ties' to the other words in the passage. Archibald A. Hill discusses applications of this principle to poetry in his *Constituent and Pattern in Poetry* (Austin: University of Texas Press, 1976). Yorick Wilks claims that this principle, unaided by syntactic information, can give fairly good parsings to sentences ("Preference Semantics" in *Formal Semantics of Natural Language,* Edward L. Keenan, ed. [Cambridge: Cambridge University Press, 1975], pp. 329–48).

7. Warren Beck, "William Faulkner's Style," in *William Faulkner: Three Decades of Criticism,* Frederick J. Hoffman and Olga W. Vickery, eds.(East Lansing: Michigan State University Press, 1960), p. 153.

8. Robert Zoellner, "Faulkner's Prose Style in *Absalom, Absalom! American Literature* 30 (1959): 490–91.

9. Barry Menikoff, "Punctuation and Point of View in the Late Style of Henry James," *Style* 4 (1970): 29.

10. Jane P. Tompkins, " 'The Beast in the Jungle': An Analysis of James's Late Style," *Modern Fiction Studies* (1970): 187–88.

11. Helen Vendler, *On Extended Wings* (Cambridge, Mass.: Harvard University Press, 1969), p. 306.

12. Ian Watt, "The First Paragraph of *The Ambassadors:* An Explication," in *Contemporary Essays on Style,* Glen A. Love and Michael Payne, eds. (Glenview: Scott, Foresman and Company, 1969), p. 273.

13. R. W. Short, "The Sentence Structure of Henry James, *American Literature* 18 (1946): 71–88.

14. Walter Slatoff, "The Edge of Order: The Pattern of Faulkner's Rhetoric," in Hoffman and Vickery, p. 193.

CONCLUSION

1. Ralph Rader, "The Concept of Genre and Eighteenth-Century Studies," in *New Approaches to Eighteenth-Century Literature: Selected Papers from the English Institute* (New York: Columbia University Press, 1974), p. 89; cited in Stanley Fish, "Facts and Fictions: A Reply to Ralph Rader," *Critical Inquiry* 1:4 (June, 1975): 888.